Cuba: The Truth, the Lies, and the Coverups

Based on a True Spy Story

Dr. Julio Antonio del Marmol

The Cuban Lightning

© Copyright 2016 Dr. Julio Antonio del Marmol.
All rights reserved. No part of this publication may be reproduced, stored in a retrieval system, or transmitted, in any form or by any means, electronic, mechanical, photocopying, recording, or otherwise, without the written prior permission of the author.

ISBN: 978-1-68588-007-1 (sc)
ISBN: 978-1-68588-006-4 (hc)
ISBN: 978-1-68588-008-8 (e)

Because of the dynamic nature of the Internet, any web addresses or links contained in this book may have changed since publication and may no longer be valid.

Any people depicted in stock imagery provided by Thinkstock are models, and such images are being used for illustrative purposes only.
Certain stock imagery © Thinkstock.

Cuban Lightning Publications, Int rev. 12/07/2016

Acknowledgements

I am a very lucky man because I have a great group of people by my side that I not only consider my friends but also who are the most capable, sacrificing professionals equal to the ones I've risked my life with over the past 50 years in their dedication and values. This group has made possible the publication of this book. To them, with all my heart today, I give the best of my love, gratitude, and sincerest thanks to every one of these fantastic warriors. In order of seniority, I would especially like to thank O'Brien: a great friend, a great individual with extraordinary values, thank you for your contributions you have made in many different ways to this project, as well being loyally by my side and watching my back for almost all of my career. I know for a fact you have never done that before for anyone. To my right arm and great friend, Tad Atkinson: for your dedication to every detail in research and many hours of hard work with me, never hesitating to sacrifice even your personal and private family time in order to make this happen. To Steve Weese: thank you for the many pieces of computer and graphic work as well professional enhancement of photos to improve the quality of the book. To Carlos Mota: my thanks for your dedication and multiple contributions and sacrifices you have made in order to make this happen. To Gervasin Neto: for your constant loyalty and many hours standing on your feet or hiding between cars in order to maintain our security with your group of people you've coordinated to watch our backs, continually keeping us informed of any suspicious activity that occurs in our surroundings. To Chopin: for your great companionship, loyalty, and support for the last 50 years with me in our fight for freedom and that beautiful, generous letter you wrote in behalf of the project. To our editor, Jen Poiry-Prough: who managed to make this book as easy to read, using her magic touch to polishing this piece of coal and bring to you, the readers, what I consider to be a very rare diamond. It makes all of us very proud to be involved in this project. Your professionalism, vast knowledge, and dedication, has made this book a great piece for future generations. To all of you, my friends who remain in the shadows, who contributed in one way or another in making this book and help me to bring the truth to the public, you have given the best of yourselves, putting forth your best effort to educate future generations. God bless you all. I embrace you as the Christian warriors that you all are.

Dr. Julio Antonio del Marmol

Dedication

Young Julio Antonio with his parents, Leonardo and Verena

I would like to dedicate this book to the memory of my parents, Leonardo and Verena del Marmol. My father was my role model, my hero, from whom I took my qualities of patriotism, loyalty, honesty, honor, and sense of ethics. From him, I learned never to lower my standards of conduct, no matter how low my enemies might go. As he put it, "If a dog comes and bites you, and you bite it back, what does that make you? A dog, as well." My mother was my unwavering supporter, the one person I could never fully hide my clandestine activities from. Even when she knew I was doing something dangerous, she unfailingly gave me her total backing, even to the point of endangering herself by assisting me in keeping my secrets. She taught me to love and respect every woman I meet, because—as she put it—"Without women, where would any of us be?" From her I learned to view women as the main source of life in God's creative process within nature. It is from her I received my sense of morality, concern for the wellbeing of others, ability to see things from another person's perspective, and unfailing optimism.

I loved both of my parents deeply, and it is one of the greatest satisfactions in my life that we were able to pull them safely out of Castro's "communist paradise" and bring them to the United States, where they were able to live out the rest of their lives in this genuine paradise of freedom. My thanks to you both for what you instilled in me and for making me into the man I am today. I pray that God has both of you seated in special places in the only real paradise in all of Creation—at His side in Heaven.

Testimonial

For those who don't know the author of Cuba: the Truth, the Lies, and the Coverups, Dr. Julio Antonio del Marmol:

I mean this with utmost respect, but you don't really know who he is. It has been the most profound honor in my life to work with him by his side so closely than I have become his personal confidant. It is a level of trust unheard of in his life and one I value more than my own existence. I have been a beneficiary of his vast experiences and generosity, and have gotten to know his character, a man of such exemplary moral decency that he can at times seem to belong to a time long gone by.

And yet, I have only known him, relatively speaking, for a short while, a decade or so. Who then, could claim an even more intimate knowledge of who Dr. del Marmol is? The answer lay in Dr. Hector Zayas-Bazan y Perdomo, who in these histories is referred to as the Professor. Dr. Zayas-Bazan has known Dr. del Marmol since he was a youth, helping in the formation of Dr. del Marmol's character in those critical teenage years. He became Dr. del Marmol's mentor and grew to love him as a son. They have remained at each other's side, no matter where in the world their journeys took them, growing older together. Dr. Zayas-Bazan, a fervent patriot and respected intelligence adviser, was the main contact between Dr. del Marmol and the rest of the intelligence community while they were in Cuba. He wrote the following letter in 2014 on his 100th birthday, at long last emerging from the shadows, placing his personal security at great risk. This letter was a gift to Dr. del Marmol, intended as the strongest testimonial for the world before Dr. Zayas-Bazan passed away, instructing all of us who this man, a master spy at such an early age, had grown to become as an adult: best pupil, the best and most loyal friend he ever had. This letter is a statement to future generations. I was able to meet Dr. Zayas-Bazan on a few occasions, and I can say with absolute certainty that I could see not only where he had left his stamp on Dr. del Marmol, but also could see the mutual father-son bond the two shared. Dr. Zayas-Bazan passed away peacefully in his sleep early in 2015. Rest in peace, Professor, secure in the knowledge that your great work will be carried on by your greatest protégé, Dr. Julio Antonio del Marmol.

Tad Atkinson
20 April, 2015

Introduction

At the young age of twelve, the author, Dr. Julio Antonio del Marmol, found that his destiny took him through extraordinary circumstances that happens only a few times in history during widespread social chaos, like that seen in the deranged turmoil of the Cuban revolution in 1959. The supreme leader, Fidel Castro, nominated this young boy to be the Commander-in-Chief of the new army for the future. As Fidel Castro went through his own changes of heart at that start of this tumultuous time, the youth went through his own conflict as he watched his childhood friends abandon the island, discontented with what looked more like a complete disruption of democratic establishment and institution of Marxist ideology by the new leaders. Julio Antonio del Marmol, the Young Commander sadly saw himself remain behind and observed daily the freedom of the Cuban people evaporate as promise after promise was broken. In spite of their previous promises for equality for everyone without any distinction based on political or religious belief, the Castro brothers and Che Guevara ruthlessly hunted down and exterminated all opposition. His admiration towards the leaders turned into disappointment and frustration, watching as the Castros' forces execute and commit horrendous crimes worse than humanity had ever seen in their ambition to maintain their power.

He comes to the conclusion that this is not what the

Cuban people fought their revolution for and decides before sharing these horrible experiences to anyone, including his father, to abandon the country as his friends had done. When he does share these intentions with his uncle, he receives the most shocking surprise that his relative is an old veteran master spy. He proposes to Julio Antonio to train him to be the next in line, and Julio Antonio del Marmol becomes the youngest spy in modern history at the age of thirteen. In this story, the reader will find seemingly unbelievable and undoubtedly controversial details about the blueprints to create communist revolutions, spread corruption, and commit assassinations so outrageous that nobody ever could create this as a fiction. We are transported back to 1960, where newly minted master spy Julio Antonio del Marmol begins by stealing the briefcase of Che Guevara from inside the provincial military headquarters of the Rebel Army in Pinar del Rio. This action propels him into a new, more dangerous sphere of operation as a spy, as he works his way into the inner circles of the most paranoid mind of the leaders of the Cuban revolution, Che Guevara—who seeks to groom the young man as his own protege as a KGB agent!

The author tells the story not merely as a narrator; he was an active participant in these events as part of his first steps in his life as a thirteen-year-old spy, as he tried to retrieve what he felt to be important documents for his friends in his intelligence network. The reader will draw their own conclusions and put the facts together. He perceived the relevance and import of what he had obtained. Only when the author's friends reviewed the data did he realize the sheer magnitude of what he accomplished as he exposed in this one act what really lies behind Cuba: the truth, the lies, and the coverups.

The Cuban Lightning

Volume I of Rites of Passage of a Master Spy

The Truth: A Lonely and Ugly Being

"The truth is like an ugly, lonely lady standing on the dance floor while everyone prefers to dance around her, because no one dares ask her to dance."

Under God's Flag

My heart has love for many lands and flags. All the countries in the world that embrace dignity and respect for our loving God and let their people live in peace, happiness, and freedom, these are the countries that earn and maintain my respect, and I keep a special place in my heart for them. I have not a single doubt in my mind that I will defend the freedom of each and every one of these countries with the last drop of my blood. I am committed to continue my fight on a daily basis, without rest, until my last breath of air. I make this my universal duty under the only ultimate Commander-in-Chief: Almighty God. I feel I was born on their soil, and I am in my heart a small piece of every single one of them. These countries Satan tries to steal from us to bring evil into the world in his drive to finally conquer our souls. He seeks to completely destroy peace, happiness, freedom, and love through his hateful armies of ambitious and unscrupulous men, who will not stop until they see the world go up in flames like the Hell they left behind. That is why each one of you should be involved in stopping these horrible forces once and for all. We need your help to defeat the evil and powerful enemy before it's too late. This could be your last call to fight under the flag of God and unite to defend from these horrible enemies what is left of this wonderful world which is the greatest and most precious gift to us from God.

Dr. Julio Antonio del Marmol

Prologue: The Terror that Comes with "Freedom"

Pinar del Rio, a Small City
Capital of the Province of the Occidental Side of the Island of Cuba
Avenue Cabada

The charcoal man and his family with their cart

My friend Tite, the son of the charcoal man, told me of an incident that left a terrible impression on him. It scarred him with a physical disability for life in that it was the cause of his stutter. It was in the early morning hours of 1959, the first months of the Revolution being in power, and a crowd ran through the avenue, ignoring the picturesque boulevard lined with its old, tall pine trees, burning cars and looting. A man in his late twenties was running from the mob. From the opposite direction, an old horse-drawn wagon containing a couple of middle-aged blacks with a young kid riding in the coach that was filled in the back with all kinds of scrap wood slowly plodded through the streets. The wagon was forced to stop due to the press of the people, and the mob caught the young man as he attempted to dodge under the horses' legs. The leader of the mob, a red-headed woman dressed in the olive-green khaki uniform of the militia, screamed, "We've got him!" She turned to one of the men in the mob. "Are you sure this is the man?" A young girl of about nine years of age stood next her. The girl's hair was the same shade of red, and her eyes were a peculiar shade of light green. Nearly half of the right side of the young girl's face was covered by a red birthmark. She wore no shoes, was very dirty, and dressed in rags. Two of her front teeth were missing. She clasped in both her hands a large pickle jar filled with liquid that had some objects floating inside.

"Yes," the man replied, "this is the man I saw several times coming out of the dictator Batista's intelligence headquarters to inform them of our movements as rebels in the city and the mountains."

"Tie him up," she ordered.

Some of the men that were holding the prisoner proceeded to bind his arms and legs. All the while, the man screamed, "I'm innocent! I'm with you guys! Maybe he saw me in that place, but all I was doing was delivering food to them, which I was paid to do. At the same time, I was looking in there to see what new weapons they had and what people they had there and passed the information along to Captain Clodomiro Miranda. You can ask him—I'm not a *chivato*, an informant for Batista! I am an informant for the Rebel Army, for you guys!"

The woman screamed, "Bullshit! You are a liar—hold him down for me! Pull his tongue out." One of the men used some pliers to try to pull out and hold the unfortunate man's tongue. The man continued to struggle against the mob. She pulled out a large pair of scissors as the black family looked on in sheer horror from the coach. Helplessly, they watched as the man continued to scream his innocence and pleaded with the mob to check with Captain Clodomiro until at long last, they were able to hold him so that the woman could cut out his tongue. She threw the man's tongue into the air, and the family watched in revulsion as the bloody meat landed on the ground right next to the wagon. The woman declaimed, "This is what we will do to each informant for the Dictator. Let's find some more!"

The small girl ran towards where the tongue had landed. She put down the pickle jar and opened it. With her hand, she picked up the discarded tongue and plopped it into the jar, where other amputated tongues floated. She screwed the cap back on and then spat into her hands. She rubbed her hands together in an attempt to clean them off, and then rubbed them on her ragged dress. The woman led the mob off into the faint light of the dawn. They streamed past and away from the wagon and its sickened occupants.

The husband and wife looked at each other, terrified. The mother looked at her son, and saw tears streaming down his cheeks. She put her arm around his shoulders tenderly and said, "That's OK, Tite. That is the evil some men have. I'm sorry you had to see this, my son." She pulled him in, and he lay his head against her breast.

The red-headed woman called to the little girl,

"Maggie! Let's go!" The little girl looked up at them, and her eyes looked into those of Tite's. She smiled strangely, the oddness coming from the level of cynicism displayed in one so young. His mother held Tite protectively and looked at her husband. She rubbed her arms as goose bumps made her flesh crawl. The young girl turned and scampered off to join her mother and the mob. Tite's eyes followed bobbing of the tongues inside the jar as she left.

His father crossed himself, and said, "May God forgive these people for the evil they do." He got out of the wagon and knelt down to try and help the profusely bleeding man, an old family friend. He pulled out a handkerchief and put it in the man's mouth. "We have to stop your bleeding. Put the pressure of this against your stump and bite down." He then proceeded to untie the poor man's hands and legs. "Don't worry, Ruben." Compassionately, he put his arm around Ruben's shoulder and helped him to stand up. "We'll get you to the hospital. You'll be OK."

Chapter 1: The Discovered Treasure

Julio Antonio del Marmol in his Young Commandos uniform

A year later, I was dressed in my Juvenile Commandos uniform in my house on Avenue Cabada, 116. I had dressed hurriedly, because I was supposed to be at the local military regiment for an important meeting with the chief of the province, Commander Dermidio Escalona. He had informed me of the meeting the previous day. It was important, because Commander Ernesto "Che" Guevara wanted to inform us of the new orders the Maximum Leader, Fidel Castro. This had originated because several groups within the army were in mutiny. Some of the officers had even taken their troops into the jungles to fight against the emerging Socialist regime. These were the last measures the government had developed as a result of Captain Clodomiro Miranda's rebellion. After this event, Fidel Castro started to doubt his Rebel Army; even though the Revolution was a triumph, he knew most of them were peasants, students, and intellectuals that had abandoned their normal lives. For these people, the Marxist ideology they were indoctrinating the army with was a very hard pill to swallow. Some of them, at least, didn't even know what Marxist-Leninist meant. But some of the more educated officers had knowledge, and didn't like it one bit. They had fought to re-establish a free democracy, not to set up a communist dictatorship that would be even worse than the corrupt dictatorship of Batista. In consequence, similar rebellions had erupted around the island, especially in the central mountains of the Escambray in Santa Clara.

The whole Revolution had by now been divided into two groups. In the one group, Fidel Castro, his brother Raúl, Che, and the other big commanders wanted to remain in power perpetually, and were aligned with Che and the Castros in creating a communist future for the island. The other group felt betrayed by these ideas and had rebelled, and so had been persecuted and forced back into the mountains. The situation was extremely tense inside the armed forces, and this tension spilled out into the general public, poisoning the overall atmosphere of the island. In reaction, the Castros and Che implemented even more extreme measures, seeking to root out any opposition and brutally put it down. Even the simple expression of displeasure or doubt could lead to the firing squad, so intense was the witch hunt they had embarked upon in seeking out any anti-communist sentiments. For this reason, a few months before, the men with Captain Miranda were either executed or given between ten to thirty years in prison. Even one of the major Commanders, Huber Matos, received a sentence of twenty years simply for sending a letter to Fidel asking when free elections would be held. No one was exempt or excused.

By this time, I had been trained by my uncle and the man we codenamed the General. I had been taking my first steps into the spy business and slowly discovered that this was a very dangerous game. With very little experience but very good, solid training, my position as the Commander-in-Chief of the Juvenile Commandos was the perfect one in which to learn as I went. I was primarily guided at this point by my own instincts because of my limited experience. When my instincts told me that Che would be back, even though he had recently left the province, something important had to be going on, and so I didn't want to be late to this meeting. As soon as I was dressed, I rushed through breakfast and walked to the front door.

The front of Julio Antonio's house

Julio Antonio's sisters Disa and Elda with a friend on their front porch

After I said goodbye to my mother, Mima, and my nanny, Majito, I passed by a man of about 45 coming into the house with a teenaged boy. This boy looked as if he had Down syndrome. They both brought poles with empty five-gallon cans hanging from either end. Both greeted me in a friendly manner: "Good morning, Julio Antonio."

I nodded affably. "Good morning, Don Pascual; good morning, Tobito."

Don Pascual said, "Your driver, that big black guy, has been waiting outside for you for a while."

I replied with a smile, "Really good. Daniel is early today. Thank you, Pascual."

"Have a great day. *Valla con Dios, mi niño.*[1]" He waved goodbye to me. Don Pascual was a tall man, stooped over at the shoulder. He had a large, Greek nose, a very ruddy complexion, and very straight salt-and-pepper hair. We called his type *isleño relloyo*, or "island Creole", because he was pure Spanish in ancestry but born on the island. He spoke with the Castilian lisp, but more exaggerated and used the "z" even when it wasn't really applicable. As a result, this group of people were the subject of numerous jokes by the majority of people in Cuba. They were stereotyped as slow, inbred, but otherwise generally likeable.

Tobito was very tall, about six foot three inches, with red, curly hair, freckles all over, complexion like his father, and buck teeth. In that time, the trash sometimes accumulated for a month before someone came by to pick it up. Public service was very deficient, with many public employees at the beginning of the Revolution being accused of collaborators with the previous regime. They were constantly understaffed, and in consequence the trash became a problem.

Cuban ingenuity created a solution for this. Many

---

[1] Go with God, my boy.

people raised farms in the surrounding countryside. They offered to pick up the trash in exchange for any food leftovers from the city dwellers' meals for their pigs. The leftovers that they used to feed the pigs were called *sarcocho*. They would have fifty-five-gallon tanks on their wagons, and bring five gallon cans into the house, collect the *sarcocho* from a family, and empty the cans into the tanks.

When I left the house, I smiled because Daniel had parked the jeep a little distance from the wagon and was holding a handkerchief over his nose and mouth due to the stench from the tanks. Despite the tarp cover, the flies swarmed around the wagon and disturbed the horse's rump. After I greeted Daniel, I jumped into the jeep.

Daniel said to me, "How is it possible that Don Pascual and his son could tolerate that stink all day long?"

I smiled. "Daniel, everything in life is just a question of getting used to something. Good or bad, we get used to everything in life. If you asked Don Pascual the same question, he would probably ask you 'what stink?' because they've been doing this for so long that they don't smell it anymore."

The good black man shook his head in bewilderment and made a sick face. He crossed himself and said, "Thank God I don't have to do that kind of work. I hear the Devil has a sulfur-smelling ass. But this Goddamn smell from Don Pascual's wagon is a thousand times worse probably than the Devil's butt."

"That's got rhythm," I said. We both smiled and drove to the military compound.

A few months before, I had been taking pictures in San Cristobol of the first boxes of missiles that had arrived from the Soviet Union when I visited this facility with my brother-in-law, Canen. Of course, he had no idea of what I was doing; but he had been assigned the command of overseeing all of the new installations. I was very anxious to know what Che was bringing to us in this meeting, information that could be of very great help to my uncle and our associates in global intelligence. When we arrived at the compound, I realized that Che had not arrived by himself: he had also brought along a couple of other big names in the communist government. One was Ramiro Valdez, the Minister of the Interior and the DTI, the internal police of the island. The other one was Commander Piñeiro, the head of the G-2, or Red Beard, as we called him.

We spent all day from meeting to meeting, first with the officer in charge of the troops, then with the other junior officers involved in the military training programs. Che explained to us that we have to observe closely every single officer and NCOs in our army, because they are the only ones capable of converting entire platoons into Counterrevolutionaries. After interviewing them, he would nominate some to be political "orientators," who would be responsible for detecting and catching in time any discontent or signal that any officer, NCO, or soldier was resisting the socialist indoctrination. From this, Commanders Piñeiro and Ramiro conducted interviews for many hours, and out of the hundreds of men they only selected a small group—the most loyal and accepting of the communist doctrine. Later in the afternoon, Piñeiro and Ramiro informed me that my Juvenile Commandos would become the Young Communist Union.

With a pleasant and big smile, I replied, "Great! We will continue to work with the same objective, to create the best results for the Revolution."

They looked at each other in wonderment, and Che smiled broadly. Escalona took the credit and said, "You see, Che? You see, Ramiro, Piñeiro? That is the good ideological work I've done with the Little Commander." They were all fascinated with my answer, and gloated at my apparent enthusiasm. Escalona continued, "I've given a few books to him, and he's been doing his homework."

Che looked a little unconvinced with Escalona's boast. He held up a hand to stop Escalona. "What books did he give to you?" he asked me.

I stroked my chin. "Well, he gave me a few. In between those, he gave me The Bolshevik Revolution, he gave me both Marx and Engels, and some of Lenin's essays about the effect internationally that the Bolshevik Revolution can have."

Che stood up from his chair, walked over to me, and clapped me on the shoulder. "You see? This is good ideological work. I congratulate you, and I'm going to give you one of my books." He opened his briefcase and pulled out a book. "I don't give a signed book to anybody, because I don't like to brag. But for you, I will sign it, since you are an example for the new generation." He signed his book and handed it to me. "The book is *War of the Guerillas*. You will learn from this book how we fight the capitalists and imperialists all over the world with a very small group of men. This is a military combat book."

"Thank you," I said. "It's a great honor."

"No, it's a great honor to have a young man like you at such a young age to have these great political views. Take the time to educate yourself." He closed his attaché case and put it down on the floor by Escalona's desk. I glanced back and made sure that Che had left his case there. Then we all left the office, Escalona coming last to lock up. We went to the officer's mess in different vehicles to have dinner. We had a great meal of fried chicken, black beans and rice, fried yucca and plantain bananas, and green salad. We all sat at a long table. I excused myself and used the opportunity to go to a chef I knew well, and asked him if I could take a few of the rations.

"Sure, Commander, no problem," he said.

The food had started to grow short in Cuba, and every time I went to the military compound, I always tried to get some extra to take home with me. All of the other officers did this, as well. I said goodbye to Che and the others, and told Daniel to pick up the extra rations. He touched his belly in a very satisfied fashion. "Did you eat too much?" I asked him.

He smiled his broad grin. "I ate for today and tomorrow, just in case we don't come back here tomorrow."

I told him, "Take one of those rations to your house, and take the other to Mima, and tell her I sent it to her."

He looked at me and said, "Thank you! Thank you very much. But aren't you coming with me?"

I drew close to him and looked into his eyes. "No, I will stay here, but you will tell my mother that I will be coming later. And under no circumstances tell anyone that I didn't leave with you."

He raised his hand. "I understand. If anyone asks, I tell them I drove you home and then went home myself."

"Whatever happens," I repeated, "remember—for your security and mine, you stick with that version, OK?"

He nodded his head. "I got it."

I smiled and walked away from the jeep. He closed the zipper on the plastic cover of the jeep, got in, and drove towards the guard point of the compound. I started to walk on the sidewalk. Once in the shadows, I left the sidewalk and entered a grassy alley between the military buildings. From there, I made my way back Escalona's offices. It was about 8:30 in the evening. There was no moon, and the stars were concealed by the overcast. The slight breeze and smell indicated that rain was near. I watched Don Pascual's wagon roll by en route to the officer's mess. I smiled, thinking about Daniel's observations. I went behind the building, and found a three inch drainage pipe hanging down. I noticed that it crossed the building close by a window just outside of Escalona's office. I unwrapped my cartridge belt, put it around the pipe, and tied myself to the belt, so that I would have some support. I slowly started to make my way up the pipe like a mountaineer. A couple of times, I had to stop, untie myself, and rethread the belt around the pipe whenever I ran into a support bracket mounting the pipe against the building. When I got close to the window, I supported myself on my knees, took out my commando knife, and pulled out the aluminum frame of the window. I worked the blade back and forth until the latch clicked open. With the window free, I sheathed my knife around my waist. I carefully slid inside, taking care to make no noise. I unwrapped my belt from around the pipe and retied it around my waist, and then jumped into the corridor. I used my knife once more to carefully force the lock on the door to Escalona's office. Everything was where it had been left when we departed—including Che's attaché case. I grabbed the curtain cord, cut it with my knife, and opened the window in his office. Without wasting any time, I tied one end of the cord to the case's handle, and slowly slid it down to the grass on the other side of the building where I had already planned my escape.

I had been tracking all the movements for the last eighteen months in this military camp, and knew where I could get out with minimal danger, and where the patrols would be lightest: by the storage for all the heavy equipment.

There were always two guards at the entry point to all buildings in the compound. Ironically, there were no guards on the backs of the buildings, as there were no rear entrances. The two guards on duty this time were two big black men, deep in conversation, a couple of men I had grown to know, and so I was able later on to get their accounts of what happened next.

The largest one had a pleasant, jovial face, and he said, "You know, man—I have to go pee, and I've been holding it for so long. But you know, the bathrooms here are all blocked."

The other answered, "What the hell are you holding that for? For God's sake, just go upstairs to the Commander's bathroom."

The large man shook his head. "No, I don't want to use his bathroom. They might come back at any moment and catch me there. You know we're not supposed to use it."

"But this is an emergency. If you don't want to go upstairs, at least go behind the building, and find a corner and go there. The dogs are smaller and they pee everywhere, and nobody notices."

"Wait, wait, wait—what kind of comparison is this? You think I look like a dog?"

The other guy paused and looked at his friend closely. "Well, looking at you carefully—you look like a Goddamn bulldog!"

The large man put the rifle behind the chair and hit his friend jokingly on the shoulder. "Well, if I look like a bulldog, you look like a Goddamn chimpanzee, with long lips that look like bacon that hasn't been properly cooked." He smiled, left, and started to unbutton his pants even as he walked, so urgent was his need to relieve himself. He found a bush out of sight from the front of the compound and sighed with relief as he started to urinate. As he emptied his bladder, he looked into the distance. A series of lightning flashes illuminated the night and revealed to him a small man crawling down to the ground along the pipe about one hundred feet away. At first, he did nothing, watching in confusion and silence. It looked like the silhouette he saw in the distance didn't see him. The small man walked in the opposite direction and apparently reached down into the grass for something. He looked up and saw that the curtains in Escalona's office were blowing gently in the breeze, billowing out like sails, plainly indicating that the window was open.

He reacted immediately, yelling, "Hey! What are you doing there? Identify yourself!!" The silhouette ran towards the heavy equipment storage. The large man tried to cut his stream short, swearing as urine spilled over his pants. "Stop!" he yelled, "Stop, or I shoot!" It was an empty threat, as he had no pistol, and had left his rifle by his post. As soon as he realized he was unarmed, he turned and ran to the front of the building, screaming to his comrade, "Sound the alarm! Sound the alarm! There is an intruder in the building!"

The other was immobile with confusion, unable to hear very well at the distance. The only movement he made was to sit up in his chair. At first, he thought his large friend might be pulling a joke on him, and so held a hand up to his ear. "What did you say?"

The large man didn't even stop, but ran into the

building. He was worried, as they were solely responsible for what happened in that building, and knew they were both looking at prison time. "God damn it! Sound the alarm!! Somebody just climbed out the window in Commander Escalona's office."

The other man noted the urine covering his comrade's pants and reacted by running inside and slamming his hand against the glass covering a button marked in red and black letters, "Use Only in Emergency. General Commander Alarm." Immediately the very loud siren sounded through the compound.

I kept running, trying to escape the military fortress. The powerful reflector lights turned on everywhere throughout the compound. I told myself that I had to change my plans and improvise another escape route. The place I had picked unfortunately had been burned when that soldier discovered me there. I needed to get away from that building as far as possible before the general alarm sounded and the compound was completely sealed. I ran in the dark through the tall grass. I could hear some soldiers close by screaming about seeing a silhouette. "Over there! I see him over there!"

I got to a clean area with a large concrete wall that I was able to immediately identify. It was the wall they used for the firing squad executions of those disaffected with the new socialist regime. Out of the blue, big spotlights turned on around the wall. I threw myself flat on my belly onto the ground, still clutching the attaché case. I lay there motionless and silent, in the tall grass. I could observe the metal doors of a subterranean installation open vertically into the air. From there, a group of soldiers with four bound prisoners emerged. The prisoners were wearing surgical scrubs. The soldiers conducted the prisoners to the wall, moving uncomfortably close to my position. One prisoner caught my attention. He had long, straight hair—because he had no beard, I at first thought he was a woman. But I realized it was a young man when I heard him scream, "I am innocent! I'm not a Counterrevolutionary, or anything like! I only went to the mountains to bring food to my brother. Please don't kill me!"

The soldiers that were conducting him had neither pity nor sympathy, ignoring the young man's pleas for clemency. They shoved him to walk in front of them. The young man tripped and fell to the ground, and began to cry like a baby. He once more begged for his life. One of his fellow prisoners stopped by him and said, "Stand up, Fernando. Don't give these sons of bitches the pleasure to see you begging. Behave like you're the man you are." He bent over and tried to offer his shoulder to help the young man up.

Before Fernando could reach up to him, another soldier hit the prisoner in the back of the head. The other man rolled to the ground by Fernando's side. Two or three soldiers kicked both of them, forcing the two prisoners to their feet. The solemn procession continued to the grim wall full of bullet holes. The four were lined up and rags tied over their eyes. The soldier in charge stepped back and barked the orders: "Ready! Aim! Fire!"

Before the last command was uttered, the tallest yelled in defiance, "Death to the communists! Long live Jesus Christ!" However, before he had completed the last word, his voice was cut off by the hail of bullets. I swallowed down the knot in my throat as I realized that this could easily be me. A strange tickling sensation in my stomach heralded the wave of nausea this sight provoked in me. I clamped my hand over my mouth and blanked my mind from the vision, lest the noise of my retching would give away my position. My mind tried to control the situation and overcome my emotions, but my body had broken out in a cold sweat from head to toe. I managed, thanks be to God, to control the nausea and not vomit.

Some of the other soldiers opened a few stretchers. While they did this, the soldier in command pulled his pistol and went over to the four bodies. Pointing the muzzle at the back of each head, he administered the coup de grace. The bodies were placed on the stretchers, and dragged by the soldiers back to the same entrance from which they had emerged.

I stayed there in hiding, petrified. The silence was total. I might have been in shock, as I didn't even hear the sirens from Escalona's office any more. I don't know for how long I remained there—it might have been ten or fifteen minutes. My grip on the handle of the attaché case was unrelenting. I knew if I was caught at that moment, my destiny would be exactly the same as Fernando and his three friends.

The lights turned off, restoring the compound to pitch darkness. It started to sprinkle, which returned me to reality. I heard once more the sirens. I pulled myself together, rose from my hiding place, and looked around for a refuge, someplace where I could hide while I reorganized my escape from the compound. Not even a few minutes later, the general siren began to sound, alerting the entire compound beyond the complex around Escalona's office. I saw a squad of soldiers with dogs and powerful flashlights headed in my direction.

I ran toward the heavy equipment storage facility. When I got to the other side, I saw another squad of soldiers similarly equipped converging on my location. I looked toward the other side of the building, and saw a small parking area. I decided to cross the street and attempt to conceal myself inside that parking structure. When I finally reached the other side of the installation, dragging the heavy attaché with me, I kept running, sweat streaming profusely down my face, mixing with the rainwater. At that moment, I could hear in my head the echo of my uncle's words during my first month of training as a spy: "Never lose your calm. You have to be able to improvise in the most difficult and dangerous moments. No matter how difficult the situation seems to your mind, the only thing that can help you is if you can concentrate, reorganize your thoughts, and find an exit." But the image of the firing squad was still too fresh in my mind, especially the youngest one. When they received the deathblow shots, I could still remember in slow motion the pieces of brain and fragments of skull flying upward through the air. That horrible image was a nightmare burning in my brain; even as I tried to forget it, that vision kept running through my mind. I knew I wasn't going through a bad dream, that I was fully awake, and I had to watch my steps, or the pieces of brains and bones that fly into the air next would be mine.

    Huge goose bumps covered my body at the thought. For the first time, as I began to act as a spy, I realized the tremendous risk and danger involved in playing this game, with my very life as the primary stakes on the table. Right now, my life depended on how I reacted to defend myself and keep from getting caught. In the dark night the loud barking of the dogs could be heard from a great distance, mixing with the alarm sirens screaming through the compound. The noise was winding up my nerves even more tightly. I thought for a minute, "Those blasted sirens and dogs. Why don't they stop, once and for all?" The normal monotony of the military compound's nightly routine had been disrupted by my actions. I heard voices, and the powerful lights of the search lights started to get closer, as more instruments were turned on to circle the area, trying to find the audacious intruder or intruders in the darkness.

From different angles, I could see various groups of soldiers with flashlights and dogs looking everywhere. My training with both my uncle and the General had meticulously indicated to me three things are the most important in our business of intelligence and espionage: the first was whatever the circumstances, you do not let yourself get caught red-handed. If this happens, and you have no other alternative, you have to eat the evidence. I looked at that immense, heavy portfolio in my right hand, imagined the value of those documents, and rubbed my stomach with a very unhappy expression on my face. It made me nauseous to think of having to eat all that paper. The second and most important thing they taught me was that, even if they catch you red-handed, have in your mind prepared a good excuse before anything happens. Unfortunately, I didn't have a single excuse prepared; on either account, I was completely out of luck. The final one was that you deny to your death and never, under any circumstance, admit that you are a spy. Use any other motivation, but confessing to being a spy was going to result in your immediate death. So long as doubt exists in your enemy's mind, you will always have a hope that something unexpected can happen that will save you.

I looked down and saw the golden letters embroidered on the leather of the attaché that clearly spelled out the owner's name: "Commandante Doctor Ernesto Guevara." There were also, in small red letters beneath, the word "Che." I swallowed hard, as I heard my pursuers getting even closer. I looked towards the approaching commotion, glanced back down to the attaché, and came to a quick decision. Since I couldn't eat the evidence, I would hide it. I searched frantically for a piece of rope, but instead found a piece of wire near an armored tank. I quickly wrapped it around the attaché case and crawled under the tank. I looked around for a place to tie the bundle; between the chassis and the transmission, I found a space by the engine. I quickly crammed it into the nook and fastened it down. To be sure, I pulled and pushed on it sharply, to make sure it couldn't be easily dislodged. As I did this, a book fell out of one of the side compartments and hit me in the face. I tried to shove it back in, but it continued to slide out and fall. It looked like a campaign diary; the cover was too slick, and with the angle at which the case was tilted, it simply wouldn't hold. I thought I should untie the wire, take it down, stow the diary, and put things back at a different angle. However, the lights and sounds of dogs were now so close that they couldn't be more than fifty feet away from me. I abandoned the plan, unbuttoned my shirt, crammed the diary inside, and rebuttoned it. I patted my abdomen to make sure the book was secure. When I realized all was good, I rolled over in the grass, and crawled out on the opposite side from the approaching soldiers. I looked at the number of the tank before leaving: "2047." I made it a point to burn that number into my memory, so that I could find it again at a later date. I crouched between the tanks to remain unseen and tried to put some distance between myself and the soldiers. They appeared to be concentrating more in that area—

probably because the potential refuge for someone to remain hidden in between the vehicles and inside the various parking structures.

In my rush to get out of there, I tripped on something on the floor and lost my balance. I had to brace myself with my hands against the ground, so that I didn't fall flat on my face. I looked down, and saw that I had tripped on the handle of a metal door. There was a large padlock on the door, but it was extremely corroded with rust. I checked the handle, trying to avoid making any noise. The soldiers were taking their time to look both under the vehicles as well as inside them. Because the clearance of the chassis for the vehicles were so high, they didn't crouch all the way down to the ground, but only stooped about half-way to shine their lights underneath. Most of their searching was concentrated on each vehicle's interior.

To my surprise, the rust had completely eaten through the lock, and the door was open. It had only appeared to still be locked. I had no idea where this door led to, but I saw it as the gateway to Heaven. I could hide there, and no matter where it led, I would be in a better place than where I was currently. I carefully kept the lock in place as I slowly closed the door behind me. It was completely pitch-black inside. I felt around with my feet until I found the first rung of a metal ladder. Holding myself steady as the best I could, I felt around my pockets and pulled out my pen with multiple uses that my uncle had given to me. This pen concealed a camera, a knife, and at the bottom, a powerful, focused blue light. I turned the light on and took a few seconds to try and figure out where I was. The ladder didn't go down very far, only about twenty-five feet or so. I climbed down. When I finally reached the bottom, I saw a tunnel with a lit outline of a door that had a porthole about fifty feet away. The light came from whatever lay beyond the door, and I surmised that the porthole must have a curtain in front of it, as the light coming through there was dimmer than the light coming around the edges of the door.

The tunnel was full of oxygen tanks, wheelchairs, IV stands—it looked like the hallway in a hospital. I walked to the end of the corridor with extreme caution. I could actually hear my heart beating with jackhammer force. I put my hand on my chest over my heart, as if I could try to stop it, out of fear that someone else could hear the drumming beat. My right hand was sweating as I placed it on the .38 Special pistol Fidel had presented to me almost a year before. My conscience was bothering me. I felt bad as I walked through that door, thinking, I'm only thirteen years old, and I have great moral principles taught to me by my parents to not steal, to not lie, to deal straight and never be a hypocrite, and here I've been doing the exact opposite for almost the last year and half after my training as a spy. No matter how much I could justify what I was doing in my mind, my uncle and the General had taught me a thousand times to fight fire with fire. At the same time, I could also hear the very loud voice of my father inside my head, from when I was only eight or nine years old saying, "If a dog bites you, and you get on the floor and bite him back, you've just come to be a worse dog."

In the midst of all these contradictory thoughts, the entire corridor was illuminated by the Freon lights turning on when I was only a few feet from the door. I jumped behind the oxygen tanks and pulled my pistol out, ready to defend my life. To avoid making noise, I slowly brought the slide back to chamber a single round in the pistol. The door opened completely, and a woman dressed as a nurse appeared. She paused to latch the door open with her foot, which gave me more time to conceal myself further behind one of the room divider curtains that were stored against the wall behind the tanks. She was dressed in full surgical scrubs and was still masked and gloved. She passed by me to the IV racks and wheeled two, one in front of her and one behind, and went back through the door. She unsecured the door and closed it behind her.

I didn't move for a few minutes, and waited for the lights to turn off once more. I moved out of my hiding place, and crept over to the porthole. Though it had a nylon curtain in front of it, it was very thin, and with the pitch blackness behind me, I could see through it perfectly. The first thing I saw repulsed me to the pit of my stomach.

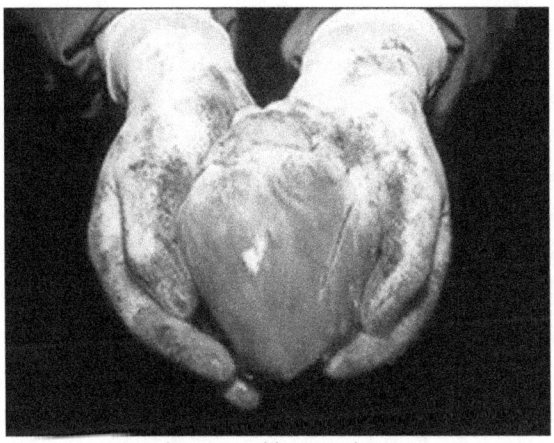

A harvested human heart

Dr. Julio Antonio del Marmol

Chapter 2: Human Organs on Demand

On the other side of the room, a man dressed completely in surgical scrubs worked under huge surgical lamps on a completely naked body. With a surgical saw, he was cutting into the pectoral cavity of the young, long-haired man who had just been executed. There were other gurneys with the bodies of the other men on them. I could see that the rest of the plasma was being drained from the bodies while he worked on the one corpse, while another nurse washed the bodies with a scrub brush. To clean the bodies, she was using a spray hose like the ones used in stores to clean vegetables.

The man finished cutting open the chest cavity and used an expander to hold open the chest. He cranked the handle on the expander as one works the jack to change a tire. The sound of bone cracking as the expander did its work grated on my nerves, and my face pinched tight as I could almost feel it being done to my own chest. As soon as he had enough room to work, he began to cut free the internal organs, passing them to a nurse who then placed them in dry ice storage containers. They emptied the body like one would empty a grocery bag, placing the organs in different containers.

At the other end of the surgical room, two men were similarly dressed, but all in white and with machine guns slung from their necks. They brought in four men in handcuffs and leg irons, dressed in green hospital gowns. They were the same kind of gowns the men I had previously seen executed dressed in. It was clearly a continual process, like some kind of gruesome factory. As they crossed through the divider curtains, they pressed a button and opened a steel door. The condemned men were handed off to another group of waiting soldiers, and the door closed, like some macabre garage door. The men in white came back inside, and disappeared through another door.

I couldn't understand why they would dress men about to be executed like they were in a hospital. I felt depressed and sympathetic to the poor wretches who would shortly be returned, only to lie on those cold stainless steel tables. We soon heard the gunshots, and then I saw the door open again. The bodies were brought back in, undressed, and placed on the gurneys in the place of the already processed corpses, and then rendered into spare parts, like meat in some butcher's shop or a meat packing plant for human organs. I broke out into a cold sweat, and my stomach started to churn as I thought about the horror perpetuated by these people. I turned around and started to walk away from that sinister place. At this point, I had two choices: get out of there the same way I came in, through the door, or come out of there in pieces through the dissecting room. My decision was very abrupt and quick—the back door I had come in through. It seemed much better to me at that point to take my chances with the soldiers.

I got back to the ladder and climbed up. With great caution, I opened the door slowly to see at least whether anyone was standing around or in front of the door. Gradually, I opened it further and further so that I could get a greater view of the surroundings. The first thing I heard was the sound of horse hoof beats on pavement and the familiar jangle of the bell of the trash man. I never felt so happy to see, a short distance away, Don Pascual's wagon stopped by the Recruit's Mess. My heart accelerated as I saw my ticket out of there. I thought to myself, God has given me an exit! I rushed to get out of that underground lab of spare parts that would please Dr. Frankenstein. Rapidly, I looked for tank number 2047. I located it right away, threw myself under the tank, untied the wire, removed the diary from under my shirt, and replaced it inside the attaché case.

I ran across the street to where Don Pascual's wagon was stopped, not far away, directly underneath a light pole. With extreme care, I checked the area. I heard the voices of the soldiers on the other side of the compound, but all was quiet in the immediate vicinity. Finally, I reached the wagon. I heard the sound of soldiers' voices coming out of the mess hall. I rushed to the other side of the wagon, hugged the side, and opened the tarp. I dropped the case inside, and, placing my foot on the spoke of one of the wheels, and slid into the stinking garbage. The soldiers crossed very close by, smoking and talking. Through one of the many holes in the tarp, I saw one of them stop by the wagon, put his foot on the same wheel I had just used to jump into the wagon, and used it to tie his boot. I stayed absolutely still; considering my current location, holding my breath was already a given. I watched them leave with the greatest of pleasure, throwing prayers of thanks to God upwards to Heaven. After they disappeared, I immediately buried the case in one of the corners under the trash near the front of the wagon. The garbage smelled so bad that it was almost intolerable. I got my handkerchief, folded it into a triangle as an improvised muzzle to cover my nose and mouth, and tied it behind my neck. I shifted the rubbish around and tried to get as comfortable as possible. I had to shift a couple of old cans out of my way that I had accidentally sat on, and settled in to wait. In the time I waited, I prayed to Jesus and God the Father that everything would go okay and that I could get out of the military camp in one piece.

I didn't have to wait too long. A few minutes later, I heard voices. I looked through one of the holes, and saw Don Pascual and Tobito coming out with the pails of *sarcocho* and garbage. I tried to cover myself the best I could in refuse in one of the corners, remaining as still and quiet as I could. Don Pascual opened one of the corners of the tarp and started to empty the contents into one of the tanks. On the other side, Tobito did the same. After they did that, they began to empty the trash from the other containers. Don Pascual said to his son, "You better hide that melon, because you know they don't allow us to take food from here. It's extremely possible that they will check us on the way out. These guards that are there today in the entry gate, they are dogs—very strict. I hope they already relieved them, and that there are different ones. If not, they will check even our asses and make us lose a lot of time. They'll use those metal rods with the sharp points to search the wagon, and then we'll have to go to one side while they conduct a secondary search. And that will be the entire night shot."

My face grew long, and I swallowed nervously. If that happened, it wasn't going to be as easy to get out of there as I had thought. I had no other choice, however; if the soldiers checked the wagon meticulously, they would find me. This completely changed my plans, and I began to think in a supersonic way. I couldn't get out of the wagon; it was too late for that. They would see me and be able to identify me. The only thing that I could think of was the worst nightmare anyone could ever conceive of: I had to get into one of the tanks of *sarcocho*. I shook my head and silently asked God why He was making it so difficult for me. But at least I had a choice. In the same corner, I saw that Tobito had hidden his melon in exactly the same spot I had concealed Guevara's case. I thought to myself that if they searched there, they would get two thieves for the price of one. I saw him try to disguise it by placing some trash on top. From my hiding place, I smiled, because of the four corners of the wagon, he had to choose the same one I had concealed my own treasure. I figured that, if the guards found the melon they might not search too deeply and so not find the case. I heard dogs barking once more, and looked out of the hole. In the light of the streets, I saw a group of soldiers—this time, they were the ones looking for me. They were coming in our direction.

I heard Don Pascual say, "Let's get the hell out of here as soon as possible. I don't think something is right in this place today. First the sirens and the movement of soldiers everywhere, now a group of soldiers with dogs. It's not a good day to be here." He clicked his tongue at the horses and started the wagon in motion. As soon as it started to move, I wormed my way into one of the tanks in the middle. I looked through the trash and found pieces of toilet paper. I managed to find enough clean pieces from the edges of the feces-stained toilet paper to create plugs for my nose. I made sure to keep my handkerchief in place, no matter what. I wasn't going to submerge myself the entire way; my plan was to simply breathe in the air space between the level of the disgusting fluid and the cover.

I finally managed to get inside the tank of *sarcocho*. It was pasty and smelled like diarrhea. I pulled the cover on top of me, and trusted to God to get me out alive. We were perhaps half a kilometer from the entry, and I thought to myself that it wouldn't be that bad, that I wouldn't be in there for too long. Shortly after, I heard Don Pascual slow the horses down, and the wagon finally stopped. In a friendly voice, I heard him say, "Good evening, *compañeros*.[2]

Several voices replied to his greeting with condescension. The guards began to unwrap the tarp as I watched through a small crack I created by holding the cover up slightly, giving me a minute field of view between the lip of the tank and the lower edge of the cap. As two of the four guards on the other side started to stab the metal pole, thrusting the sharp point deep into the trash, the other two climbed into the wagon and began to remove the covers of the *sarcocho* tanks. As soon as I saw the hand coming towards my cover, I took a deep breath and dove into the tank. The light changed as the lid was taken off. I felt a cramp in my left side. I shook, but

---

2 *Compañeros* is the Spanish word for "comrades."

otherwise did nothing. Almost immediately I felt the same sensation in my left arm and ribs. Everything went by so fast that I couldn't even think of anything, and the light disappeared as the cover was replaced. I continued to hold my breath and remain submerged, and could feel the jarring of the wagon as the soldiers climbed out of the wagon. I could no longer hold my breath, and slowly emerged. Much to my relief, I felt my head brush against the cover—it was indeed in place, and I could breathe again, even in such a stench. I listened to the voice of Don Pascual bidding the soldiers farewell. I had to unplug my ears from the leftover rice, beans, and other goop. In spite of my improvised nose plugs, I had to do the same to clear my nose of residual muck. I maintained my position in the tank until I could see complete darkness and feel the wagon accelerate to its full speed. At that point, I knew we were away from the military compound and on the main road through town. Only then could I feel safe enough to slide out of the tank, soaking wet with that pestilent liquid and clean myself as best I could with the trash, which seemed luxurious after the stuff I in which had just been immersed.

    I felt an extremely painful cramp in my side, and began to massage the muscle, assuming that my position had caused my leg to fall asleep. The military compound was only about four or five miles from the little town of Pinar del Rio. The main highway connected Pinar del Rio with the capital in Havana. There was a bridge over the River Guama. I noticed the wagon began to slow down, and heard Don Pascual order the horses to stop. I opened the tarp a little bit, and saw a line of cars creating a checkpoint into and out of the city that had not been there before.

There were thorough checks of all vehicles going on. I was not about to endure the tank again, so I quickly through the trash, felt around with my hands underneath the watermelon to find the portfolio, and pulled it out. I slid the case outside the wagon on the side by the curb and let it fall to the ground. I held on to the edge of the wagon, and stood in preparation to jump. Extreme pain shot through my left arm, almost causing me to fall to the ground, since I could not hold on. I grabbed on with my right arm to steady myself. The wagon by now had stopped, and I managed to climb out. I staggered back to where I had dropped my prize along the shoulder of the road, and began to climb down the ravine to the river. When I bent over to pick up the case, another pain checked me, this time in my ribs. Once I got to the bushes near the river bank, I pulled out my flashlight and raised my shirt. I could see in my left side a hole that bled profusely. I sat down on the ground, took off my shirt, and used my knife to cut away one of the sleeves at the seam. I improvised a bandage to wrap around my wound and stabilize my ribs. Then I pulled down my pants to see the same kind of hole in my left leg, also bleeding badly. I cut off one of my pants legs for another bandage and tied it as tight as I could to attempt to staunch the bleeding. I proceeded to inspect my arm to corroborate that I indeed had a third wound. I realized that I had been stabbed during the search of the *sarcocho* tank. Fortunately, I thought, it hadn't hit any of my bones or he would have discovered me. In my rush of adrenaline, I probably didn't even feel the stab of the dagger point of those rods. That triple stab had, instead, in my tense and frightened state, had felt more like someone had hit me with a hypodermic needle.

I climbed down the ravine with great difficulty, clinging to the bushes for support, until I got to the riverbank. I removed all of my clothes, entered the water, and tried to wash my body as best I could. I then washed my clothes to the best of my ability, to try and remove that terrible odor that I was sure was impregnated in my very brain. The more I rinsed the clothes, the more I seemed to smell the stink. Evidently, water was not sufficient—that smell was going to require strong detergent, which I did not have at that moment. I squeezed the water out of my clothes the best I could, and pulled on the still wet garments: my shirt with one sleeve and my pants missing half a leg. I walked for a while along the riverbank and all of the detritus lining the ground. Once I found what I thought to be a strategic place, I used my knife to try to dig a hole deep enough to hide the attaché case. I tried working at this for a while, but the rocks and sunbaked dirt made it very difficult. It could also have been my body was weakened from blood loss, reacting in an adverse way, like a motor sending a signal that it is running out of gas as the pistons begin to misfire. I had a terrible migraine and a very cold sweat rolled all over my body. Once again, I tried to dig that hole. With the sleeve I had left, I tried to mop the sweat off of my face, only to have my face get soaked immediately again with sweat. It got into my eyes, making it difficult to see. Like I was in a frenzy, I didn't stop. I knew at any minute I could lose consciousness, and the only thing that was compromising me at that moment was that attaché case. If only I could hide it and walk to the highway, or even if I passed out still on the riverbank, I could always create a story. More importantly, I would then be able to come back later and retrieve it without wasting all the effort I was currently taking. The worst was past; I had gotten it away from the military compound.

That idea kept pushing me to get that hole dug so that I could hide it, and prevent someone from taking it away from me. Like in a nightmare, my arm kept getting heavier and slower, like it didn't want to respond. The pain in my side began to throb. I opened my bandage for a few minutes, and it was absolutely soaked in blood. The blood was clearly not coagulating like it should. I had to stop that blood loss. I ripped one of the cargo pockets off of my pants, and folded it to make a stronger bandage to try and stop the blood flow. After I finished, I began to dig again, but my head began to spin with dizziness. First I looked far off, and saw a light moving along the riverbank, coming in my direction. It was very similar to the flashlights used by the soldiers back in the military compound, and I started to get a really bad feeling. My headache grew stronger, and I rushed to hide that briefcase. I began to think the hole I was digging was getting smaller, or the case was getting bigger. In a final effort to hide it, I left it lying there and began to simply cover it with any loose sand I could find nearby. I could hear not too far away what sounded like a helicopter along the riverbank, approaching in my direction. It still wasn't close, but I could see the searchlights as well as hear the motor. The noise got stronger as it grew closer. In my bemused state, it seemed like it was over me. Finally, the powerful flashlights of the soldiers were only a few feet from me. A tall, powerfully-muscled black man with long dreadlocks and a teenaged boy only a few years older than me approached.

The man put the flashlight in my face and said in surprise, "What the hell are you doing here at this time of night, kid?" His voice came to me like it was in slow motion. He pointed the flashlight at the attaché case, and his eyes bugged out as he read the golden letters on it. He looked up, saw the approaching helicopter, and immediately snapped off the flashlight, like he had been bitten by snake. He dropped it on the ground, grabbed the kid, and said, "Get down! Now!" He pulled his friend down into the snarl of dead wood. "Don't move. No one move!"

The helicopter was moving right along the river itself, while we were further up in the ravine. The lights were never projected that far up—clearly, they were only searching the river and the immediate riverbank. After a few minutes, it had gone right by us. I pointed to the case and tried to speak. In my mind, I was going to tell him that I worked for Che, but the words simply wouldn't come out. It was like I had a paralysis in my vocal cords which kept me from being able to say anything.

Once the helicopter had left, in his slow motion voice, the man said to the kid, "Come on, help me. We should drag him to the wagon where we have the wood. This kid is wounded really badly." The boy helped him sling me over the man's shoulders like a sack of potatoes. "Take that bag," he said to the boy. That was the last thing I heard with any clarity. His voice seemed to come from a distance, until it was lost. From then on, I could only hear pieces, like the tide coming in and out.

They put me in the wagon, and off and on I heard the noise of the wheels of the wagon. The boy sat by me while the man drove. They turned onto a dirt road under the bridge with their wagon full of drift wood. They took me to an old, wooden house not too far away from the river. I heard the voices of the two of them and a woman like a short-wave radio signal fading in and out. They took me out of the wagon and took me inside the cabin. I could not see their faces clearly; my vision was like a fun house hall of mirrors, all distorted in odd ways. The light from a small oil lamp in that humble cabin was reflected on the ceiling made of palm tree fronds. In my uncertain vision, the reflection created an illusion of the palm fronds dancing along the ceiling like a Dance of the Dead.

A black, heavyset lady wearing a turban, her smiling, oily facing shining in the lamplight, gently placed one of her arms behind my neck and lifted me up. She put an aluminum cup to my lips. "Drink this, my boy," she said in a caring voice, "this will make you better." After I drank that tart liquor, she lowered my head back down onto the bed, and I must have either fallen asleep or passed out.

Many hours must have passed, I started to have a strange and bizarre nightmare, maybe related with my birth, as my mother and Majito had told me many times over the years. I was completely naked and covered in blood and the goopy liquid from the placenta, as I was just recently born. But strangely, I was the same size I was at the age of thirteen. Kids, men, and women from the black race dressed in native clothing were dancing to very exotic African music on bongos all the way around me, smiling and happy. Three young, beautiful mulattas, almost naked, were cleaning up the placenta fluid from my body with banana leaves and palm tree fronds. They opened glazed containers which held what looked like water with rose petals. An ancient lady with an extremely wrinkled face, all dressed in white with a matching turban came close to me, and with a white linen blanket covered my body. The beautiful mulattas that had previously bathed me started to dry me with the blanket. The music continued and the huge multicolored fire that they were dancing around blazed cheerfully. Everybody looked very happy, laughing, and the sound of the bongos grew increasingly louder.

Suddenly a man appeared, coming from the sky, screaming like he was coming out of Hell itself. Until that moment, everything was in perfect harmony, and everybody was showing great joy, celebrating what looked like my birth. But after that figure appeared, the music stopped and every person that had been dancing around that beautiful fire halted, their faces bearing expressions of extreme terror. The man pulled a sickle out of a sack over his shoulder. In slow motion, he dropped the sack to the floor, and all the people present watched the sack until it hit the ground, spewing up dust from the impact. The man was dressed all in black and wore a red hood. Until that moment, the face of the man could not be seen, as it had been covered by the hood and the shadows. As he raised the sickle into the air and began to decapitate people, the hood fell away and I could clearly see his face by the light of the fire: it was the face of Che.

He was laughing demonically like a man possessed. He was enjoying his executions, cleaving into men, women, and children like a farmer harvesting corn. I was completely petrified. I tried to get up to defend myself from the altar built of wood and dead leaves on which I was lying. I felt like I had been tied, and I realized I had been tied down by umbilical cords. Everybody was screaming and trying to get away from the scene. My heart was pounding ever harder as I thought I was going to die. Che finally got to my side and looked into my eyes, his own blazing with hatred. He screamed at me, "Shitty traitor!" He raised the sickle high as I looked up at him in speechless terror.

I thought that these were my last moments; but from behind Che, a hand with a very sharp machete cut off the arm holding the sickle at the elbow. His hand fell to the ground, still gripping the weapon, streams of blood spurting out of his elbow. A scream of pain broke the silence of the night. The silhouette behind him that bore the machete stood forth into the light from the fire. It was the blessed and beautiful face of the black lady, Majito, my good nanny. She was dressed all in white with a black hood. She screamed at him, "How dare you call my boy a traitor? The only traitor here is you! You have stolen our freedom, our harmony, our love, and you bring with you only death and hate with your atheist ideas and destroy the beautiful Paradise of our island. You converted it into an Inferno."

The diabolical being that resembled Che had fallen down to his knees, and he tried to take his shirt off. Once he got it off, he wrapped it over the stump of his arm, trying to stop the bleeding. He tried to hold himself with the other arm to prevent himself from falling over. Looking from the ground to Majito, he screamed, "You nigger Imperialist! You will die, like all my enemies."

Majito raised the machete high and yelled in a deep voice that sounded nothing like her own, but sounded more like the echo of a supreme being that made me shake in ecstasy, "In the name of all the gods of the world, Yemaya, Chango, Elegua! From heaven and joy and from the gods' Supreme Architect of the Universe, death to this demon! Take him back to the Inferno he came from and where he belongs, and let him take with him our suffering, our hate, and death." The infernal being tried to stand up. Once he was almost fully standing, the machete started to do its work. With precision like a surgeon, first his other arm came off, flying to lie by its mate. With another swipe, she took off his head. The voice of Majito could be heard again as an echo. "Damn you—die! Die! Die!" The headless, armless corpse still made a couple of steps forward. Majito grabbed a bottle of rum and started splashing the liquid on the body in an X pattern. She grabbed a brand out of the fire, flipped it onto Che's body, and lit it on fire. The burning cadaver fell by my altar, which then started to catch on fire itself. I struggled in vain to free myself. I could see Majito try to reach me to get me out of there, but she was too far away. I could see her weeping at the sight of me going up in flames, as well. I screamed three times from the depth of my lungs, "NO!!!!!!" I woke up to find the black lady, the black man, and the boy all holding me down to my bed. Finally, they pulled me down. The lady tried to put a towel on my head that smelled like alcohol.

    She said to the man, "He has a very high fever. I hope he doesn't die." She leaned over me and tried to comfort me, saying, "Drink this. You will be fine." She put the aluminum cup to my lips. Even though the liquid was so tart, I drank it thirstily. She lay me back in my bed. The position they had me in to drink aggravated the pain in my ribs, and so she helped shift my position, elevating me slightly. As she raised me up, I could see from the expression she gave to the man that she didn't think I was going to make it. I groggily relaxed back onto the bed and drowsed. I remembered for many years afterward with unbelievable clarity that strange nightmare.

Many years later for reasons I cannot explain, a part of that nightmare became a strange reality when Che tried to convert Bolivia into another communist state like Cuba. After his capture and execution for his actions in that country, a man of high position in the Bolivian government, who was also a double agent for us, cut off the corpse's arms and brought them back to Cuba along with Che's campaign diary. He needed the arms to confirm to the Castro brothers that the diary he was giving them did indeed belong to Guevara. This extraordinary plot completely fooled Fidel; in the heat of the moment, they did not even bother to read the diary to ascertain its contents. The Communist Party rushed to establish small printing presses in the capital of the island to distribute free copies of Che's diary to the general population along with a red beret. This last was a symbolic gesture in opposition to the Green Berets of the United States Army, who were responsible for the death of so many of Che's comrades in Bolivia. In the midst of this euphoric hype, a member of the Communist Party took a break to read the diary, only to realize the huge political fiasco the document represented. He discovered that Che openly blamed the failure of the Bolivian adventure on the Bolivian Communist Party, the syndicated unions and their peasants, as well as the lack of resources promised by Fidel and his brother when Guevara left the island—resources that never arrived. Che mocked Castro very openly in his diary because Fidel, in one of his big speeches on the Plaza de la Revolución in Havana, announced that he was completely in contact with Che and his international guerillas, assuring the Cuban people that Che and his comrades had all his support in their international fight to free the people of the world. Che called this a telepathic miracle, because there had been no contact since Guevara had left Cuba months ago. For this, among other reasons, the diary disappeared from the public view so completely that no matter how much money was offered, one could not find it anywhere. It had been classified as a seditious document that could be used as propaganda against the communist regime.

Many weeks must have gone by; I could not be certain, as I spent it fading in and out of consciousness. The only reason I had any idea of how much time had passed was that, at the beginning of my convalescence in that rustic cabin, I could see through my window a huge tree that was part of the scenery outside. The big tree had grown so tall that it practically covered the cabin, giving partial shade to the entire house in the small family farm. On one of the branches I observed a couple of small hummingbirds making their nest, growing daily from small branches and leaves to a completed nest. The high fever combined with the infection my body was fighting rendered me unconscious when I wasn't sleeping half of the time. In my lucid moments, though, the first thing I always saw when I opened my eyes was the progress those small birds had made in building their nest. I even noticed, when it was completed, how the female laid her eggs and, later on, how she stayed in the nest incubating her clutch. Finally, one day, I saw four tiny heads popping out of the nest as she flew back and forth, bringing food to the chicks. From these details, I could estimate the amount of time I had lain ill in that bed. Once in a while, I vaguely heard voices having conversations, a man and a woman speaking to each other. The woman's voice belonged to the lady who had been spoon feeding me soup and taking my temperature as well as taking care of my daily hygienic needs. Later on, as I grew stronger, she assisted me in my toilet, an assistance I took mechanically with little or no memory of what I was doing.

Early one evening towards twilight, I heard their voices arguing. I could definitely tell I was getting better, as I could hear and put together complete conversations. The lady said, "Marcel, I just came back from town. I found my friend, Majito, in the line at the butcher's shop. They are really concerned and scared for this boy. The authorities are looking everywhere in town, and have issued a national bulletin. They assume that this boy has been kidnapped. Everyone believes that counterrevolutionaries have taken him and will probably kill him as an example to the other kids who don't want to join the communist organizations and military service. She begged me and asked if I knew anything about the whereabouts of this boy. She raised him and loves him like a son."

Her husband replied, "What did you tell her about the situation?"

"Nothing—what do you think? Everybody knows in this town that you sympathized with the dictator, Batista. I prayed to God all the way here that they don't find him in our house. We'll all be shot if they do, including our boy, Tite."

Marcel tried to calm her down. "Don't get hysterical, calm down. Fraya, this night we will move him to the *boio*[3]

---

3 A subterranean shelter

under the barn. I assure you, nobody will ever find him in there."

Fraya started to cry. In between sobs, she said, "God protect us, Marcel. I think the best thing is you tell the authorities that you found him by the riverbank, wounded, and we brought him here to help him. That's only the truth—all we've been doing is helping him and try to make him better."

Marcel replied irritatedly, "For God's sake, Fraya! The truth? How many times do I have to tell you? Do you remember what that lady, Maruca, did to Ruben? Do you remember what we watched in the middle of the street, how she cut his tongue out and accused our friend as being a *chivato*? You and I know better than anyone that it wasn't true, because he came to our home, arguing with me in defense of the Rebels. The truth doesn't work with these people, especially when everyone knows that I supported the Dictator."

She replied, "What if he dies in our home? What a major problem, Marcel!"

"Don't even say those things, woman! Don't bring bad karma. This boy is very strong, and he will be well very soon."

From my bed, I felt so sorry at that moment, as full understanding of the situation in which I had put those people, and I was consumed with guilt. I tried to raise myself out of the bed. Laboriously, I stood up and searched around in the growing darkness for my clothes. I began to dress myself, and had just gotten my pants on before in my weakness I tripped against the table on which Fraya had all the aluminum cups she had been feeding and medicating me with. With a loud clatter, they all fell to the ground, which attracted their attention. They rushed into my room to see what had happened to me. Half-naked on the floor, I tried to get back to my feet, my shirt in my hands and pants half-way put on. They each grabbed me by an arm and carefully lowered me back onto my bed.

"I just want to go home," I said weakly. "Don't worry, I can walk to my house. I don't want to create any more problems for you."

Marcel shook his head reproachfully at Fraya, who felt very bad. "No," she said, "you're still very weak, and you can't walk that distance to your house. It's a long way from here. I'm sorry if you heard our argument, but don't worry—we will put you in a safe place in a little while. Probably in a few days or a week, you'll be able to walk home by yourself."

Marcel gave me a big smile, showing his brilliant, white teeth. "You see? I told you, Fraya. This kid is very strong. Very soon, he will be able to go back to his family. He won't tell a single word to anyone that he's been here with us all this time. Is that not true, my boy?" he finished in a loving voice.

I looked straight into his eyes and said, "*Claro, chico. Desde luego, señor*[4]. You don't have anything to worry about. I will never say to anyone where I've been."

"Thank you, my boy," the big man said with gratitude.

Fraya, overwhelmed with emotion, embraced me and gave me a kiss. "Thank you."

"I am the one who has to thank you, all you guys," I said. "You put yourselves in danger to take care of me for the past few days like a member of your family."

---

4 "Of course, sir."

Marcel said, "It's lot more than a few days."

Fraya said, "OK, OK, OK! You shouldn't talk that much. You're still very weak. Save your energy; we'll need it in a while to transport you to a safe place. All the police, the army, and everybody else is looking for you everywhere. We don't want them to find you here, under any circumstance, that is for sure!"

I held her by the arm and asked, "The attaché case—where is it?" I began to try to rise again from the bed. "I have to go and get it. It's possible it's still there by the riverbank!"

She looked at me in surprise. I could tell she didn't know what I was talking about, and she shook her head in perplexity. Marcel held me gently by the shoulder and tried to calm me down. "Don't worry about it, kid. It's in a very secure place."

I moved my hand from her to Marcel. "Be extremely careful, because if they find me here, I can tell them a story that will save you. If they find that portfolio, we're all dead."

The good old black woman looked back and forth between us, her mouth half open in utter incredulity. She threw a recriminatory glance at Marcel. "What did you do this time? Why don't I know anything about what this boy is talking about?"

"Woman," Marcel said, "pick up all these cups. I'll explain it to you later. Do you want to start another argument in front of our guest?"

I looked at them, and he glanced at me. We remained absolutely silent, and I realized that he hadn't spoken a word about the treasure he had found me trying to bury. Evidently, I had not only brought them a headache politically, but now was the heart of a domestic rift. Marcel must have realized how dangerous it would be for him to have that case in his possession, didn't even mention it to her, and put it in a secure hiding place. Obviously, they knew me as the Little Commander in town; he evidently knew for a fact that I didn't have any business to be in the possession of something so clearly the personal possession of Che Guevara's. He knew they were looking for me, but they had no reason why—he had only been thinking of being the Good Samaritan and helping a young boy who obviously needed aid. Even though he knew it would put his family in danger, he chose to do the right thing, and bring me home in an attempt to heal me. I thought I definitely was feeling better, as I felt a strong sense of remorse, sympathy, and gratitude, that despite the fear and confusion that man must have in his head, he didn't betray me by turning me over to the authorities. That told me what kind of decent human being this man is. On the other hand, he might have thought that if he went to the authorities, he might get accused based on his past as being the one who inflicted on me my injuries. He had, I could tell, decided to do what he thought was best for everyone involved.

In the early morning hours, I heard the noise of trucks and voices coming from not too far away. Still half asleep, I looked out my window. In the darkness of the room in which I lay, I couldn't find it. Where there once was a window, there was now a wall. In my semi-awake state, I came to the conclusion that I was no longer in the same room. I must have been moved to a different place. In a flash, I had a vague memory of the couple transporting me to their place under the barn. I could hear voices upstairs and a noise like the door was being opened. I jumped back into bed. I heard footsteps on the flooring above my head, and froze in my bed, scarcely even daring to breathe. Pieces of dust and hay sifted through the cracks in the floor and fell down onto my face. I didn't even move my hand to brush the stuff away. After a few minutes, I could hear a man's voice.

"It's all clear in here. It's only junk and fodder for the animals," it said.

I could hear others still moving things around as they searched the barn. Finally, after they were certain that there was nothing in the barn, and I could hear them walk out of the barn and the squealing of the rusty hinges on the old barn's doors. Everything remained silent. I sighed deeply in relief, still taking care not to make any noise. It had flashed through my mind that I could be discovered there.

The sun started to come out and shone through a tiny window high above the floor under which I was concealed. It was an unglazed window with a chain link grating covering it. By this light, I could see across the room from me, right by the wall, was Che's portfolio. I jumped out of bed and hugged it to me in joy. "Yes!" I said quietly in exuberance. "Yes!" I felt a great relief, as this was proof that I hadn't endured everything I had gone through in vain. I had the fruit of my labor safe in my hands. My happiness vanished, and the exuberant expression faded as I thought about what would happen if the soldiers found me there. This was a double-whammy: me and the portfolio in the same room. There was no way I would be able to get out of that one. I thought of Marcel with gratitude, because he chose the right place to hide us both.

I heard a voice behind me stuttering. I jumped and whirled around in surprise. "H-h-how d-d-do you f-f-feel t-t-today, J-j-julio Anton-n-nio?" In the shadows, sitting in an old rocking chair, was the same black teenager I had vaguely seen that night on the riverbank. He wore an old farmer's hat of woven palm leaves. "I am T-t-t-tite," he stammered his introduction.

I was surprised, since this is the first time I had seen him in this room—or since that night, for that matter. I replied, "I'm Julio Antonio." I could think of nothing else to say in the awkwardness of the moment.

This time, without a stutter, he replied, "I know who you are. I slept here last night, watching you and taking care of you."

"Thank you. Today, I feel a lot better." I noticed he had a blanket over his legs and a pillow behind his neck. I felt bad, thinking that this kid had slept all night in that old rocking chair. This motivated me to reassure him. "Really, I'm OK. You can go and get some sleep."

He smiled. "Everybody knows you, the Little Commander. Everyone knows you in the city and everywhere. I saw you once on television by Fidel, in the Plaza de la Revolución. You're a famous guy. Can I ask you a question?"

"Sure."

"Are you a communist?"

Without even thinking, I quickly replied with determination. "Communist? Never! A Revolutionary, yes." I realized that what I had just said wasn't really prudent, so I tried to correct it by saying, "Well—people try to say the Revolution is communist one, but I don't want to believe so." I remembered my uncle telling me to never reveal my true feelings to anyone, especially to a stranger. "I am a very good Revolutionary, and will be that way until I die, because I don't like dictators and injustice."

"W-w-well," he said, stuttering once more, "if you d-d-don't like d-d-dictators, in a very short t-t-t-time you will realize that we will have the b-b-biggest d-d-dictator in C-c-cuba. According to my f-f-folks, in the c-c-communist system the government takes the sons away from their relatives. That way, they can indoctrinate them with their ideological ideas. If this is true, then the d-d-democracy we b-b-built here is ended, because c-c-communism is the end of d-d-democracy."

We both sat in silence after he said those final words. I looked up and saw my uniform on a hanger. It was apparent that Fraya had been fixing it—my pants were no longer missing a leg, and my shirt had both sleeves. It looked cleaned and ironed as well. Tite noticed that I was looking at my uniform. "My mom fixed and cleaned it for you."

I asked him, "Why have you told me all this? About the communists? You know I'm a Commander in the military, and sympathize with the Revolution."

He smiled cynically, and tried to shift position in the chair, like he was suddenly uncomfortable. He pointed to the attaché case. Once more without a stutter, he said, "I don't think Che loaned his personal military portfolio to you. What are you doing with that?"

"I can explain," I said to attempt to interrupt him.

He raised his right arm to cut me off. "You don't have to explain anything to me. But I can tell you one thing very clearly: I've got a stutter for sure, I'm not too brilliant, and maybe to a point a little slow in my brains, but for sure, one thing I'm not. I'm not a *come mierda*—I'm not a fool. I can tell you for certain that the panicked expression I saw in your face when the soldiers were searching the barn upstairs that, while you may have an excuse in your head prepared in case they catch you with that thing. But I believe strongly that you prefer not to be in the position where you have to explain that to the soldiers." He stayed silent after that. I stared at him, trying to get the time to answer carefully what I was going to answer to him.

After several seconds, he broke the silence in an attempt to assure me that I had nothing to worry about from either him or his family. "A few months ago, we used to live in the city," he said, "in a nice place. After so many years of my father going to school, he became an English professor. In a single day, this Revolution kicked him out of his job, confiscated his house, and we had to move to this little shack where my grandparents used to live, before they left for Miami. Now we have to sell charcoal in order to make a living, the one thing my grandpa didn't want him to do and sent him to school to avoid. My parents want to send me out of the country, but I don't want to leave them behind. They've made arrangements with my grandparents to send me over there, because there are rumors that the government wants to implement mandatory military service. I will be of military age next year."

I thought it was kind of strange that he sometimes stuttered, at other times seemed to labor to finish the simplest of sentences, and yet would have moments of seemingly effortless speech. I had never encountered anyone like this before. I thought how lucky I was that when I was born, I had no physical impediment like this boy had. It would probably trouble him, I thought, for a long time. His friends probably made fun of him all his life growing up. It looked like he read my mind, for he then said, "I'm s-s-sorry for my s-s-stuttering. People s-s-sometimes d-d-don't understand what I s-s-say."

In an exaggerated way, I brought my hands up to my ears, and said, "What? What stutter? I've understood everything you've said to me."

He smiled happily. "Thank you."

"Thank you for what? I'm the one who has to thank you for staying here all night and watching over me." I asked him then something more important: "How long have I been here in your house?"

"Seven weeks. We thought you were going to die. We couldn't get rid of the fever. My parents were so scared that they didn't even sleep most of the time. They made such a big thing about your disappearance. Thank God you're getting better."

"Oh, my God! You're kidding me? Seven weeks?" I immediately thought of Majito, my poor mother, and the rest of my family. "Seven weeks," I mumbled, "almost two months."

Tite nodded his head affirmatively. "We don't have television, but my father and I delivered charcoal to one of their clients, and we watched your picture on the TV and said that the kidnappers hadn't yet asked for any ransom. That is why the government think that the Counterrevolutionaries are behind your kidnapping. They assumed you would be killed as a few others have been killed in the juvenile organizations, as an example to other kids."

"Oh, my God," I said. "This is getting more and more

serious. If they find me here, for sure you're all dead."

He could see I was very agitated and tried to calm me down. "Don't worry about it—they'll never find you here." He touched the wall near where he was sitting a metal door. "And even if they find you, you have an emergency exit here that will take you almost all the way to the riverbank. It comes out in a cave in the ravine where we found you. This farm in the eighteenth century used to be a clandestine moonshine distillery. When the ancestor of my grandpa emigrated here from Jamaica, they bought this property a long time ago. Nobody knows this subterranean place exists, because my parents don't want me to tell anyone about it."

I smiled. "Why are you telling me this, then, if it's supposed to be a family secret?"

"Well," he said with a smile, "I like you. Besides, we have mutual secrets. I don't believe you're going to tell this to anyone. This makes you a part of my family; I don't have any brothers and sisters, so you're now the little brother I never had."

"Don't worry about it—I'll never let anybody know about your secrets. From today onwards, you will be my brother, even though I have three. You will be the fourth."

"Are you hungry?"

"Yeah, I kind of am."

"Well, I'm going to go to the house, and will tell my mom that you're better and are hungry. She'll prepare some food for you, and it will be good for you. She's been worried about you, and had been feeding you on milk and chicken broth for the last two months."

"No wonder I'm so hungry!" I exclaimed. "My stomach is howling like a cat that's had its tail stepped on!"

He smiled and straightened his hat. He went to a crank and lowered the stairs from the ceiling. He climbed the stairs and disappeared.

The KGB badge of Ernesto "Che" Guevara

Cuba: The Truth, the Lies, and the Coverups

Chapter 3: KGB Agent 066614 (Che Guevara)

I started to do an inventory of the portfolio. After I got Che's personal diary, I took out first the documents that said in bold red letters "Top Secret Classified Operation", and then later schematics for different plans and projects. Then I took my camera from my uniform and started to work, taking pictures of everything I found in there. I also wrote notes about everything I could understand. Anything I couldn't understand, such as cities and names in Russia, I marked with a question mark to highlight my lack of understanding. At the bottom of the case, I found a black plastic bag with lots of money—not only Cuban pesos, but all kinds of international currencies, US dollars, Bolivian bolivianos, Venezuelan bolivars, Chinese yuan, Soviet rubles, as well as Central and South American currencies, even some from Europe. Another envelope contained many 8x10 headshots of different people, including John F. Kennedy, Richard M. Nixon, Hubert Humphrey, Adlai Stevenson, Nelson Rockefeller, Robert Kennedy, Nikita Khrushchev, and Commander Camilo Cienfuegos, as well as Camilo's lieutenant and pilot, Luciano Fariñas. I of course knew Camilo very well, owing to the several conversations we had enjoyed, and Luciano was one of his most trusted men. There were also several other individuals I did not recognize. What really caught my attention was a small envelope that was attached to these photos by several paperclips. It only contained two smaller 5x8 photographs that looked like the same man. However, when I turned them over, I saw that one had an X, another had an X with a circle around it. I flipped them back over, placed them side by side and looked at them closer. As I scrutinized them, I could tell that they were not the same individual. The photos had been taken at the same angle, and the facial structure was slightly different. The image marked with the circle had along the border an L marked in red ink. The other one had a Y inscribed on the border. To indicate my lack of understanding and to highlight the need for further analysis, I wrote a question mark on them.

    I made notes to make sense of it all later with my uncle and the General. I took from one of the compartments what looked like a normal man's wallet. To my surprise, it was completely empty, and had something like a police officer's badge affixed by a clip on one flap inside of it. It was shield shaped with a sword running through a red pentagonal star that bore the Soviet hammer and sickle. In gold lettering on a red scroll draped by the sides and beneath the star were VCK (translating the letters into common English equivalents), USSR, and KGB—I did not know what the first referred to. In white enamel and gold lettering above and to the left and right of the shield were Cyrillic lettering which spelled out the motto of the KGB: "Hot heart, cold head, clean hands." Underneath was the name: "Ernesto Guevara." There was also an ID card in a window on the other flap of the wallet, which read, "Doctor Ernesto Guevara de la Serna," and in large letters below, "KGB Special Agent 066614." All of the writing was in Russian Cyrillic, and I rubbed my chin, finally closing my mouth. I had been completely surprised for several seconds, like I had found the lost city of Atlantis or something equally momentous. My heart was beating rapidly, because I knew that my uncle and the General would never believe me that Guevara was a KGB agent, unless they saw this with their own eyes. I took several pictures in different positions. The plate had another inscription behind it, but my Russian was very limited, so I took a picture and made another question mark in my notes. After I had inventoried everything, I put it all back the way I had found it, just in case I found myself in the dilemma of having it in my possession; I could at least now say that I had discovered it somewhere.

I lay down on my bed and started to read the diary, anxious to know its contents. It was written in Spanish, so I was able to read most of it. However, there were notes and some writing in Russian and Egyptian that I was unable to understand. The more I read, the more urgently I felt the need to make contact with my uncle. My primary fear was that, were something to happen to me, that this incredibly valuable information would not reach the proper channels. The blueprints and plans I had seen were for national and international covert operations of a startlingly vast magnitude, things that would radically change a single country and or even history on a global scale. These were things that would achieve their political agenda, but in ways that no rational mind would ever believe. I wondered as I read why Che would carry all of this valuable information with him at all times. I smiled as I thought about how crazy all of this must be driving him. Almost an hour later, the clanking noise of the stairs caused me to jump out of bed. I grabbed my pistol and prepared myself for anything. My wounds were almost healed, and the scar tissue looked healthy; the only injury that still bothered me was the one in my ribs. It felt like an electrical shock when I moved so rapidly. I placed my hand against the wound, and it came away wet with blood. I looked down at my white t shirt, and could see a widening bloodstain in the cotton tissue. I immediately realized that I must have opened the wound when I jumped out of bed.

Tite came down the stairs with a tray of food. His eyes grew wide when he saw the bloodstain, and said, "You have to lie down immediately. Put your hands over that wound and put pressure on it. I'll go and get my mom." Without wasting a moment, he ran back up the stairs.

Before he left, I called out, "Please don't take too long. I'm very hungry, and the food you brought has an irresistible smell."

A few minutes later, he returned with Fraya. She lifted my shirt and looked at my side. She said, "You are a very lucky boy. If I hadn't been a nurse in the hospital for many years, until your friend Fidel kicked me out for sympathizing with Batista, I wouldn't be able to properly treat your wounds."

I hung my head, feeling sincerely ashamed. For nothing more than their political ideas, these two good people had been ousted from their respective livings and forced to live in utter poverty. For the first time, I was genuinely embarrassed by my association with Fidel and his elite group.

After she put some antiseptic and medical herbs into the wound, she dressed it with a clean bandage. She looked at me sadly and said, "This is the one injury that has given us the most trouble. Even though it's not too deep, this is a very delicate part of the body because it is so close to your stomach. There are many nerves and muscles there. But it's good that it opened, because the scar tissue on top concealed that the deeper laceration was still open. You've accumulated pus in your deep tissues, which explains the fever you've had. Now that this is open, we can let it drain and begin to truly heal. The last thing we want is for your body to get attacked by such an infection again. It will be more difficult for your body to fight it off the second time. Let's hope that in a few days now, you'll be able to walk around with no problem. The other two are almost healed now." She put her hand on my forehead to test my temperature. "You don't have a fever anymore, so you can eat solid foods and drink all that milk we brought to you." She pointed to the large aluminum jug on the tray Tite had brought down. "Your poor mom and Majito are both ready to die of sadness, thinking the worst has happened to you. I beg you, please, never tell her that you were here all this time. I don't think they would ever forgive me." Tears filled her eyes then. "God knows that I only kept my silence to protect my family," she added, biting her lip with remorse. She dried her tears with her sleeve.

I grabbed her hand and kissed it. I looked into her eyes and said, "This is a family secret. Nobody will ever know where I've been all these weeks. I swear in the name of God, I will never betray your trust."

She looked at me sadly, but smiled nonetheless. She touched my face and answered, "You don't have to swear, my boy. I know though you are young in years you are strong in heart. I know you will grow up to be a great man, one day. You come from a great family, and Majito is your mentor and has groomed you. She is a very great woman and friend of mine. That is very important, because your environment provides the examples which shape you as a person. It should not be important what political ideas one has, the greatest thing in life is to look at people as individuals with respect and love, because we are all brother and sisters. It shouldn't matter what the color of one's skin is or one's ideas, you should never hurt anyone."

I nodded in agreement. "My lady, you are absolutely right. The respect to others is the most important thing in life."

She smiled. "Well, I have to leave you alone so that you can eat in peace. If you need anything, tell Tite. I'll leave him in here for a while."

"Thank you very much, for everything. There's no need to leave Tite. I'm fine. Let him go and rest—he practically didn't sleep at all last night."

"Thank you, my boy. You're very considerate. I'll let him rest and come to check back on you later."

They both left, leaving me to eat all my food. I then returned to my reading of the diary. I started to take pictures of each page of that valuable document. He had over 600 pages filled, and it took me three days to read the entire thing. Finally, after I had reviewed all of the schematics, maps, and diagrams he had in it, I tried to memorize as much as I could, in case I got into a predicament which necessitated destroying it. I started to walk around the room two or three times a day to build my strength back up, while doing light calisthenics. Nearly a week later, I felt that I would be able to go back to my house and family. I told Tite that morning to tell Marcel and Fraya to come over, because I wanted to leave that day and wished to say goodbye to them.

We all gathered in my hiding place, and I reassured them once more that I would keep their secret, no matter what happened. I pleaded with them to maintain the same story, no matter what happened, so that they wouldn't contradict me. "No matter what anyone says to you," I advised them, "say nothing until they bring me to your face or you hear from me. Never admit to anything until you hear something from me directly." Once I felt we were all in mutual understanding of what I was saying, we said our farewells.

At the last minute, Fraya said, "Julio Antonio, forgive me, but I wanted to ask you something. You don't have to answer me, if you don't want to, but I won't see you for a long time, if ever again, and I want to keep this inside of me."

I replied, "Remember what we talked about before? We are bonding now as a family. You can ask me anything you want. Go ahead."

"When I was cleaning your wounds the first day you were here, I found an olive pit in the wound by your ribs. Then, to my surprise, some pieces of black beans and something that looked like a piece of chicken bone in your arm and leg." She raised her arms above her head and said, "I've asked myself many times these past weeks where the hell you got those wounds, and why you smelled like a dead animal when you arrived, and whether someone had done some voodoo on you. I washed your body for three days with alcohol, and still you stank."

I shook my head and smiled, understanding her curiosity entirely. "I was inside a *sarcocho* tank for almost half an hour. That's how I escaped from the military headquarters with that portfolio." I pointed at the attaché case, which lay on my bed. It was now empty. I decided at the last minute to carry all of the documents in a plastic bag. I looked at Marcel. "I want you to burn that in one of your charcoal ovens, immediately, if you please. Don't leave any traces."

She smiled and exclaimed, "A-ha! No wonder you smelled that way."

Marcel smiled. "Thank you, that leather is going to make a better-quality fire, and a better quality charcoal. At least Che is finally going to contribute to the poor and make that better quality charcoal with his fancy portfolio."

We laughed and hugged each other. I picked up the plastic bag with the documents, threw it over my shoulder, and started towards the stairs by which they had brought me into this room.

Marcel stopped me. "No, no—don't go out by there." He opened the metal door. "Leave this way. This tunnel will take you all the way to a cave in the ravine, close to the riverbank. Follow the ravine until you reach the bridge and the main highway. You will pass the soda pop factory, Jupiña Montes. From there, it will be easy for you to find your way to Avenue Cabada and your house."

Tite and I looked at each other and smiled. Tite had already told me about the tunnel, but I kept his secret. We hugged each other. He said, "Take care, my brother."

"You do the same, brother," I replied, "and thank you— all of you guys—from the bottom of my heart."

Marcel gave me a small kerosene lamp. "Leave this on the other side, when you get out. It's pitch black in there."

I left. Once I was in the tunnel, I heard the metal door

close behind me. I walked with the bag over my shoulders, and continued on by the dim light to the end of the tunnel. As I approached the other end, I could see a light that grew in intensity. It was sunlight shining through the overgrowth that covered the mouth of the cave. I got to the cave's mouth, extinguished the lamp, put it down, and wormed my way through the scrub brush. I discovered was at the top of the hill that everyone in Pinar del Rio called El Cerro de Cabras, or the Goat's Hill. I could see from that height the river and its surroundings. There wasn't a single soul in sight. I looked for a strategic place in the dirt to hide the plastic bag and its contents. The only things I did not leave there were the diary and the KGB badge. The diary I concealed inside my t shirt, tying it securely to my chest. The badge I hid in my sock along the inside of my leg, and pulled the elastic band of my pants leg down over my boot to complete the camouflage. I checked myself to make sure the book didn't create an unusual bulge around my stomach. I began my descent from the hilltop to the river, and followed the riverbank until I crossed under the bridge and entered the area close to the city. I smiled, as I recognized the landmarks in the area—I was coming close to terrain I knew well. Mima never let us go by ourselves to the river in her desire to protect us. My big brother and his friends, however, always enjoyed my company because of my sense of humor, and would take me with them to go fishing without telling her. I spent many great times with them by that riverbank. As memories of those times flooded my mind, I remembered how happy they were, in spite of the dictatorship under which we had lived at that time. I felt everything in our childhood was harmony and happiness without so much convulsion and killing as we now were living. Even our neighbors had been arrested under accusations of helping Counterrevolutionaries.

Distracted by my memories, I hadn't even realized how close to the city I had come. I heard a voice behind me as I crossed a small creek. It was a female voice. "Julio Antonio! Julio Antonio—is that you?" I turned around. There was a very small hill just behind and to the right of me. I saw my friend, the blonde-haired, blue-eyed Yaneba with her ever-present beret, a butterfly net, and a basket of glass bottles. She put them down in the grass and ran down the hill to meet me. She was about two years younger than me, but her body save for her breasts had matured early. She had a young, attractive woman's form, and enjoyed her older appearance. Her long, wavy hair flew out behind her, her smile was broad and beautiful. We always got along well together, and even though we would have arguments and differences in opinion, they were always resolved in a friendly way because of the sympathy we had for each other. She never hid her regard for me, and whenever she saw me with Sandra, who was more my age (in spite of the vast difference both in look and personality), Yaneba would grow extremely upset. She never really liked Sandra, especially when the two of us were together. Out of breath, she ran up to me, hugged me closely, and kissed me on both cheeks. She held me at arm's length, looked me up and down, and asked, "Where the Devil have you been? We all have been thinking you were dead! My God!! I thought I would never see you again." Her eyes filled with sudden tears. She caught me completely by surprise as she grabbed me and kissed me full on the lips. After a few seconds, she grew red, moved quickly away, and looked down at the riverbank in embarrassment. "I'm sorry," she said as she dried her eyes.

"It's OK, don't worry about," I said.

She wiped her index finger under her nose. She stamped her foot angrily on the ground. "Can you imagine it? They've been looking for you all over the country, your picture is in the newspaper, on television, they've asked after you on the radio—we all assumed you had been killed!" She shook her head in frustration.

I smiled in gratitude at seeing this gesture of affection, the sincere love she was displaying in her apparent disturbed state. I took a couple of small steps towards her, took her in my arms and hugged her, a long hug of thanksgiving. When we parted, she again surprised me with her perceptiveness. "Why is your stomach so hard?" she asked with a mischievous smile.

I touched my stomach and replied, "Oh, just a very important book. I just put it in there so that I would have my hands free, and be able to walk and get through the scrub brush easier."

She took my answer at face value, grabbed my hand, and took me to a large rock by the river. It was a very beautiful corner, where several creeks met above the river, forming a small waterfall. We sat down on the rock, and she repeated her questioning. "Really—where have you been all this time? Do your mom and dad know you're OK? Everybody's been looking for you!" she said once again.

Before she could ask any more questions, I took her by the shoulders and said to her, "The truth? I cannot say it to anybody, but I like you very much, and if you really are my friend, you have to repeat what I'm going say to you, the version I'm going to give you right now, and don't ask me anymore questions. Please. I want you to realize, if I told you the truth, not only my life, but also your life will be in danger, as well as another life if you are indiscreet and tell anyone what's happened to me these past few weeks."

She looked at me in surprise, a little scared. Her blue eyes opened wide. "It's that bad? Don't worry. Of course I'm your friend, and I'll never repeat what you tell me, unless you tell me it's OK to tell somebody. Whatever you entrust me with I will take with me to my grave. You don't have to tell the truth to anybody, but you can tell me."

I smiled and shook my head. "Evidently, you didn't listen to me. I know you're strong-headed and very young, still a little girl, and you can't understand the gravity of what I'm telling you."

She slid back on the rock away from me. "Ha! First of all, I'm not a little girl." I could see her white skin turned red. I clearly had lit a match in her and hit a hot button.

"Well, I didn't want to say that. I'm sorry—what I want to say is that you are too young, and you don't understand what I'm trying to tell you."

She jumped up onto the rock and into the sun. "Ha! You think you are so very adult? You're only two years older than me. What is the big deal?"

"OK," I replied placatingly. I patted the rock next to me. "Come on, sit down again. I already said I'm sorry. In the past, you told me when I was defending the Revolution and Fidel that your father told you that all these people in the Revolution were a bunch of bandidos and opportunists. I got pretty pissed off then, too—all we have to say sincerely is I'm sorry when someone says something to offend us or hurt us, as I just did to you right now. So, calm down, sit over here by me, and I will confess to you something completely unbelievable."

Full of curiosity, she immediately calmed down and jumped back down beside me. "What?" she asked, full of eager interest, "What? I forgive you. Will you tell me where you've been hiding all these weeks?"

"No, I already told you I cannot tell you that." She grimaced unhappily. "But I'm going to tell you something better than that, and you cannot tell it to anyone."

"OK, OK—what's up? What is that?"

"Your father really is right in everything he said. In reference to these people, the leaders of our government have completely turned this Revolution around and are trying to convert all of us into slaves. But, please, don't repeat this to anyone, because if you tell anybody I said that, not only can it get me in trouble, but it could get my whole family into trouble."

She smiled in pleasure as she heard me say that. "I will never tell anyone what you just entrusted to me. Thank you for trusting me," she added, touching my shoulder. "Let me tell you something, I've been telling my mom and dad that you, before we leave Cuba, will realize the truth behind all these people, and you'll wake up to the reality. You don't know how happy you've made me, because I've told them you're too smart to follow a dictator. But what are you going to do with your father? He's completely brainwashed by these evil men."

"Don't worry. God is very big and powerful, and I have faith he will react the same way I did as soon as he realizes what is behind all of this. He is a great man, the only man I admire on this Earth. He is a just man and so he could never be a communist, because they don't care about justice."

"OK, I understand. And since you told me this great confession, and something that could get you into a lot of trouble, I will give you a confession myself, that equally could get me into a lot trouble, and I think my father would kill me if he ever found it out, especially to you, since everyone thinks that since you are with the Revolution, you must be a communist. Not counting your being on television and everywhere with Fidel, Raul, Che, and the other leaders of the government...."

I interrupted her at that point. "I am a Revolutionary until my death, but I will never be a communist."

"Yes, but only you know that, and maybe some very close to you. To the rest of the town and the entire country, you are a part of this socialist system. But don't worry about it—what I want to tell you is that my father has a plan to get all of my family out of Cuba, and they're preparing a small boat. As you know, we tried to legally leave, but the government wants to put my father to work for two years in the agricultural programs, practically for free, in order to qualify to get the stupid passports. Imagine it—after he's been working for twenty years in his own business, but this government has made it like a crime to want to leave your own country to go anywhere. It's like a punishment to obtain permission to leave. My parents wanted to send me and my little sister through the 'Peter Pans'[5] until they can get out and be reunited with us. But

---

5 Fearing the loss of young children to the communist state, the CIA and the Catholic Church successfully created this clandestine operation in which 14,000 boys and girls were saved.

I'm completely against this. I told my father that we all go together or we all stay together here in Cuba, but we will not divide our family. My mother completely supports me and told my father the same. That settled the matter, and my father decided that we all will leave together. But you cannot tell this to anybody, because my father is clandestinely putting together the details and food." Her face grew long in sadness. "I know I won't see you for a long time. But one day, even if you marry that flat-faced, half-breed lowlife, brunette communist, who will only give you kids born with bones in their noses, and I will wait until you divorce her, and then I will marry you."

"Come on, don't be like that. You don't even know her that well. She's a nice girl."

"Sure, sure," she said sarcastically.

"Changing the subject, if your dad needs any gasoline, tell him I can get that for him. They may have rationed the gas, but I can get it through my contacts. If he needs anything else, those same contacts in the government can get them for me, and no one will know anything about it—spare parts, food, whatever."

"Thank you," she said with a look of gratitude. "I knew I could count on you." She leaned in and gave me a kiss on the cheek. "You're sure? This won't create problems for you?"

"That is the smallest problem I could possibly have to worry about." I raised my arm as if taking a vow. "Believe me."

"Very well. Thank you, very much. I never had a doubt that you are a great friend." She clapped her hand on my shoulder, and I winced and moaned in pain. "What happened to your arm? Did I hurt you?"

"Nothing—it's just a scratch. It's already healing, but it's still sore. Please, pay attention to what I'm going to tell you. This is very important, because you are the first person to see me and talk to me after my strange disappearance. It's very important that, if anybody asks you, that you say exactly what I will tell you to everyone, including my family."

"Not even to your family? You won't tell them the truth?"

"No," I replied sternly. "To them, even less than anybody. Remember what I told you before: I could put in danger the life of everyone who knows the truth."

"OK, OK." With an impish smile, she said, "If you're not even going to tell the truth to your family, that makes me feel a little better. Does that include Sandra?"

I shook my head. "Oh, God!"

"I'm just joking," she reassured me. "Don't be so touchy. Where's your sense of humor?"

I pointed to the hill. "I left my sense of humor buried in that hill." Without telling her the meaning of those words, I added, "My humor disappeared when I confronted a horrible reality and see how morbid, ugly, and scary the dark and degraded mind of some human beings can be. I lost it when I faced the death and horror that has been prepared for the future of some of the good leaders of our country and many other countries around the globe."

She looked at me in surprise, wonder, and semi-comprehension. It was clear she didn't understand the full import of my words; however, I knew she could feel my emotions. "I'm sorry that at such an early age that you have to go through this painful experience and deception. This could psychologically damage you and could create a depression in a spirit as young and pure as yours."

I smiled. "When you talk to me that way, I forget your age. That is the reason that I like you so much. You are very intelligent and mature for your years, as am I. Someday, you will make the man you pick to be your husband very happy."

She smiled impishly. "You mean to tell me that I will make you very happy one day?"

I shook my head and smiled. I stroked her beautiful, white, freckled face with my right arm and sighed deeply. "I wish you were a little older, because I know I would fall in love with you."

"Don't say that anymore!" she scolded. "You always blame my age!"

I decided to change the subject again. "Remember, don't tell anyone that you've seen me yet. I have to still complete my alibi. For that, I need a couple of days."

She looked at me in surprise. "What? You mean to tell me you're not going to your house?"

"No, not yet. I don't have a complete excuse that I can give my family for this long absence. That is why I need you to keep your lips sealed until you see me back in the neighborhood in a few days. You will tell everyone that we met and that I told you I spent almost two months with my half-brother in the Occidental side of the island in the town of Las Martinas. You must tell people that I told you beforehand that I was making this trip, but you completely forgot about it."

"Fine—don't worry about it. If that is the way you want it, I will do it the way you instruct." We both got up from the rock, and I helped her to clamber down. We hugged each other. She tried to kiss me on my lips, but I turned my face so that she kissed my cheek instead. "Take care of yourself, and God bless you."

As I walked away, I said, "You take care of yourself, too, and remember what I told you." She said nothing, but nodded in acknowledgment and waved to me. I continued walking to the riverbank until I reached the soda pop factory. Instead of turning to the left and towards home, I turned to the right and continued on to the street that went directly to the bus terminal on Veles Caviedes Street, trying to avoid anyone seeing and recognizing me by crossing on the far side of the sidewalk. After I passed by the police station on this street, I felt a great weight lifted from my shoulders, as that was the place that held the greatest risk of identifying me. It was early in the morning, and so people were still getting out of bed and going to work. By great good fortune, I made it to the bus terminal without running into anyone that could recognize me. I bought my ticket to Guane and went directly on board the bus, fully thirty minutes before it was supposed to depart. I tilted my seat back as far as I could, and spread a magazine over my face to prevent further recognition. It was a great relief once the bus started to drive out of the town. I peered from under my magazine to watch as we left the city and moved out into the countryside. I thanked God that everything, so far, had gone according to my plan.

It involved going to my half-brother, Leonardo, the product of a relationship my father had with a young girl he had when he established his business in the town of Guane before he had ever met my mother. This young lady, older than my father, was divorced with several kids. She had gotten pregnant by my father, and when the baby boy was born, she legally raised him with my father's last name without consulting him about it. It didn't make my father very happy. He wasn't really sure if this baby belonged to him or not, since this woman had relations with several men at the same time. However, because all of my father's friends thought that the baby looked like a picture of him, he took it as true and, as the decent and good man he was, not only gave her money to support the boy but also made sure that nothing that was needed was wanted. At that time, there were no DNA tests. Blood tests were known to be completely conclusive, so he never bothered to have any paternity tests done. He simply took her word as good and accepted the responsibility.

When my father met my mother, he told her the whole story. An exemplary woman who was full of compassion, she accepted it like any other mistake one may have made in the past. When she saw that four year old boy in the street begging for coins, her compassion caused her to ask my father to bring him to live with us so that he would receive the same education and love that the rest of us had as a family. She didn't want him to end up joining his brothers and sisters, all from different fathers, who lived as beggars and grew up with the terrible example provided by the greedy mother. My father did as he was asked, and brought Leonardito, as we lovingly called him, to live with us, with all the comfort my father's business provided in a middle class fashion and all the care that my mother gave to all of us. My father also enrolled him in a private school to see to it that he had every opportunity in life.

My half-brother, Leonar (which we used as a shortened name), became a rebel without a cause. He not only didn't go to school to study, but he also started to drink when he was but sixteen years old, he liked to smoke, and—

according to the stories I got from my family—he was a Casanova. He reportedly had a girl on a different corner on each street. He was a very good-looking man, and even though he didn't work, he never lacked for money, and had the best cars in town. His women always brought him gifts and saw to it that his needs were met. He had a great personality, very friendly and seductive, which he used to get out of his more complicated problems. Growing up, when he went to see his mother, he became very street smart. He knew that the police were very corrupt. Every time he got into trouble, if they were involved, he knew he just had to give them enough money and they would let him go. Even as a minor, he was driving the flashiest cars, even the one owned by the mayor of the town.

Of course, having the same first and last name as my father was an advantage, one he knew how to use quite well. My father, a businessman, well-known throughout the city, a Free Mason, and successful as well as honest—those weapons my brother learned to use with significant effect. When he couldn't get out of a problem that was too big for bribery, my father was the one who would come to his rescue and do whatever was needed to get him out through his relationships and influence. Leonar became at a very early age the black sheep of our family. Normally, when we are young, we do crazy things that we regret in later years as we settle down and become more responsible; in his case, the older he got, the crazier and more irresponsible he became. I can say for myself from when I was a little boy and he a teenager he was a great brother and always tried to protect me. In spite of his craziness and irresponsibility, he always gave me great advice and helped me to stay away from the bad things he was doing. He defended me whenever I needed it.

The straw that broke the camel's back of my father's patience was when he had sex with the daughter of one of my father's Masonic brothers. Her story was that Leonar raped her, pure and simple. Leonar maintained always that it was not true and insisted that she tried to blackmail him into marriage. I never saw my father as angry and ashamed as that time, and the argument ended in the ultimatum of marrying the girl or leaving the house. Leonar chose to leave the house, expressing a desire that he would rather live under the bridge than to marry that girl. Extremely upset, he left, and with his drinking friends and went to the mountains to join the Rebels and fight against Batista. There, he was distinguished for his bravery and heroism, and rose to the rank of Captain in the Rebel Army.

It didn't last very long; though he had an ample supply of courage, he was short in the areas of discipline and obedience. After a fight with some officers who didn't want to play cards with him, he was demoted to Lieutenant. After another encounter, he was further demoted to Sergeant, and then again as a result of disobedience demoted to Corporal. By the time the Revolution had won, in order to get rid of him, they sent him to the small town of Las Martinas. Once the indoctrination to communism had begun, he hung his uniform up, handed it to Commander Escalona, and told him he no longer wanted to be in the Army. He found a beautiful school teacher and married her. He bought a small piece of land in the middle of the jungle along the coast. It was practically inaccessible: no roads, and so no access by automobile. He built his own rustic cabin out of trees he felled himself, fifty kilometers from civilization, with no electricity and no telephone, and a single CB radio in case of emergencies. That might be the way he protested the treason of the Castros against the Revolution Leonar helped to build. From that time, far away from the world, he lived in splendid isolation. I had only been there once, and knew it to be a beautiful place with a scenic view of jungle flora and waterfalls. That is why I had conceived the plan to convince Leonar to be my alibi and say that I had been there with him and his wife for the two months of my disappearance.

Some of the young children preparing to leave Cuba

Chapter 4: My Brother, the Greatest Alibi

When I reached Guane, I had to transfer to another bus. It was a downgrade to a country bus that also had passengers who were bringing chickens and pigs with them as they headed to market. Night had fallen by the time I arrived in the small town of Las Martinas. I had to use all of my skills in persuasion and bargaining to convince a local guide, offering him double his normal fee, to take me to the remote area in which Leonar lived. He insisted that it was very dangerous to move around that area at night due to Counterrevolutionary activity; additionally, the jungle was so dense that it was easy to become lost. It very easily could have been an excuse to charge me more, but I didn't care. I paid him, and we arrived at my brother's house around midnight.

When I knocked on the door, Leonar was completely surprised to see me, but he and his wife, Blanca, received me with great joy in spite of the late hour. I let him know how disappointed I had become with the Revolution, and how I had found out for myself that despite Fidel's promises to never break bread with the communist murderers of the Hungarians, he was still disguising with words the direction in which he was steering the Revolution. He declared It was a progressive or nationalist movement, but never a socialist or communist one. Only our enemies, he said, were trying to dress the Revolution in red, but the reality was that it was as green as the palm trees. I reassured them that, even though I had known for a while what they planned to do, it had become more obvious now because Castro's emissaries, Che, Piñiero, and Ramiro, had told me to my face that they were going to begin Marxist-Leninist indoctrination of the armed forces. I told them that they had brought to me orders directly from Fidel to convert my Juvenile Commandos into the Juvenile Communist Union.

"I know," Leonar said. "That's why I left the army. They had been doing this slowly for a while; now they're just doing it more openly."

We talked until very late by the light of the kerosene lamp. The next day, we rose late in the morning. I walked around before they rose to explore my surroundings. I had forgotten how beautiful the property where my brother had built his house was. There were several creeks and fountains that formed lovely waterfalls, hot mineral water springs, and he had planted around the water features different varieties of banana trees. From the highlands, I could look down and watch as the creek emptied into the rough waves of the Atlantic Ocean. I returned to the house, and saw that my brother was awake. I used the opportunity of Blanca's taking a shower to share with Leonar the real reason for my visit. "I can't give you too many details, my brother," I explained, "but could you back me up and say that I have been staying here for the last two months?"

"That is extraordinary," he said with smile, "because actually, around that time, I visited Pinar del Rio to buy provisions and a new emergency generator—you know they're much cheaper to buy there." He reassured me, "Don't worry about it at all. If anybody asks me, I will tell them exactly what you tell me to say. And if you need to hide for any reason at all in the future, the door of my house is open to you."

This made me happy for the rest of the day. After I thanked my brother, the three of us went to the coast. We found in the rocky, rough coast a small cove along the sandy beach. We dug for clams.

Home of Leonar, Julio Antonio's half brother

Area near Leonar's house

Blanca put our clams in a five gallon bucket, and we picked up a couple of conch shells. We then went back to the house, and while she prepared a fresh clam soup, Leonar killed a small pig. In the ground in front of the house, he slow roasted the meat in a rustic barbeque. By sunset, the pig was fully roasted, we set up a table outdoors before a bonfire and we consumed a delicious jungle dinner. That night, I slept very well. He and his wife were insisting that I stayed a few days to recuperate from my long trip. However, I told them that I had to return as soon as possible, because I was very worried about how my mom and dad might be going crazy over my continued absence. I only spent one day with them to rest. The next morning, Leonar and Blanca took me into town using three of their horses. They gave me a few presents to give to my relatives, as well. I thanked them and said goodbye as they rode back into the jungle with the horse I had borrowed between them. From Las Martinas, I took the bus back to Guane, and then got on the upgrade bus to take back to Pinar del Rio. As I sat down in that nice, air-conditioned bus, I felt a vast wave of relief and a great weight lift from my shoulders. I knew that, no matter what happened now, all of my bases were covered. More than anything, my greatest worry had been to avoid creating any problems for Marcel and Fraya.

When I arrived in Pinar del Rio and got out of the bus, my heart started to beat harder. I walked down the Calle Real, or Royal Street, which was the street that led towards the road my house was on. I was about a block from my house when the first person recognized me. It was my girlfriend, Sandra. She lived close to us, and so was an old friend. She jumped off of her bicycle and hugged me very emotionally. "For God's sake!" she exclaimed. "Where have you been? We've all been thinking you were dead!" She looked me up and down, as if to reassure herself that I was still in one piece, and that it was indeed I. She put both arms around my shoulders and hugged me again, and then planted a very passionate kiss on my mouth, completely without care about how close we were to her house. In those days, it was a very unseemly thing for a girl her age to do. "Have you been by your house already? Do they know you're OK?"

"No," I replied. "I'm on my way there now. I just got back into town. I've been in Las Martinas with my brother, Leonar."

"My God!" she said again, her right hand raised to her mouth. "They've been looking for you everywhere. They posted your picture all over the place, and you've been on the radio and television. Your mother, Majito, and everyone in your family have been crying all the time, because they think you're dead."

I felt really bad, but acted completely surprised. "But I told Daniel to tell my mom and my dad that I would be leaving town with my brother for a few weeks. It just took a little longer than I expected. You know how it is with family; when you're visiting them, they don't want to let you go. And you know where Leonar lives, there's no TV, no radio, no phone."

"Oh, maybe Daniel forgot or something."

Even though I knew that this wasn't the truth, but I knew for a fact that Daniel would support whatever story I spread around. "Or maybe he didn't hear me clearly. You know how noisy those jeeps can be when they're moving."

Sandra shook her head. "Well, well—that is not important anymore. The important thing is that you're OK. Let's rush to your house to let everyone know you're OK." She pedaled ahead of me on her bike, yelling "Julio Antonio is OK! He's OK!! He's right behind me!"

My sister, Disa, was outside on the porch. She screamed into the house through the front door, "Mima! Majito! Everybody!! Julio Antonio is here—he's alive!!" She came out to the sidewalk when she heard Sandra's screaming and then ran to meet me in the street. She was the sister who was, at that time, the fiancée to Canen, who had just been promoted to second-in-command of the army forces in the province. They had arranged to get married in the next few days. She looked at me with both hands over her mouth and eyes full of tears. She hugged me fiercely and kissed my cheeks. Calming herself down, she asked, "Where the hell have you been? We've been going crazy, looking for you everywhere!"

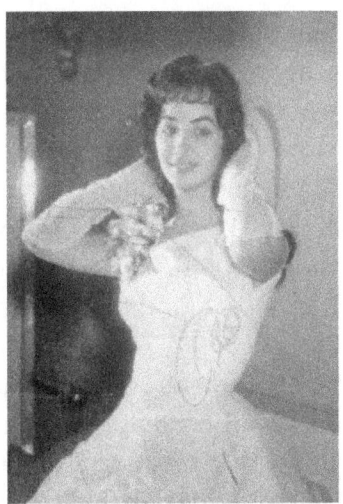

Disa, Julio Antonio's sister

I told her, "I'll explain later." I pulled out of my bag a large jar of honey. "Here you are—honey for your honeymoon. I wish you great happiness in your marriage."

She smiled and said, "Oh, God—you never change. The best present you could have given me for my wedding is your being OK." She kissed me once more on my cheek. She hugged me again and whispered in my ear, "How the devil do you manage to keep us from getting angry with you? None of us have slept for weeks, not me, not Mima or Papi, Majito, or any of your brothers and sisters."

Mima and Majito were the first ones to come out of the house. Mima didn't get a chance to come close to me—she collapsed in Majito's arms as soon as she saw me. Disa ran back to help Majito, and with help from my other brothers and sisters put my mother in one of the chairs on the porch. Majito ran into the house to get some smelling salts. That was the saddest moment in my life, to see my mother there like she was dead. I thought for a moment that she might have had a heart attack—certainly the extreme sadness turning into such ecstatic joy could have caused one. I thought for a moment that my heart had stopped, and I stood there for a few seconds, paralyzed. Finally, I breathed deeply as I saw her recover consciousness. I realized, starting with that day, how valuable life is, how easy it is to lose it, and that we have to treasure every moment.

A few hours later, after the excitement over my return had calmed down, I explained my absence. Disa came to me once more and hugged me with a broad smile. "You know, we almost postponed my wedding. Thank God you came back, because Canen didn't like the idea very much. But because of the entire family's emotional state, we were seriously considering that."

I smiled in return. "Well—you don't have any excuse now, unless you're having a change of heart."

"No, no," she replied with great assurance. "Canen is a great man, and I'm positive we'll be very happy and have many sons."

I stroked her face and asked, "Are you in love with him?"

"*Claro*[6]!"

---

6 "Of course!"

"Well, this is the most important thing. Where there is love between two people, the rest is all a complement. Where there is no love, nothing functions properly, and your marriage will become a miserable."

She smiled. "You're always giving advice, as if you were an old man." She stepped back from me. "Do you realize that I'm older than you, or have you forgotten?"

I held up a finger. "Ah-ha—but your spirit is very young, while mine is a hundred years old. Do you remember what Papi has said? I'm a reincarnation of our great-grandfather, General Donato del Marmol."

"Oh, my God—I forgot, you're an old man and a lawyer, too!" She mockingly saluted me. "You are already a Commandante, maybe if you're lucky and Fidel comes back to the old rank system, you'll make it to General yourself and repeat history. After all, your third name is Donato."

I smiled again. "Maybe in another government; not with Fidel Castro."

She looked at me in surprise. "What are you trying to say?" she asked curiously.

I shook my head, my face serious. "Don't worry about it—it's not important."

She continued to look at me askance, but she didn't press the issue any further. I left her room and went upstairs to my own room. I locked the door behind me, pulled out the diary, and lay down on my bed to read it in greater detail. The more I read, the more surprise and doubt gathered in my mind with every page. It was simply unbelievable, but here were his plans, clearly spelled out in black and white. As I read, I thought about my older sister, Elda, and her fiancé. They were getting married two weeks after Disa, and he was a lieutenant in charge of the

Transit Authority in Pinar del Rio. In reality, that was a cover-up; he had told me himself that he was in reality the chief of clandestine operations for the G-2. I couldn't help but compare him to Che, and how both of them appeared to be one thing, but in reality were both something very different. I felt responsible for all of this; these marriages were of great benefit to my sisters, as both fiancés were highly placed in the government, and it was because I was always bringing these men by the house that my sisters had met them. It gave me comfort to know that they had made their own decisions.

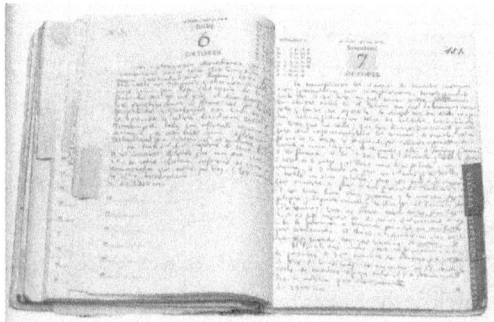

The diary of Ernesto "Che" Guevara

Of course, my father welcomed these choices with great joy, since both of them were so prominent. At the beginning of the Revolution, I embraced it with joy, as well; at that time, I had no inkling that I would one day become a professional spy against them, one that was starting to become the most wanted spy in their circles. The Cuban government was in no doubt that the United States had to have a spy placed with them somewhere through the classified information they had obtained from Soviet intelligence that the US had suspicions that the USSR was transporting nuclear missiles to Cuba. The only way that information could have been leaked to the US is if someone within the highest military circles in Cuba had been passing that knowledge to Western global intelligence. It never crossed anyone's mind that it was I who had taken those pictures nearly a year before. We asked ourselves why it was taking so long for the North Americans to send a spy plane to corroborate this data. We came to the conclusion that the bureaucracy in the intelligence community and that of the US government found the very idea that the Soviets would bring short, intermediate, and long-range missiles to Cuba unbelievable. Such an act was in direct violation of every agreement between the US and Soviet governments. I never realized until much later the complexity of the espionage machinery, and how all of this had to function in mingling with diplomacy in democratic countries. We had to play a game of cat-and-mouse with the Congress, while our enemies were breaking established laws in conducting their clandestine operations and creating a political scandal. With the precise caution of a tightrope walker, in order to protect the people, it had to be played out so. It was a dangerous game, full of obstacles, in many cases winding up with many years in prison and in the worst case in front of a firing squad as the penalty one paid if caught.

After several hours of writing notes and taking more pictures, my mother called me for the second time to come to dinner. I didn't want to keep her waiting after my absence, and so decided to stop for the day. I concealed the diary like part of treasure in the closet underneath my socks and underwear. After I finished dinner, while the rest of the family was distracted in the living room by the TV, I made a phone call to the capital and my uncle. I simply said a code word that indicated an emergency need to see him. He replied to me in our code that my contact would be in touch with me the next day and tell me the place in which we would meet.

The next day, I met with Daniel and briefed him on the whole situation, so that he would know the story and be prepared to answer correctly the questions that might be put to him correctly, using the same cover I gave to my brother. My good friend smiled and said, "I will say exactly what you tell me to say. Don't worry about it at all."

I smiled and thanked him for his loyalty. I knew for a fact I could trust him with my life. I gave him a pat on the shoulder and said, "I know, brother. I know I can depend on you."

We went in the jeep to the military regiment. It was a beautiful day with the sun shining in the blue sky. When we got inside, I didn't see the normal routine. It was practically desolate. The soldiers on guard at the gate were overjoyed to see me alive and well. I asked them, "What's going on here? Where is everybody?"

One of them replied, "Oh, the troops are out on training exercises. Some of them are in San Cristobal. Commander Escalona and Che are directing the exercises. Captain Canen is in command of the base right now."

We continued to the General Headquarters. When we got to the building, I exchanged salutes with the guards at the door and went inside. I noticed the guards were different, a pair of soldiers who normally didn't have this post. I went to the stairs, and once I reached Escalona's private office, I saw that the door was open. This was unusual, since this door was normally closed and locked. I smiled as I observed the new lock on the door; but to my surprise, the office was completely empty. I used the opportunity to look over Escalona's desk and through his folders lying on his desk. Under the folders, I saw a book. I was shocked to see that it was a Bible, and looked at it incredulously. I knew for certain that Escalona didn't have a Bible, let alone one on his desk so poorly concealed underneath some folders. I picked it up and opened it, still standing by his desk.

It had several ribbons of different colors. I opened it to the first ribbon, a green one. It marked Exodus Chapter 6, verses 10 and 11: "Now the LORD, spoke to Moses, saying, 'Go, tell Pharaoh, king of Egypt to let the sons of Israel go out of his land.'" I closed the Bible and opened it to a white ribbon. John Chapter 15, verses 1-4: "I am the true vine, and My Father is the gardener. He cuts off every branch in me that bears no fruit; and every branch that does bear fruit, He prunes so that it will be even more fruitful. You are already clean, because of the word I have spoken to you. Remain in Me as I also remain in you." I closed it once more, and opened it to a red ribbon. Revelation 22:15: "Outside are the dogs and the sorcerers and the immoral persons and the murderers and the idolaters, and everyone who loves and practices lying." I closed it again and stood there for a few seconds in thought. I wondered who owned this Bible. Clearly, this person was very remorseful, and that his good spirit might be noble and full of love for God and the good things God represents. It was a terrible contradiction with his own principles that communist ideology preached. He had underlined the words "murderers," "idolaters," and then double underlined "lying." These were the routes along which the new tyrants in Cuba were bringing the Revolution. Completely distracted by my thoughts, I didn't even realize that Canen had quietly come into the office behind me.

In a strong, authoritative voice, he asked, "What the hell are you doing here?" Without even allowing me to reply to him, he continued irritatedly, "Where did you get that book? Have you been snooping, and in Commander Escalona's desk?" He snatched the book out of my hands. "I don't know where your manners, but when we come into a place and the person we're looking for is not there, we don't stick around snooping around the place. For courtesy, you leave, and you come back when that person is present." He added harshly, "You really disappoint me." I could also see nervousness in his demeanor. As I looked into his eyes, I could also see a redness there, as if he were either intoxicated or had been crying.

I held his gaze without saying anything. I let it show in my face and eyes that I didn't like the way he had been talking to me. I was accustomed to being treated with respect; and especially by him, who only a year and a half before had been a mere lieutenant. He had always been cordial and educated, and we had become friends. We had even had intimate conversations in which he had confided to me that for many years he had studied accounting and had worked at night as a conductor for the bus to pay for his schooling. It had crossed in front of our home, and he had been in love with Disa since she was about fourteen years old. As it drove by our house, he would think about her, sometimes even hearing her play the piano, and dream of one day when she could be his wife. It had given him the inspiration to study hard and improve his position in life so that he could one day successfully court her. At the beginning of the Revolution, it was not yet a crime to believe in God, and he confessed to me that he was an Evangelical, rather than a Catholic, and had been a youth leader in his church. For that reason, I decided to bring him with me and introduce him to my sister. I repeated many times later to my friends, "It is a lot easier to find a man without principles who doesn't believe in God than to find a man who believes in God with a lack of principles."

For this reason, among many others, I was extremely irritated. I straightened my uniform cap in silence. I looked at him once more, and my jaw tightened. I turned around, left the office, and slammed the door behind me so violently that I felt that perhaps I might have broken the pane of glass in the middle of it. I was not yet on the stairs when I heard the door behind me open and his voice yell out, "Commandantico! Wait! Come back here! I've got something for you from Commander Escalona."

I didn't know if that was true or not, or simply an excuse to get me back there. I looked over my shoulder, my left hand already on the bannister. "I will tell Daniel to come up and get it from you." I started rapidly down the stairs, without even waiting for his reply.

He evidently didn't want me to leave in such an angry state. He knew that the way he reacted was abrupt and highly improper. He ran to the stairs to try to stop me. I was almost to the bottom of the stairs and heard him running down the stairs. He said to me in a conciliatory tone, "I'm sorry. Please, I need to talk to you before you leave. Come back here, and we can talk in the office."

The two guards at the door could hear him, thanks to

the echo from the stairs. They turned and looked at us curiously. They knew that something was wrong, and they both looked at me directly. I didn't want to create a scene, and looked at Canen's sad-puppy eyes, and felt sorry for the commotion. I turned and went slowly back up the stairs. I was still unhappy. He waited for me to join him inside the office, and then closed and locked the door. He picked up the Bible in his right hand and said with moist eyes, "What I'm going to tell you can create a lot of trouble for me. I could even lose my position. But I have to tell this to somebody, and since I trust you and know you are a real man, in spite of your youth. If I don't tell this to you or someone I will explode. But please, before I tell you, promise me that you won't tell this to anyone, not even your sister."

I looked at him and shook my head unhappily. "You know better than anybody that I don't repeat what I hear to anyone. We've been close for a long time, you should know that by now. And you're going to become a part of my family in a few days."

"OK. The first thing is that I want to apologize to you for my conduct before." He raised the Bible high and then put it close to his chest. "This Bible, not 'the book,' as I referred to it before, is mine. Because all of this ideology and the turn the Revolution has taken, it is now considered a seditious document. Only our enemies are supposed to have a Bible with them. My preservation instinct caused me to react violently a few minutes ago when I saw you find it there." We were facing each other; he looked me full in the eye as he stepped towards me and put his hand on my shoulder. "I'm up to my neck in this government. But at the same time, I repudiate with all my heart the bullshit, the killing, and the lies we've been feeding people. Even after we executed our supposed enemies, we emptied their bodies like vultures to sell their guts to the highest bidders on the black market." I remembered what I had seen two months before, realizing that he probably had seen this every day. I remained silent.

He took a couple of steps away and sat down in a chair. He rubbed his chin. "You know how many days I haven't been able to sleep? They have given me another 'promotion'. They now want me to be in charge of the Revolutionary tribunals, and send to the slaughter my own brothers, my friends. Can you imagine it?" he added in a voice filled with sadness and frustration. He shook his head despondently.

I took a few steps towards him, pulled up a chair, and sat down in front of him. I stroked my right ear and crossed my leg, thinking about everything Canen was telling me. I had some doubts—he might have been sent by somebody, he might be a trap, he could have left that Bible on purpose there. All of these things flashed through my mind. I had no doubt that he was deeply religious, because I knew about his past before all of this happened. On the other hand, he could be going through a great deal of agony in being the executioner. There still was the chance that this could still be a well-presented theatrical trap.

He smiled ironically. "Can you imagine? This is the wedding present that son of a bitch gave to me. On top of it all, I had to smile and thank him for the 'honor' of being promoted! As Escalona says, not every officer is given this distinguished position. They've given me a small booklet from the Military Tribune, telling me the guidelines I have to follow. A minimum of ten years for any act, even a simple student protest in the street. Twenty to thirty years to anyone who takes up arms against the government. Death penalty for any other major act of terrorism against the interests of the People's Republic." He waved his arms in frustrated sarcasm. "The People's Republic. Ha! Who believes that? Not even an imbecile."

I kept silent this entire time, holding back a very powerful desire to scream to him that I was a spy, that I agreed with him completely, and to invite him to come work with us. Instead, I bit my lip and remembered my training. My uncle and the General had repeatedly warned me to be very careful, especially with my own family and everyone close to me. It was through these associations that they worked to get to someone—it was how both sides worked. For instance, under no circumstance, I was cautioned, could my father ever even dream about what I was doing.

Because Che, Piñiero, and Ramiro had recently been in the camp, and the recent burglary of Che's case in that exact same office in which we were talking, goose bumps went through my body. I felt that Canen's emotions were sincere, but my gut also was concerned that all of this could be a very sophisticated trap. I tried to get all of this out of my mind and reorganize my thoughts; in doing so, I shook my head so violently that he looked at me in surprise and a little frightened. "I'm sorry," he said quickly, "I'm sorry. Maybe this is too much for you. But please, keep it to yourself, even if you don't agree with me. Please, please—don't repeat anything of which I've told you, to anyone, or your sister will be a widow very shortly after her marriage." Evidently, he repented very quickly what he had told me only moments before.

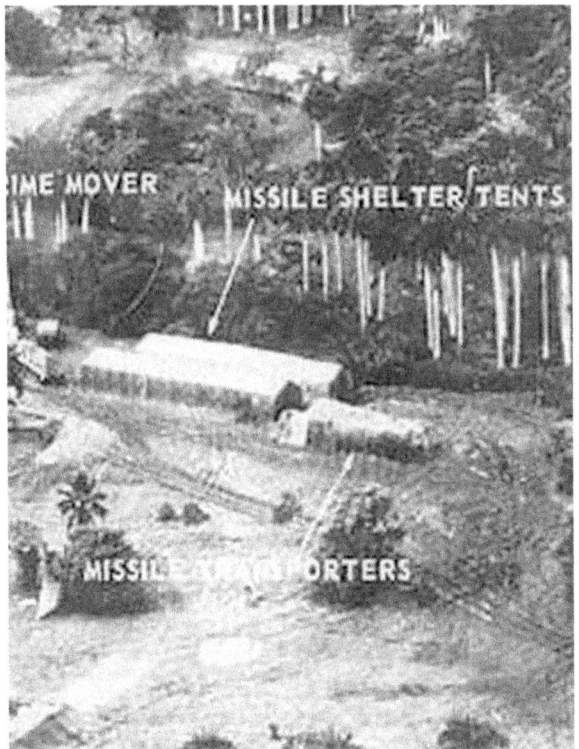
Intelligence photo of the missile base

Chapter 5: The Declassification of the Treasure

I rolled my chair closer to him and gestured for him to sit down. He looked at me nervously. I smiled calmly at him and said, "Maybe you don't even realize it yourself, but they say that God moves in mysterious ways. Maybe He put into your hands this extraordinary power by placing you in charge. You may be able to save lives this way, instead of taking them. I'm not too religious myself, and don't read the Bible very much, but I remember one passage I read. One of the characters in it was betrayed by his brothers, who first tried to kill him, but then instead sold him into slavery. He became a high minister in Pharaoh's court. He later saved his brothers from hunger and protected their lives."

"Oh!" he exclaimed, "That is Joseph."

"OK," I acknowledged. "There was another book I read about the Nazi persecution of the Jews in Germany. There was a Jew who worked undercover with the Nazis, and he became a wealthy man. He used his prominent position with the Nazi government to protect the lives of hundreds of thousands of his Jewish brothers, keeping them out of the concentration camps and the gas chambers, using his astute intelligence to keep himself secret. No one even knew that he was actually a Jew; everyone thought he was a Nazi. He suffered more than many of his brethren, watching it happen to those he couldn't save, but he kept his silence and did the best he could to save those he could reach." I stroked my chin in thought. "Remember, you're marrying my sister in a few days. I will never betray you, but you have to control your nerves and try to be happy in your marriage. Use this power they've put into your hands to not only help your family and friends, but also those your authority can reach. Every time these Marxists order you to give the death penalty to somebody, use your intelligence to manipulate things so that you only give them twenty or thirty years. You can save an innocent person that way—they're still alive, at least. It's the same way that Jewish man saved all those people from the concentration camps. When they tell you to give someone twenty or thirty years to someone, give him ten. You'll be giving back to him days of happiness and freedom that he wouldn't have otherwise had."

He looked at me and slowly nodded his head. "Maybe you're right. But when that poor devil gets twenty years, he'll hate me for the rest of his life. Who will convince him that I saved him, when in fact they want to kill him?"

I stood up, walked the few steps over to the table, and picked up his Bible. "That is not the only thing you have to worry about, brother. No matter how shrewdly you act, there will be situations in which people will be executed in spite of your efforts. But, to those you save, and to your conscience, you know you did your best. Even when some have to die, you at least will know you did your best to save their lives. And the poor devil you referred to—it might be his destiny to die, but in God's eyes, you will be forgiven because you actually put forth your best effort to save that man's life."

He stood up, walked to me, and opened his arms to give me a bear hug. My ribs creaked, and I grunted in pain. "Oh, I'm sorry," he apologized. "Thank you for your words. Believe it or not, you've made me feel a lot better. To hear you talk about it that way, I sometimes forget how old you actually are. Now I realize why everyone in your house calls you 'the old man.'"

I shook my head. "Don't give me so much credit. All I did was listen to you and was patient enough to let you spit out everything you had on your chest and in your soul."

He smiled again. "Modesty is a great virtue."

I smiled. "Thank you. God helps those that help themselves." I pointed to his Bible. "Put that where someone cannot see it. Put it under your pillow in the house you'll live in with my sister, but keep it someplace out of sight of those who don't know your real feelings. Bringing that here is like taking a lamb to the lion's cage. Carry the Bible instead in your heart and head, if you need to carry it with you."

He looked at me shrewdly, nodded, and picked up the Bible. He concealed it inside a folder. I was almost ready to leave when he stopped me. "By the way, I'm really glad to see that you're safe and OK. We all thought something horrible had happened to you."

I grinned. "Don't forget, I'm like a cat."

"Yeah, you've got nine lives. You still need to take care of them, because you never know when you'll be on your last one."

We both looked at each other, he with appreciation, and I with pride. He could not know that I had passed my first test. I had controlled himself and kept my mouth shut about my double life, even though I had wanted to fairly scream it to him because we were obviously in sympathy with each other. My uncle and the General had both been very clear and firm on that point. He handed me a document that had been signed by Commander Escalona. It authorized me to requisition a large truck from the Transportation Department, so that I could transport my Juvenile Commandos to a large building in which they would become transformed into the Communist Youth Union.

He asked me ironically, "Are you accepting Fidel's offer to study in the Soviet Union to become an intelligence officer for the proletariat in Cuba?"

I nodded cynically. "Claro. If that is what the Commander-in-Chief and Che want, then I will do it. Remember, the walls have ears. In the future, when you want to share your personal feelings with me, don't do it in a place like this. If something is repeated or something happens to you, I don't want you to have any doubts, because you know that you entrusted it only to me. You are now the second-in-command of this province, and even your dear friends among your fellow officers will be envious."

He nodded again. "You're absolutely right. Thanks again."

"No problem, brother. It will always be my pleasure to listen to you and help in whatever way I can. By the way, what happened to the two guards that were at the front door before? I noticed that we have new guys on duty there."

"Oh, they got thrown in jail after Che's briefcase was

stolen out of this office. They were really lucky—only six months for negligence. They kept repeating that all they could see was the lightning in the sky, poor guys. The silhouette that was seen got lost in the night, and they started to doubt them. They didn't find a trace of anybody that supposedly crawled down the wall like a spider. According to Che, there were some incredibly important things that were stolen. Even Fidel flew over here to investigate the situation personally; that's how grave it was. They've been going crazy, moving troops, equipment, even the missile camps to other places. I believe Fidel classified this spy that stole the attaché as a very sophisticated one. In our paperwork he is codenamed iel relampago[7]."

I asked in surprise, "Why that name?"

"Do you remember that first night when we brought the boxes with the missiles from the Mariel Pier to San Cristobal? It was a night of torrential rain, and we had a lot of lightning. They know this spy took pictures that night and sent them to our enemies. And now, he's repeated himself the same way."

---

[7] The Lightning

I looked at him in surprise, as if I didn't know anything about this. "It couldn't be coincidence? How do they know that pictures were taken that precise night when the missiles arrived?" I knew for a fact that my uncle had told me that the pictures were clear because they were illuminated by the lightning flashes. The photos were so sharp that even the serial numbers could be seen. I had joked with him at the time that God had sent the flash for the photos by His Providence. I thought now that, if that were the case, the flashes that had exposed me the last time must have come from the Devil, since I went through Hell that night.

"No," he replied. "According to Soviet counterintelligence, they have one of those pictures. They know that someone here must have taken pictures."

I thought for a moment that you never know who you're working for; clearly, the Americans had Soviet spies planted deep within their own intelligence network. I nodded thoughtfully. "Hm, that means that someone that night with us was the spy."

He rubbed his face. "Yes, and you know how they think—something like that happens, and they immediately look at the senior military officials. I was in charge of that operation at that time, and so had to answer a bunch of questions."

I felt a little guilty about that. To comfort him, I said, "You don't have anything to worry about. Your loyalty has been proven to this government. Keep your feelings to yourself, and you'll be OK."

I left the building and headed over to the Transportation Department. I took the jeep and let Daniel drive the truck to my Commandos HQ with his instructions. I told him that I would meet him later, and drove to the center of the city.

I went to the Office of the Revolutionary Directorate of Students, which had been the headquarters for the March 13th Movement before Castro started his own revolution. I parked the jeep by the door in the rear. I took a key from its hiding place beneath a planter, opened the door, and walked into the building.

It was full of furniture—desks, typewriters, and other office equipment—but it was otherwise empty. I turned a single dim light on. I had been there recently, about five months ago, with Commander Cubela. It had been closed, and everything inside was left exactly the same. The last people had left abruptly, as some typewriters still had partially typed papers still in them. I pulled up one of the chairs. After dusting it off, I sat down to wait. I looked at the wall that was covered with photographs of the student martyrs who had been killed, all young university students and those who joined them in the March 13, 1957 attempt to kill the Dictator, Fulgencio Batista. Hundreds of people died in that effort, as many had joined the students and intellectuals in the endeavor to take down that regime. One of the pictures on the wall was of my father's cousin, Menelao Mora Morales. He was the planner behind the whole attempt. I breathed deeply in that lonely building filled with furniture, and thought about how many young lives had been wasted for naught. We had a new dictator in this country now, and he didn't even care about those who had died in that attack. The Revolutionary movement that had organized this attack was led by José Antonio Echeverría, the President of the Federation of University Students. He was supposed to be the next President of Cuba, but Castro's 26th of July Movement took over their attempts. Since it wasn't his movement, Castro cast those survivors out, accusing them of being traitors. Those who didn't end up in jail were left with insignificant jobs and were utterly forgotten. The only memorial they had was to have their photographs hanging on the wall in an empty office building, gathering only dust and cobwebs. Every organization that was not a part of the 26th of July was declared illegitimate and unnecessary, since the Castro Revolution had already won.

Thinking about all of that as I sat in that chair and looked at those pictures, I could no longer hold it in. I said aloud, "What a son of a bitch that Fidel Castro is."

A voice behind me said, "There's no doubt about that."

I was so surprised that I almost fell out of the chair. The General had completely taken me by surprise. I hadn't heard him even enter the building. "I was only thinking aloud."

"Remember what we've told you," he said very seriously. "Keep your impulses and emotions to yourself. They are luxuries that those in our line of work cannot afford to have."

I replied with equal gravity. "Yes, you're right. I'm sorry. You took me by surprise."

He smiled to ease me past my embarrassment. I realized that, for all I knew, that building might not have been empty, and it could just as easily have been someone with the G-2 as the General who had come in and overheard my outburst. He could see I felt ashamed. "We're all guilty of that. The trick is to control them. Just remember that when you sit down to wait for somebody, always sit facing the door. If there are two doors, sit in the corner and face the doors. In fact, it's best to find the darkest corner so that you can control the whole room. Don't rush to meet them, but let them find you and come to you. That way, you will always be the one to surprise the others."

"Very well, I will do that always in the future."

He put his arm around my shoulder. "I know. You're very good at learning. From now on, I know I will be the one who gets surprised every time we get together."

"Thank you." I pulled Che's diary out from inside my shirt as he sat down opposite me. I held it out to him.

The light was too dim for him to see what it was, and so he pulled out a flashlight to read what it was I was giving him. He started to turn the pages with a small smile on his face. After a few pages, his smile grew broader. His eyes widened in surprise, and he frequently glanced up at me in astonishment. Finally, he asked, "Where the hell did you take this from?" Without waiting for an answer, he continued. "My God—this is for real? You don't think they planted this in order to throw us off? Are you sure they didn't try to catch you with this? Do you know the magnitude of this information, and I've only gone through a few pages?"

"Slow down, I know your concern, and I appreciate it." I leaned back in my chair. "In reply to your first question, I took it from Che's personal attaché case. To your second question, I will tell you that he didn't even dream anyone would take it. The office was perfectly secure when we left it. And to your third question, I've read this more than ten times. This might be written this way to throw people off or make it difficult to understand certain things, but it's obvious that he didn't even dream that it would leave his hands. There are clandestine plans to assassinate leaders that have already taken place here and are in process both in Cuba and in different countries, as well as other Machiavellian games around the world. We now have in our hands irrefutable proof of this."

He looked at me in surprise. "How did you get to that conclusion? Just by reading his diary?"

"No, I have schematics, maps, graphics, routes, dates and places, weapon receipts and deliveries, the caliber of the weapons they have used and for those they plan to use in those assassinations, and much more."

He shifted in his chair to look at me incredulously. "This is can't be all you got from his portfolio."

I reached into my pocket and handed him my pen. "Everything is on here"

He grinned from ear to ear. He stood up and embraced me warmly. "How did you do this, kid? My boy, you don't even know what tremendous importance this has!" He put the pen in his guayabera and returned to his seat. He opened his briefcase, took out another pen, and handed it to me. "I will stay here for a few days to analyze all and digest all of this. Do you have the originals?"

"Yes," I replied. "They are in a safe place. I will retrieve them pretty soon, but I did what the circumstances required at that moment. I left them behind."

"You know, you should destroy those."

"Yes, but I didn't consider it prudent. You told me that the pen doesn't need absolutely bright light, but it does need some kind of light. The place I was in was extremely dark, and I'm afraid that some of those documents may not have come out, and we may need to photograph them again. I decided to be extremely cautious and hold on to them until you verify to me that the pictures came out OK."

He nodded and touched my shoulder approvingly. "Very well done. Sometimes, we have to improvise based on the particulars of the situation…"

I leaned back again. "You have no idea how much I've had to improvise in the past weeks in order to save my skin and get that portfolio out of the regimental headquarters."

He looked at me in surprise, closed his left fist, and brought it to his mouth in thoughtful curiosity. "How is that? You got that portfolio out of the HQ and nobody saw you?"

I smiled. "I've become not only a spy; I've become a magician." Then began to describe to him in greater detail my narrow escape on that dark, lightning-lit night, the emotional trauma and physical injuries I had sustained, and the resulting infection that nearly took my life. He listened to my account with increasing astonishment. I told him about my conversation with Canen in detail then.

"You've become a complete professional in a very short time. You followed your instincts without violating any security protocols. When you have any doubt, you stop and proceed with caution once circumstances allow you to do so. We will observe Canen and put our attention on him. We will find out if he is sincere and what is behind all of this." He touched the pen in his pocket. "Your future brother-in-law could play an extremely important role in the verification of the information we're getting right now because of his clearance. I spoke with your uncle, and he'll be here in a couple of days for the wedding. We will have a meeting, the three of us, and we'll see what kind of conclusions we can draw from this buffet we have before us." He stood up to say goodbye. "I'm very proud of you." I stopped him with left hand raised as my right hand reached into my campaign pants. He looked at me in surprise once more. "There's more?"

I took out the wallet with Che's badge inside. "The best for last. Your friend, Che Ernesto Guevara, the international revolutionary, is nothing more than a KGB agent, paid for and trained by the Soviets."

"What?" He took the wallet from my hand. After he recovered from his surprise and sat back down in the chair as he examined the contents closely. "Oh, my God! You hit the jackpot! The only reason he has this in his portfolio and not in a security box or safe is because, when you took that case, he had come just the night before from the Soviet Union on one of his trips. He might need that to identify himself to his other comrades in the game in Central and South America. It's incredible that you took the whole attaché case!" He smiled again from ear to ear. "For the first time, I will agree with Fidel. You are *el relampago*! No doubt about it—you burned their asses. The most amazing thing is that it doesn't even enter into their wildest dreams that it's you."

I replied with a vague expression, "Let's hope it stays like that for many, many years." We stood up and gave each other a big hug.

"Remember your training," he said seriously. "Watch your back."

I left the building from the rear while he left by the front. As I drove across the city in my jeep, heading towards the outskirts, I encountered a large crowd in the streets. I could no longer move through—it was like there was some kind of celebration going on. I saw a sign that said "*Camilo vive*[8]!" Another read, "You are the best of us, Camilo!" People all over the place had stopped their business to come out in the street to scream the chant, and the crowd began to increase by the minute. Traffic was entirely paralyzed, and people climbed on top of cars with Cuban flags. Women wept at the news. I had no choice but to stop the jeep.

---

8 "Camilo is alive!"

Someone screamed to me from one of the balconies, "Julio Antonio, I'm here! Look over here!!"

I looked around. In that crowd, it was difficult to pinpoint a single individual. From the balcony, dropping flowers and waving at me, I saw Sandra. She gestured for me to go down to the front door so that I could meet her. I got out and went over to the front door of the building. Finally, she burst out of the door, gave me a hug, and kissed me on the lips. "Where are you going?"

I looked around at the crowd and gestured. "It looks like I'm not going anywhere right now, with all this craziness." We decided to sit down in the jeep. She explained to me that a little while ago the radio and TV had reported that they had found Commander Camilo Cienfuegos alive and well.

Crowds thinking Camilo still lives

Camilo had once been Fidel's right arm. He was well-loved by the people, with his Texas ten-gallon hat, his long beard, and crucifix. He looked like one of the Apostles, and was becoming more popular than Castro was himself. He had mysteriously disappeared not too long after Fidel had sent him with the sad mission to arrest Camilo's best friend, Commander Huber Matos, in the central province of Camagüey. The government's official story was that the Cessna he had flown in had disappeared somewhere off the coast. No trace was found of any accident, plane, or Camilo's body, even though they had searched for months. But the Cuban people were not resigned to the idea of losing that charismatic character, and several times rumors were spread that he was alive. The reaction was inevitably identical to the one I was witnessing now. The rumor throughout the whole island was that the Castro brothers, along with Che, had plotted his assassination because he didn't sympathize with the communist ideas they wanted to plant in Cuba. Those closest to them reported several confrontations, especially when he mediated in Huber Matos' behalf, persuading them to sentence him to twenty years instead of the firing squad. This irritated the trio immensely, and so many thought that this incident had cost Camilo his life.

Evidently, this demonstration had been repeated so many times in the past few months, that it had become an unspoken protest in Camilo's memory. It was almost mocking the government, and so it bothered the Castros and Che. It was almost twenty minutes after this latest demonstration started that cars arrived with loudspeakers on the roofs, telling the people to disperse and return to their homes, stating firmly that the news was false and that Camilo was dead. The people ignored the edicts and continued their celebrations, with more people continually joining in with this disguised protest.

This angered the new dictator, since he saw it as the people rising up against his power. Two hours later, as Sandra and I listened to the jeep's radio, the emergency broadcast relayed the news that Fidel was about to address the nation. Sandra pointed over to an electronics store. "Look—they're putting TVs out on the sidewalk. Let's go and see what Fidel has to say." I looked, and saw the tables that were being set up for the TVs to sit on.

"Sure," I replied, "let's go over and take a look."

We walked over to the store. A crowd was already gathering, and we managed to squeeze in between the people to be able to see. Castro finally came onto the screen, and said in an irritated voice, "The rumor that Camilo is alive is an outright lie. It is nothing more than the deceiving way of the Counterrevolutionaries to interrupt the good function of the workers for the Revolution. Every one that listens to this falsehood has been part of this sinister, absurd stupidity, because there is no basis at all for it. This has been created by the worms," he paused here, touching his beard. "Camilo, unfortunately, is dead. It is a sad reality that we must all accept. Everybody should return to their homes and places of work. This is what every true Revolutionary will do right now!"

Like a magic wand had been waived, people began to disperse in utter silence. There were a few that tried to gossip, but they were abruptly ignored. We waited for a few minutes until the crowd dispersed. Sandra asked me, "Could you please take me home?"

"What the hell were you doing in that building?"

"My aunt lives there. I had just come from the militia headquarters. This whole commotion trapped me here."

"I can take you home, but do you mind if we stop someplace? I have to go pick up something."

"No, no problem. I'm in no rush."

"Very well. It won't take me too long."

"Isn't it funny? This is the third time this month that someone's been spreading this rumor. Fidel has a reason to be angry." She also appeared irritated. "This has to be the Counterrevolution, trying to create problems." I smiled ironically and shook my head in disagreement. She looked at me in surprise. "You don't believe so?" I didn't reply, but continued to smile cynically. "Julio Antonio—you and I, we have complete trust. You can tell me what you think, what kind of idea you have about all of this. You know better than I do, because you're inside the military, you know for sure better than anyone what the truth behind all of this is."

I shook my head, my ironic smile still on my face. "If you only knew. Let's leave it like that for now. But do you know, the first time I met Camilo and spoke with him, he didn't even ask me how old I was? That took me by surprise, because every single one of the Commanders and the ministers, or anyone else introduced to me by Fidel, Raul, or Che, the first thing they asked me was my age. They wanted to be friendly with me to keep on Fidel's good side, but clearly, they didn't want to talk to me much. Camilo came close to me, and said, 'Who is your favorite hero? Mine is the Lone Ranger with his friend, Tonto.' I told him with a big smile, 'Mine is Superman.' I asked him if that was the reason he wore the cowboy hat, and he didn't even say anything. He just nodded and winked at me. He was like such a big kid, and I'll never forget that in my life." I tapped my temple with my forefinger. "Then he invited me to eat *funche*[9]. I smiled and said to him, 'Only *los guajiros*[10] eat that.' He said, 'I was born here in the

---

9 Ground corn with milk
10 Country folk

capital, and grew up in the suburbs. I feel, though, that I am a *guajiro* in my heart, since from my earliest youth I loved the country. This is my favorite dish: fresh, warm milk added into this corn meal.' I made a sour expression and told him I didn't really like that stuff. He smiled and said, 'Come on, be a *guajirito* with me.' I didn't want to disappoint him, and agreed to eat it. I almost threw up, because the corn grains caught in my throat and made me gag. I tried to conceal it from him so that I didn't look like a wimp in front of him." My eyes grew moist as I drifted down my memories of that time. I shook my head and said to Sandra, "I know for a fact that we'll never see Camilo again. Fidel knows that better than anybody."

I stopped at that point, because I was about ready to weep in my grief over the loss of this good man. I couldn't take the chance of saying something that I shouldn't say to her in my emotional state. I knew the truth almost from the beginning behind Camilo's death, as my friend, Commander Cristino Naranjo, Camilo's second-in-command, had been extremely disturbed by the official version of the disappearance. He had started his own investigation with a group of officers. It was never completed, because a few weeks afterward, while driving into Havana's Columbia Regiment Headquarters, he had been confused for somebody else. He was gunned down with an automatic weapon by the captain in charge at the gate. The officer was exonerated for the incident, which had been deemed an accident. The strange part in this situation was that everybody in that compound knew him on sight. Stranger still was that the officer involved, Captain Manuel Beaton, was arrested a short time later and tried for treason. He and a group of officers were charged and found guilty of plotting an attempt on Fidel's life, and were all executed. I could not forget how, a year before, Che had made the toast to the death of all the enemies of the Revolution.

I shifted uneasily and cleared my throat. If I had any doubts of Commander Naranjo's suspicions, I had in black and white from Che's diary how the Argentinian had explained how and why they had planned to get rid of both Camilo and Huber Matos for the good of the Revolution. It was the same way so many other leaders in the Revolution were handled. Sandra could see how tense I was, given my silence. She could tell I was feeling emotional, and leaned in to put her arm around my shoulder. "I know, you probably feel very bad. You've told me so many great things about Camilo, and you were very fond of him. Maybe he's not dead after all," she said, trying to give me some hope.

I smiled cynically, shook my head, and said, "He is dead for sure. Mark my words—even in a hundred years, nobody will ever find his body."

We were almost to the outskirts of the city, crossing under the bridge to the other side of the riverbank. I could see close by up ahead two jeeps with a couple of groups of soldiers, conducting a search of a wagon loaded with sacks. I crossed by slowly by to see what was going on. The sergeant in charge recognized me and greeted me. I could see Marcel, Fraya, and Tite in the wagon. The sergeant, a tall, muscular black man, was signaling to Marcel to get out of the wagon and unload their cargo. He was clearly irritated for some reason. I pulled up next to them. I wasn't happy to get involved in this situation, because behind me I still had the fruits of my labor, but I felt the obligation to intervene and see what was going on. I had hidden those documents for so many days, and I might now be handing them directly into the soldiers' hands. The irony by no means escaped me. I wondered what they were doing here. They kept gesturing me to continue on by, and were surprised when I pulled over and got out of the jeep. I considered for a minute going ahead and continuing on, but I later thanked God that I decided to stop.

"Come on with me," I said to Sandra. She was still in her uniform of the civil militia. When we grew close to the wagon, I could see that some soldiers had machetes in their hands, ready to cut the ropes. Marcel was clearly taking too long to untie them, and the soldiers were impatient. As we approached, the soldiers saluted me.

The sergeant said, "*Buenos dias, Commandante.*" He shouted to his men, "Attention!" The six men stopped what they were doing, drew themselves up and stiffly saluted. They remained at attention until I returned the salutes and gave them the stand easy order.

"*Buenos dias*, Sergeant. What's going on here? What is the problem with these citizens?"

Marcel looked at me seriously, concealing the fact that he knew me. Fraya and Tite looked scared, but followed his lead and let no glimmer of recognition show in their faces. The sergeant replied, "My Commander, we have a complaint that someone in this area is producing contraband liquor, and is selling it in town. A few people have been getting sick because of the poor quality of the liquor."

I shook my head in disagreement. "These are decent people. I know them, and know they are good, hard-working people. They provide the town with charcoal."

"Oh!" the sergeant said in surprise. "You know these people?"

"Hello, Marcel, Fraya, Tite," I said, to demonstrate my knowledge.

"Hello, Commander," Marcel said timidly. The others waved to me.

I turned back to the sergeant. "This family is a great friend to my second mother, my black nanny Majito." Marcel nervously continued to attempt to untie the ropes before the soldiers cut them. I noticed that, and said, "Marcel, don't do that." He froze. "I don't think that is going to be necessary, eh, Sergeant?" I looked at the man. "What do you think?"

"No, no," he said, "it's OK. Don't worry about it." He smiled at me. "Thank you for stopping, Commander, you saved us a lot of work. I wasn't looking forward to going through these sacks of charcoal and getting myself all filthy. If you know these people, Commander, we're out of here." They saluted me, loaded into their jeeps, and took off.

To my surprise, after the jeeps had moved away to a comfortable distance, Marcel stuck his hand into a sack. He said to me, "Bad liquor my butt! This is the best liquor anyone in this town ever drank. Take this to your Papi—he will probably enjoy it very much."

Fraya jumped out of the wagon and gave me a big hug. "How are your wounds?"

I looked at her and then at Sandra. I smiled as I said, "What wounds, woman? This is a long time ago, practically when I was a little boy and fell on the rocks in the river." I looked at Sandra once more. "By the way, this is Sandra—the daughter of the Minister of Transportation." The three of them absolutely froze at that point.

Sandra stepped forward to introduce herself. The poor black woman turned gray in the face as she realized how indiscreet she just had been. "Well, well, well—the time goes by too fast with you kids. You grow up like weeds. In my mind, it's not too long ago, and here it's been years already that you fell. I remember taking you to the house...." She would have kept going, but Marcel intervened.

"OK, woman—I can't stay here all day. People in town are waiting for me to deliver the charcoal so they can cook."

I lifted both bottles up and looked at them. "What kind of liquor is this?"

"It's the best of the best," Marcel said. It was a yellowish liquid, like honey or Grand Marnier in thickness. It was guayabita del pinar, a liquor made from fermented guava, a particular kind that grew only on the Occidental side of the island.

I was taken by surprise, since I didn't know they really were carrying contraband in their wagon. We looked at each other, the three of them scrutinizing me to see what my reaction was going to be. I smiled, and they relaxed. I lifted my bottle-filled hands, and said, "I thank God that by coincidence we crossed paths today."

"You're right, my boy," Marcel agreed. "But it's not coincidence, as we crossed paths not too long ago. What goes around, comes around."

"Amen," I said. "I have no doubt about that." Bottles still in my hands, I hugged each of them. "*Vallan con dios*," I told them very carefully. As we said our goodbyes, we heard rifle shots not too far away. We all looked around, but didn't see anything unusual. I thought the soldiers might have been indulging in some target practice.

As we walked back to the jeep, Sandra said, "My God—these people are nigger smugglers! You really got them out of big trouble. They shouldn't be doing this kind of stuff."

We got into the jeep, and I started to drive. "That 'nigger,' as you called him, is my friend. So is his family. If he is a smuggler, it is because our socialist Revolution is pushing him into that life. Not too long ago, he was a reputable professor of English. The government wasn't content to discriminate against him, confiscate his house and outlaw his way of life, all because he has different political ideas—they had to push him back into being exactly what his father didn't want for him, being a charcoal man. Our Revolution, Sandra, is supposed to protect the poor people. Look at what we do. We not only made this man a charcoal man, but we've also made him a smuggler. You see he's not driving a nice car or a jeep like we're driving; for God's sake, he's driving a horse-drawn wagon. He needs that money to support his family. On top of that, he chose to stay here when his father left to go to Miami, and look at what we've done to him."

She looked at me in surprise. She couldn't argue with what I had said, and so kept silent. She didn't say anything for a while. We continued along the road along the riverbank. In an attempt to alleviate the tension, she finally said, "You drive very well. Who taught you?"

"I've been driving since I was eight," I said very seriously. "My father taught me. I remember that I could neither reach the pedals nor see over the dashboard, so we had to put a bunch of magazines under me on the seat so I could see the road and then put pieces of wood tied to the pedals under my feet so that I could push them." I saw something in the road ahead and slowed down to a stop.

"What is that?" Sandra asked.

"I don't know. Let's check it out." I got out of the jeep.

As I got close, I was surprised to see it was a beautiful, large dog, white with black spots. It looked like an Akita. It was bloodied, with bullet holes all over its body.

Sandra had come up behind me. As soon as she saw it, she gasped and lifted her hand to her mouth in distress. Not too far away, I could see three puppies, also bullet-riddled and dead. I could see that the adult was the mother, her udders filled with milk and the body still warm.

I grimaced in disgust. "This explains the shots we heard. These were the targets for their practice. Those sons of bitches, using these beautiful animals like that. She looks to me like a cross between a wolf and a husky." I thought that this dog looked like a purebred animal, not a street mongrel. It probably belonged to a family that had abandoned Cuba. I asked myself what these animals had done to those guys to be shot in this way. I grieved in frustration and discontent, because I love all animals, especially dogs and horses.

To our right, near the river, I could hear howling and whimpering. We both looked in that direction. In the middle of the river, on a sandbar was a small puppy. It was smaller than the others, possibly the runt, and it was soaking wet and clearly frightened. Without thinking twice, I took off my boots and socks, rolled up my pants, and waded into the river. The puppy was so scared that I had a hard time catching it. It tried to bite me each time I reached for it. I spoke to it softly, and finally managed to calm it down. I quickly grabbed it by the scruff of its neck, and lifted it above the deadwood. I brought it to my chest and embraced it. As soon as it felt the warmth of my body, it stopped fighting me and let me carry it.

When I got back to the riverbank, Sandra exclaimed, "Oh, my God! What a beautiful puppy!! What are you going to do with it? It looks like he still needs to suckle with his mother."

I caressed it a little bit. This time, instead of trying to bite me, it licked my hand in a friendly way. "I will take care of him. I know I can't take him to my house, because my father gave us a dog when we were very little. A car killed it right in front of our home, and my brothers and I cried so hard for so long that he promised himself that we would never have a dog again. I will call him Kimbo. That was the name of the dog we had that got hit by the car."

"Where are you going to take him?"

"I will take him to the ranch where I have my horse. Leocadio, my friend who is the caretaker there, will look after him for me, at least until he starts to eat for himself."

Sandra cooed over the puppy. "I'd love to take him to my house, but my step-father and mother don't want any dogs or cats in the house."

"Don't worry about it. Leocadio has two cows that just had calves, so he's got plenty of milk, even for ten puppies like this." I unbuttoned my shirt and put the little puppy inside. We climbed back into the jeep and drove on in silence toward our houses.

Sandra broke the silence. "I've been thinking, in reference to what you said about your friend, the charcoal man." She put her hand on my shoulder. "I want to say I'm sorry to you. Everything in life is like the moon: it has two sides, the one that shines that we see every day and everyone likes, and the dark side that nobody cares about because they don't see it. They don't want to see it, anyway, because it's ugly and dark. We just ignore it because we don't care. I'm sorry for my previous insensitivity. That is the other side of the Revolution. Unfortunately, we don't want to see it." I smiled and nodded appreciatively. I caressed her cheek. She looked at me sadly, and I could see a couple of tears of shame roll down her cheeks. She looked straight into my eyes for a few seconds, very deeply. "You know, very soon I will leave for a while. You won't see me for a long time. My father wants to send me to the Naval Intelligence Academy."

I smiled to hear her say that and thought to myself what an irony that was, but kept silent.

She tapped my shoulder jokingly. "I've never see you so quiet. What is going on in your mind? You are so mysterious lately. You smile at everything I say, like there's something you know that you're not telling me. You're going to make me mad. Is that what you want to do? Make me mad?"

I thought to myself once more, if only she knew. Instead, I said, "Your father wants to send you to make you a spy. And you want to study arts, painting, music, and so on. I want to be an attorney, a musician, and a film maker. And Fidel wants to send me to the Soviet Union, in order to make me into a spy as well. Is this not really strange, or is it a coincidence?"

She smiled. "Yes, it really is." She placed her finger to her temple and smiled mysteriously. "You haven't been thinking that, maybe because my father is a minister that he and Fidel maybe are preparing all of this like the way they used to arrange marriages in olden days? To make us both spies and get us married?"

I smiled, this time genuinely. "Don't let yourself dream so high. We're not that important to these people. Maybe you are to your father, but I don't think I'm that important to Fidel. Besides, we're too young to be thinking of marriage."

She grinned. "Well, you have to start preparing

sometime."

I held my hand up as if to halt her. "We've got plenty of time. Don't rush yourself."

We were a few blocks from my house. I stopped the jeep close to the sidewalk. She gave me a kiss and said, "Well, we'll see each other Saturday at your sister's wedding."

"OK. It's only a couple of days." We said goodbye and I continued to my house. When I got the documents out of the back of the jeep, I went to my bedroom and put my documents in the hiding place inside my closet. However, on my way out of the house, my mother saw the puppy sticking out of my shirt.

She asked me, "What are you thinking of doing with that little puppy?"

I gave her a kiss on the cheek. "Don't worry, Mima. I'll take him to the ranch, and Leocadio will take care of him until he can walk by himself and feed himself."

She shook her head in resignation. "You always try to rescue all the animals in the world. Remember, your father doesn't want dogs or cats in the house."

"Don't worry. I won't keep him in the house." I got into my jeep, and drove towards the ranch.

Castro addresses the crowd

Chapter 6: The Abduction

As I got close to the ranch, I saw Tite coming the opposite direction on horseback with a couple of sacks of charcoal on the back of his horse. He told me that he was on his way to deliver to a customer. I told him, "If you wait for me until I saddle my horse, I can go with you when you make your delivery."

"OK, I'll wait for you here at the entrance to the ranch."

"No—tie your horse to that tree, and come with me in the jeep. I'll bring you back here."

He walked a short distance, and tied his horse under a large mango tree. He opened the gate for me, jumped into the jeep, and we drove into the ranch. Leocadio received me with a big smile on his face on the porch of the house. He was a short, plump man who was missing two front upper teeth. The rest of his teeth were in terrible shape, due to his old habit of chewing tobacco. He was sometimes unshaven for weeks on end, and loved to drink liquor, no matter what kind it was. He was the sort of drinker who preferred quantity over quality. However, he was a very hard worker, in spite of his drinking habit and his preference to sleep in a hammock on the porch of the house. He was very pleasant, very courteous, and very humble. This is why my father, many years ago, had loaned him the money to buy that small ranch. He never completely paid it back, again thanks to his hard drinking. However, he compensated for it by bringing to our house the spices, eggs, corn, milk, and other fresh produce that he harvested at the ranch. In a way, it was paying my father back with gratitude for his patience in not demanding back the rest of the loan. He took care of my horse, Diamante, without charging me a penny. Diamante was completely white with a black, diamond-shaped spot on his forehead. It was this mark that gave him his name, which was the Spanish word for diamond.

As we approached the house, his mongrels ran to the jeep, barking and attacking the tires. They followed us until we finally stopped by the porch. Leocadio was standing by one of the columns with an aluminum jar in his hand. He took off his palm leaf hat off with his free hand. With a smile, he waved it at us. He always seemed happy whenever he saw me. I always brought with me a bottle of wine or whatever I could find as a token for taking care of my horse. After I introduced Tite to Leocadio and left my new friend, Kimbo, I gave him the bottles of guayabita. I went and saddled my horse, brought Tite back to his horse, and then we rode to the riverbank toward Tite's destination. For about twenty minutes we rode, crossing small creeks that formed the river. We came to a beautiful chalet on the top of a small hill. Tite went and delivered his charcoal while I waited for him at the gate of the beautiful residence. When he came back, I handed him invitations to my sister's wedding.

"Tell Marcel and Fraya that they have to be there. I've already told my parents that you guys will be sitting at the table they assign to me and my friends. It will be a great feast—roast pigs and all kinds of food there. My family have been buying food like crazy in preparation for the celebration."

Tite smiled mischievously. "I will tell them if they d-d-don't come to the wedding that you will t-t-tell everybody our secret." He started to giggle at the expression on my face.

"No, no, no! Don't even joke about that. You want to kill them of a heart attack?"

"How can you think I would actually do that? I was just joking. If I told that to them, they would be having diarrhea for a week." He grinned broadly. "OK—see if you can catch me." He nudged his old work horse into a gallop.

I was surprised by the speed of his old horse, but I kicked my horse into a gallop. I soon caught up with him and passed him. I didn't want to make him feel bad, so I reined in my horse. I knew the old horse had to be laboring heavily, and was almost dead already from all the work Marcel made him do every day, pulling that wagon. He couldn't compete with my horse, so much younger and full of energy. I only rode Diamante once or twice a week, so he was always eager for a good run. I slowed him down so much that I practically stopped the horse. I could see he was far behind me, and I assumed that he would soon catch up. Instead of stopping beside me, however, he continued on past me like a flash, screaming, "Catch me this time, if you can!"

I smiled and shook my head. "Oh, God," I said aloud to myself. I started back into a gallop, not so fast to immediately catch up with him, but to make it more gradual. Far away, along the riverbank, I could see in the distance a group of soldiers and a military jeep. Tite had a very good head start, and so got to the group of soldiers well before me. Several soldiers ran behind a beautiful mulatto girl, with long, straight, gorgeous hair. They were trying to catch her, but she ran in a zig-zag pattern, making it very difficult for them.

Tite didn't stop, and nearly ran over the soldiers. He

would have, if the soldiers hadn't dodged out of the way to let him pass through. Almost like some American Indian, he caught her by the waist and pulled her onto the horse's back. She saw that he was coming to help her, and so she was doing her own best effort in jumping onto the horse. They kept going.

One of the soldiers had fallen to the ground. He came up, rifle in hand, and brought it up to cock and fire it. I could see the danger immediately, and I didn't stop my horse, either. I yanked on the bridle and virtually jumped over the soldier. He tried to protect himself from the horse, and jumped into the river with a large splash, rifle and all. We had caught them utterly by surprise. I didn't have any idea at all what was going on there, but instead followed my instincts to help my friend. Not too far off, I could see another group of soldiers wrestling with somebody on the sand. I heard a familiar voice screaming, "Julio Antonio! Julio Antonio! Help us, please! Help!"

The screaming voice took me by surprise, and I turned in my saddle to my left. I could see the same sergeant from earlier holding Yaneba with two other soldiers. I stopped my horse and turned towards them. I trotted the horse towards them. The sergeant had on his shoulders a sack of freshly cut grass. He immediately recognized me and pulled himself to attention to salute me. The others tried to do the same, though not as well as they were also holding the struggling Yaneba. She was kicking them fiercely in the shins and clawing at their arms. The salutes failed as they had to turn their full attention to restraining her.

I took the initiative to take command. "What is going on here? What's happened now, Sergeant?" To my right, I could see two soldiers bringing another girl by the arm.

This one looked Asian, with long hair full of sand. She was kicking and assaulting the soldiers, as well.

The sergeant took a couple of steps towards my horse. He raised the sack in the air. "These spoiled rich brats were cutting marijuana, maybe to sell in the city. They are possibly daughters of the Imperialist worms."

Yaneba screamed at him, "The only Imperialist here is you, you son of a bitch! You put your dirty, filthy hand in my private parts. That is why I bit you when you tried to kiss me by force! That grass is for my rabbit that I have at home. I don't know what the devil it is because I'm not a drug addict like you are, you moron!"

Still on my horse, I looked at the sergeant in recrimination. I could see the bite mark on his lower lip that was bleeding slightly. I could also see scratches on his face that could easily be from a girl's nails. Tite had turned around and was coming closer to us with the third girl still on the back of his horse. The soldiers in the river ran over to him and tried to bring both of them down off the horse.

I turned in my saddle and yelled angrily. "Get out of there! Leave them alone, if you don't want to sleep tonight in a goddamn jail cell." The soldiers stepped back, their eyes wide in fear and shock as they realized I was genuinely upset. As soon as I saw they were going to be left alone, I turned back to the sergeant. "Sergeant, you are a disgrace to the Rebel Army if what this young lady tells me is true."

The sergeant rushed to defend himself. "No, no, no, my Commander. When I ran after her, she fell in the sand. I tripped over her body and fell on top of her, but it was just an accident. I swear to you, I never tried to kiss her or anything that looked like it."

"What is that you have on your lip, then?" I asked sternly.

"I hit myself against a rock when I fell down. She's creating this because she wants to get me in trouble. She is a liar!"

I slid down off my horse. Yaneba screamed at full lung, "The only liar here, you son of a bitch, is you! If you don't believe me, ask my friends, Chandee and Marlina." She looked at me. "If you didn't come when you did, thank God, these sons of bitches would have been raping us. They tried to rape us!" She began to cry. "The only reason they didn't rape us is because we fought with them. No doubt in my mind that that was their intentions. Why the hell else would this son of a bitch put his hands in my parts? That was not an accident!"

When the corporal over by Tite's horse heard that, he quickly began to pull up his pants, button up his fly, and retie his belt. I looked at him in angry disgust. I said nothing to the corporal, but turned to the ones holding Yaneba. "Let her go!" They both let her go immediately and stepped back. She ran straight at the sergeant to hit him, both hands closed in fists. I quickly got between them and held her. He was so much larger and stronger that he could easily have smacked her away; it would also give him reason to detain her. "Calm down," I reassured her. "It's over. I'm here, and I won't let anybody hurt you." She measured the difference in size between the two of them, and stepped away from him.

The sergeant stepped back a few feet from her and said, "You see, my Commander? These bourgeois teenagers, they're all crazy!"

I looked at him accusingly. The other soldiers holding Chandee let her go before I could even say anything. As soon as I looked in their direction, they had voluntarily released her. I looked at them individually, shaking my head in disappointment, letting them know how I felt without saying a word. I held my hand out towards the sergeant. Without saying a word, he also handed the sack of grass to me. I could see the blades had a kind of triangular shape. After I had the sack, I gave it to Yaneba. I looked at the sergeant and said, "Take a pen and paper, and write down every single name of the soldiers here, including your corporal. When you finish your round of what you're doing here, I want you to go directly to the Regiment and leave that list with Commander Argibay, the Military Auditor."

The sergeant looked at me and said, "My Commander, but--"

I interrupted him with an upraised hand. "Here, there is no 'but' any more that is worth a shit. It's very clear to me what happened here, and I'm going to make sure a very meticulous investigation of the conduct of everyone here today, including the witnesses, takes place as soon as possible." He tried to interrupt me again, but I barked with full force, "Atten-HUT! Dismissed. Now!"

Without a single word, they turned around, got into their jeeps, and drove off. Everyone looked at me, aghast at my red-faced fury. Tite smiled broadly in satisfaction and said before dismounting, "I've never seen you in action as a military commander. Today, I c-c-can assure you that you behave like a true C-c-commandante: d-d-dignified and d-d-decent as you are." He dismounted, and held the horse by the bridle. He came close to me and put his arm on my shoulder. "You made me feel very proud to be my brother. Yessir, you made me feel very proud." He beamed broadly at me. "God knows why He made you the C-c-commandantico of this c-c-crazy Revolution, yessir. God knows what He d-d-does, and there's no d-d-doubt in my mind."

I still wasn't very happy. "I haven't done anything yet. The shit will hit the fan when I get to the Regiment. I can assure you guys that these bullies will receive punishment, even if it's the last thing I do in this goddamn army." That last I delivered with frustration boiling in me, both fists balled in fury. "Indecent abusers, and bullies." I was so furious that I could only repeat myself.

Yaneba was about thirty feet away from us, crying and wiping her face. I thought it best to leave her alone for a few minutes, and we introduced ourselves to her friends. Tite and Marlina helped Chandee to clean the sand out of her hair and clothes. Chandee had a big bump on her head, the result of a soldier hitting her in the back of the head with his rifle. It corroborated the whole story. I grew even angrier, because I could also see that she had a small cut on her face as a result of her abuses. After the two girls told me everything that had happened. There were even some details that Yaneba had not revealed. The soldiers had initially attempted to rape Chandee, but Yaneba—the smallest one in their group—had in turn attacked Chandee's molesters. That had led them to the events she had revealed. They were thankful that Tite and I showed up when we did; a miracle, they described it. They were both trembling as they relayed their story. They knew that, had the rape gone ahead, the soldiers would very likely have killed them in order to conceal the crime.

"I'll be back in a little bit." I turned and walked over to Yaneba's side. As soon as I was close, I asked her softly, "Are you OK?" She didn't say anything, but just shook her head negatively and began to cry harder.

I understood her emotional state, and my heart was completely torn by her pain. Seeing the jaunty Yaneba so crushed and vulnerable was almost more than I could bear. I took a couple of steps to the bushes, tied up my horse, walked over and gave her a big hug. Her body was trembling like the leaves of the trees being blown by a strong wind. My emotions were turbulent and jumbled, seeing her in such agony, knowing her for so long to be such a feisty and self-assured girl. My muscles grew weak, and I could sense her feelings growing into my veins. My eyes grew moist, and in spite of my self-control, a pair of involuntary tears streamed down my cheeks. In a voice hoarse with emotional intensity, I said as I touched her long hair, "Don't worry. I won't ever let anybody harm you, my love." I wasn't even thinking; it seemed to come from some deep, unfathomable place in my soul.

In reaction to those last words, she stepped away from me and looked into my eyes. She saw my tears, and a kind of joy and satisfaction gleamed responsively in hers. She wiped away my tears with one hand, while the other remained on my shoulder. Still trembling, she said, "I was so scared. So scared. For the first time in my life, that man terrified me, especially when he tried to take my underwear off. With his filthy hand, he tried to stick one of his fingers in my vagina." She sobbed. "For a minute, I thought I was about to lose my precious virginity to that foul beast of a sergeant, and my world collapsed on top of my head. I don't know from where I got the strength, because he's so muscular and much stronger than me." She paused as she sobbed again and continued, "But I got strength and remembered what you told me once. If I ever need to defend myself against a man, hit him in the testicles. You take him out of combat for a while. Thank you." She gave me a small kiss on one of my tears. "I did what you told me, and I ran and ran with all my might, but

I didn't run fast enough. The other soldiers caught me again. I don't know if it was because I didn't run fast enough because I didn't want to leave my friends behind, or if my nerves just didn't make my muscles respond. When they brought me back to that indecent monster, you appeared out of the blue like you had been sent by God." She sobbed again. Two new tears streamed down her face. She tried to smile. "I never felt so happy to see you, even when I saw you near here right after that time you disappeared recently. The only thing that came to my mind was to scream to you with all my power." She sobbed once more. "My Julio Antonio, thank you, with all my heart. Can you imagine it? I've been saving myself to award it to you, and you've been refusing to take my gift, because you haven't wanted to hurt my honor. That giant communist pig with his soiled hands tried to steal your present."

I looked at her tenderly. It was as if her warm blood had entered my body, along with her love and emotions; I could feel it all rolling through my arteries with the power and strength of a volcano or a geyser. In that particular moment, I saw her differently: beautiful both in spirit and body, adult and gorgeous. She became the woman of my dreams. She was still hugging me and looking warmly into my eyes. With a woman's perception, she could feel what she had transferred to my body and soul at that instant. Slowly, her face moved close to mine. First, our noses touched, and then, lingeringly, her lips moved closer to mine. I didn't move, as if the power of my emotions had frozen me there. She moved slowly, tentatively, as if she were afraid of rejection. Finally, her lips touched mine, and with extraordinary tenderness, I could feel the heat of her lips. As she moved in to kiss me, her body leaned in against mine. My arms squeezed her against my body, and gently we kissed. At first, it was a small kiss, but then it became a long, passionate one. For the first time in my life, I never wanted that kiss to ever end. It was the sweetest kiss, full of fire, that I had ever yet received. When we parted, we stared at each other in silence for several seconds. I thought to myself, Oh, my God. I'm in trouble.

As we looked at each other lovingly, she reached out and touched my face. "How long have I waited for this?" We were about to kiss again, when we heard the voices of our friends calling out for us. She gave me a quick kiss and said, "We'd better go find them." She giggled with joy. She grabbed my hand like a lover, and we went to my horse in the bushes. We untied him and walked back towards the group. Just before we reached them, I removed from my shirt pocket the invitation for my sister's wedding. As I gave it to her, I said, "If you want, you can bring your friends with you. My parents assigned me to a long table. We could easily have fifteen people there. They know how many friends I have."

"Very well," she answered with a big smile on her face that displayed to me her perfect, white teeth. "I'll ask them if they want to come with me."

When we reached the group, the exotic mulatta, Marlina, and the lovely Asian Cuban, Chandee, joined Tite on the back of his horse. Yaneba climbed on the back of Diamante. It began to rain very lightly, just a drizzle. We rode our horses along the riverbank towards the town, and it began to rain harder. By the time we reached the city, we were all completely drenched. We reached Yaneba's house and said our goodbyes, Yaneba giving me a soft kiss by way of farewell. I said goodbye to Tite, as well, as we were going in different directions. Because of the rain, he urged his horse into a canter. I did likewise, as I still had to get to the ranch.

As I drew near the ranch, the rain diminished, and then stopped. The sun broke through the clouds, and ahead of me was a brilliant rainbow that seemed to arch over the mountains. I was only half a mile from the ranch gates when I saw a car in the road. It was a dark green '55 Oldsmobile. It looked much like the G-2 used. I didn't give it too much thought, and continued to ride on towards the ranch. It looked like it had a flat, and two large men in civilian clothes were changing the tire. I slowed down. The road was very narrow, and I had to carefully maneuver my horse on the opposite side to avoid trampling them. As I passed, they waved at me in greeting, and I waved back. I was going to continue on by them, but before I could, two other men I hadn't observed stepped out. They had been hiding from me, crouched just behind the car out of my line of sight. They jumped forward. One held my horse by the bridle. The other tried to pull me bodily out of my saddle, yanking at me fiercely to try and make me lose my balance. I grabbed the saddle horn, leaned back, and kicked the man full in the chest away from me. The man rolled back onto the muddy road. I pulled my pistol out and cocked it, ready to shoot all four men. I pointed it at the man who was holding my horse, but before I could pull the trigger, the man behind me hit me with the tire iron in the back of my head. When I turned my head, I could only see his hand with the long metal rod. I fell slowly out of the saddle, and rolled in the mud next to the man I had just struck. I heard my horse whinny, and from my prone position I could see Diamante try to strike the two men. The one man struck my horse with his tire tool, causing him to gallop away rapidly. That was the last thing I saw before

I lost consciousness.

When I awoke, I was in a very dark place. It looked like some subterranean dungeon. I saw chains with manacles hanging from the concrete walls. A few five gallon buckets with dirty water lay on the floor next to a large fifty-five gallon tank. It looked like a torture chamber. Perhaps thirty feet away from me hung a man who looked unconscious, chained to the green, musty wall. There was a large metal table bolted to the concrete floor with a similarly bolted chair, and scissors, and a strange metal instrument on top of it. It was stained with very dark liquid that looked like blood. A very foul and terrible odor like human excrement permeated the room. It smelled like something was really rotten, and it hurt my sense of smell. I realized that, according to the new terminology of the Revolution, I was now in disgrace—that I had fallen out of favor with the government. This was how they described the disaffected: as traitors and enemies of the Revolution. Even though I had been trained for this particular moment, I had a knot in my throat and butterflies in my stomach. I expected the worst. My mind seemed to race at a hundred miles per hour as I went through several possible scenarios. The first thought that flashed through my mind was to wonder who had betrayed me.

They left me there for a while; it seemed like a long time. I could reflect on how I was going to answer the various questions that I concocted for myself, anticipating what interrogations I was about to endure. I analyzed everything, and a deep release came to me when I arrived at the conclusion that there was nothing that could have compromised me. As my reason took hold over my emotions, I came to the realization that this could be the best thing that happened to me, as I had only to make it a situation of the word of someone else against mine, and I could get free of this. The feeling lasted only a moment, as I hung my head down—and saw the pen in my pocket. Once that was discovered to be more than just a pen, I was doomed. A displeased expression crossed my face at that realization, and I gulped nervously. I tried to calm myself, reminding myself that this pen was so original and sophisticated that it would never cross their minds what its real purpose was. But if they found out the pen's functions, I determined to do what the General had instructed me to do in my training period. I would deny any knowledge, and say that I had found it in the street that same day, and had no idea what that pen was for. I had found it in the chaos of the false news about Camilo, and that someone in that multitude must have dropped it. I completely calmed down as I recalled that it was empty. The General had just given it to me recently, and I'd had no opportunity to use it. I smiled; I had the perfect alibi for it.

I heard the noise of the metal door open and close. A few seconds later, a man wearing a hood came to the man next to me. He grabbed the wretch by the hair, raised his head up and observed him for several seconds. He then said, "Hey. Hey! Wake up! The show is about to begin." The chained man's eyes didn't open, and he didn't reply. When the hooded man let go of the prisoner's hair, his head dropped back onto his chest. The hooded man picked up one of the buckets of water and dumped at least half of the contents of the man's head. I could see pieces of feces, or something similar, stick to the hair of the chained man. It wasn't too far from me, and a horrible smell of feces and urine, worse than before, permeated the room. I turned my head away, trying to cover my nose against my arm. It flashed into my mind that the contents of those buckets weren't dirty water as I had thought. They contained human excrement and old urine.

The chained man roused and shook his head abruptly, as if an electric shock had been administered. He screamed at the top of his lungs, "You son of a bitch! I'm a member of the State Security! Why the hell are you doing this to me? I'm one of you!! I would never betray the Revolution." He spat what horrible things had caught in his mouth, blew his nose as if clearing it from the pestilent smell, and continued to clear his throat.

The hooded man laughed as if he were enjoying his work immensely. Without a word, he took another object out from under the table. It looked like a portable toilet. He pulled his pants down, took a magazine off the table, and before our eyes had a bowel movement. I understood the significance of this. He whistled as he defecated. A little while later, after he had finished, he emptied the contents into another one of the buckets. He walked over to a sink in the floor and turned on a faucet. He poured about half a bucket of water and took a piece of wood that was leaning against the wall. I now saw that it showed signs of its current use as he began to stir the stool inside the bucket, all the while whistling tunelessly. He brought it over to the man and put the man's head almost fully inside the bucket. "This is your lunch," he said with a chuckle. "I've already given you your breakfast." He laughed. His laugh did not show signs of great intelligence. He walked over and put the bucket on the floor.

We heard the door open and close once more. From where I was bound, I could not see the door at all. Three additional hooded men entered the place. Two of them opened their flies and went over to the buckets on the floor. They then urinated into the pails. Clearly, this was also the toilet for this team. The third man waited patiently until his friends had finished, and then did the same. The tallest and skinniest of these men seemed to be the leader of the gang. He said to the man by his side, "Prepare everything to start." Two of the hooded men came over to the other prisoner. Ignoring his screams and protests, they unchained him from the wall and brought him to the metal table. They forced him down and tied him to chair, securing both hands and legs. The leader continued, "Today, you need to tell us what we want to know. I don't have much time. If you don't tell me what I need to know, your pain will be permanent. Today, you will lose your fingers. Maybe one eye. Perhaps your testicles." When I heard that, I swallowed uncomfortably. "But today, you will talk. Of that, I don't have any doubt." Up to this moment, they had been ignoring me, as if I didn't even exist. The leader, however, turned to the first hooded man and said, "Get the Commandantico's breakfast ready." My stomach churned with nausea at the merest thought. I kept my expression neutral and the fear out of my eyes. I looked right into the holes in his hood where his eyes would be. I was hoping to see the color of his iris or something that I could use to identify the man later.

    The man was short and chubby. He took the stick from the wall and mixed a bucket of urine and feces. "Yeah. I'm just getting it ready. It only needs a little salt and pepper." He coughed up some phlegm and spat into the bucket. "Could you guys get me some salt?" Very loudly, so that I could hear them, the other men likewise expectorated into the bucket, except for the leader. They also loudly sharpened various implements, also so that I could hear them. The leader never took his eyes from my face, intently studying my reactions. I didn't move. My legs began to cramp up and tingle from loss of circulation, but I was determined to hold myself still, not showing any fear to these men. The chubby man came over to me, grabbed my hair, and forced my head into the bucket. I gagged and very nearly vomited. "I'm just letting you smell it," he said in response to my nausea. "In a little while, I'm going to make you eat it." He laughed in his imbecilic fashion. He then yelled at me, "Today, you are going to tell us where you put the portfolio and the personal diary you stole from our Commander, Che. You're going to tell us how you took it out of the Regiment."

I felt my world collapse on me. Somebody must have betrayed me, and I reacted violently. "*Me cago en el recontracoño de tu madre hijo de puta*[11]! When I get out of here, I will be repaid by you with interest. I don't know what kind of shit you're talking about, but I assure you that out of that fat ass you have I will make a couple of filets to feed my dog with. I'll even use my commando knife to do that to you!"

The chubby man looked at me in surprise, not expecting my energy after what he had done to me. He certainly wasn't expecting that level of aggression from me. Perhaps many of the men they did this to tried to be humble or became intimidated in order to get out of the situation. He lost his own control, and he emptied the entire contents of the bucket square in my face. He grew so enraged that he struck me in the head with the bucket, and broke my upper lip with the corner. He screamed back at me, "I shit on your mother, you snot-nosed brat!"

The others realized he was losing his temper, and ran over to him as he began to strike me with his fist, hitting

---

[11] I shit in your mother's pussy, you son of a whore!

me where ever he could find to land a blow, chest, leg, or arm. Once, he tried to hit me in the face, and I moved quickly to my right, jangling the chains loudly. Instead of my face, he hit one of the links of my chain, which angered him even more. The leader bellowed, "Stop! Enough!! *Que carajo te pasa*[12]? Are you stupid or something? How can you allow this little kid make you lose your control?" He had advanced towards us, bellowing right in the face of the chubby one. They all took him outside, leaving us alone for a few moments. We could hear from a distance the group talking together, with the leader admonishing the chubby man for his attitude.

It occurred to me that this must be a prepared routine, a good cop/bad cop routine to psychologically condition us to answer their questions. If this were really G-2 professional interrogators, that man wouldn't lose control so quickly and over something as insignificant as an insult from me. I didn't know what their plans were or who was behind this, but the worst of my worries was what that man said about Che's military attaché. How could they know about this? My head spun, and I tried to maintain my calm. My agony, however, increased by seconds.

The other prisoner was still tied to the chair by metal table. He was, I could now see, about thirty years old, a mulatto, with very refined features and wavy hair. He looked at me and asked, "Did you really, truly steal the briefcase from Che, and his diary? Boy—if you did that, you may be young, but you've got really big cojones. No doubt, they're in the right place."

I looked at him in silence for a moment. Without answering his question, I asked, "What are you here for? I

---

[12] What the hell is wrong with you?

heard you tell them that you're a member of the G-2. Is that true?"

"Claro," he replied. "I'm a clandestine agent, but these crazy sons of bitches are assuming I'm a double agent. I made the mistake to tell one of my personal friends that I'm not a communist, and never will be. I believe in God and His Son, Jesus Christ. All these fucking communists are atheists." I nodded my head, but I didn't believe a word of it. "My name is Luciano," he continued. "I know who you are, the Commandantico, but what is your name?"

"My name is Julio Antonio."

We heard the door open and close once more. The group of hooded men came back and walked over to us. I was still covered in fecal matter, and felt like I had a piece in my hair that I couldn't quite shake out. Luciano, likewise, was still filthy. This time, the leader said, "OK, let's start with Luciano. We can continue later with the Commandantico."

They forced Luciano to put his right hand into the metal instrument, a machine that looked like a guillotine. There was a small opening into which they crammed one of his fingers. They ignored his screaming and protests, and began to cut his fingers off, one by one. Each time the blade of the guillotine fell, I felt like they were cutting off one of my own fingers. Until that moment, I thought that Luciano was planted there to make me talk. I became completely convinced that it wasn't possible, since I could not accept that they would cut off the fingers of one of their men, much less that one of their own would volunteer to let them do this to him. They cut off almost all of his fingers, right in front of my eyes. The table was perhaps only fifty feet from my position, and Luciano's screams of horrendous pain and the blood made me very scared. Reality hit me, and I thought that I would be next. This was very serious.

The leader said, "OK, bind up that hand so he doesn't bleed out on us. We'll continue later on his other hand. Let's give him a break and start on the Commandantico."

They took the semi-conscious Luciano and chained him back to his section of the wall. One of the other men took out the portable toilet, and pulled down his pants. "Well, I'm going to contribute to the lunch of our friends." He began to defecate into the toilet. The other two men came over and opened my manacles. They were stronger and taller, and virtually lifted me off of my feet as I struggled with them. As they strapped me down to the chair in Luciano's place, I saw with my own eyes the bloody fingers lying on the table. My stomach heaved at that sickening sight, but I tried to control my fear. The fingers looked like little sausages—except for the fingernails.

The leader leaned in close to my face and looked into my eyes. "OK, you have two choices. The first one will leave all of your fingers cut on this table. That is the stupid choice. The other one, the intelligent choice, is to tell us where you have the documents you stole with that attaché case from the Regiment. Tell us who you work for. You'll keep your fingers, you'll have lunch in your house, and you'll be able to go into the back where we have a clean bathroom. There you can clean yourself of all this shit you have on your body, and we won't hurt you anymore. We're not interested in you; we're interested in who you work for. I'm sure you'll make the smart choice—you're an intelligent boy. You're the Commandantico; there's no way you could be stupid. After all, you are Fidel's favorite. We always can say that you worked with us, and you wanted to catch those people. They are the bad people, not you."

I shook my head. "This is very simple. You will cut off all of my fingers, like you did to Luciano. And you will finish the rest of your life in jail, brother. I don't know what the *carajo* you are talking about. Remember, I'm not only Fidel's favorite—I'm a personal friend of Che. Open your ears: I will never, never steal anything, much less something of Che's. Starting with his personal portfolio? I don't know how anyone could even pull that off within the Regiment, let alone get it out of the gate while they're doing a thorough search of everyone coming and out of there. That's not a small matchbox you could hide in your pocket." I paused for a moment. "I've been around Che. I've seen that thing—it's big! There's no doubt in my mind that whoever pulled this off had to be somebody big, someone who would never be searched, a real big wig. Or somebody in cahoots with the guards at the gate—those are the ones who's fingers you should be cutting off, if it's necessary." I stared into the holes of his mask. "I am one of the favorites of the Commander-in-Chief, as you say, and he wants to send me to the Soviet Union to train me in intelligence." I nodded my head suggestively. "Or counter-intelligence. You know what that means? Do you believe that, just because you've got that hood, I could not identify you? I see those hands, and I see many other things on your body. I will be able to identify even the way you walk." I could see in his eyes wonderment, and I nodded once more in satisfaction. "I would love to see you explain to our Commander-in-Chief Fidel why you cut off my fingers without consulting him first." The leader was silent for a few seconds, and then reached under his hood to stroke his chin. I could see his uncertainty. "Imagine it—with no fingers, I cannot pull a trigger. In other words, I cannot be an efficient intelligence officer anymore. You will be in deep shit!"

He leaned back over me. "How do you know that Fidel isn't the one who ordered your arrest?"

Without even thinking, I sneered, "I doubt that very much." I realized that this could be true, but I thought it best to maintain the facade. I realized it could even be Che, since the day the burglary happened, I had been there with them.

The leader was silent for another few seconds. "Look, I'm going to go to lunch for a little while. When I come back, if you don't decide to tell me the truth—you see this funnel?" He held up a funnel like one used to siphon gas. "We're going to stick this down your throat, and you'll eat shit until you blow up. Then we'll cut off your fingers. Maybe an eye. You have an hour to think about it." He signaled to the others, and all of them followed him out of the room, leaving us alone, Luciano chained to the wall, and I tied to the chair.

As soon as they left, Luciano said to me, "Do you know, I know your brother-in-law. He is my boss."

"Who? I've got two brothers-in-law."

"Yeah, but you've only got one in the G-2, Lieutenant Guerrero." I nodded. He looked at me and shook his head. "Why don't you tell these sons of bitches what they want to know? It's not important if you stole it or not. If you truly did it, you can tell them any excuse. Your brother-in-law will intervene for you. You're too young; someone could come in and convince you of anything." He painfully raised his bloodied right hand. "Don't let these guys do to you what they did to me. This is a calamity. Can you imagine? I can't even use a fork now to eat."

"Yes, you're right. That is a calamity. What they did to you is a terrible and unprecedented abuse. But in reality, I don't know anything about this. I don't know where these sons of bitches came up with this idea and that story that I had anything to do with that burglary. I can swear by anything you want me to swear by that I didn't have anything to do with it. How can I tell these guys anything if I don't know about this? I have to resign myself to losing my fingers. That's all I can tell you. It doesn't make me happy, of course, but que sera."

Luciano looked at me incredulously. He couldn't believe how I could contemplate in cold blood losing my fingers and my calm. I sat there, trying to figure out how I could get out of that situation with them intact. We were silent; after a while the door opened, and the hooded men returned to that unclean room. Without saying a word, they untied me from the chair and, ignoring my protests and fighting, tied me by the legs to a long rope. I hadn't seen the pulley on the ceiling, and they hoisted me into the air, making me dangle upside down. They rolled the large tank under my body. Then, one by one, they emptied the buckets of body waste into the tank. They added more water, filling it just over half-full. The leader yelled at the man who held my rope, "Let it go! Let him scuba dive for turds. Let's see if the little man can stand this!"

They let go of the rope. I held my breath as they dipped me in the tank. I don't know how long they kept me down there, but I started to lose my breath. I felt like I was drowning in that toxic waste material. I thought that perhaps they were going to let me drown in that. It was one of the worst moments of my life. I couldn't breathe any more, and I swallowed some of that muck. Finally, they pulled me out, and one of the hooded men took a high-pressure hose. He sprayed the water full in my face, forcing me to gag and cough. They effectively prolonged my drowning sensation, as I couldn't breathe under that high pressure. By moving my head from side to side, I could catch a little breath, but the pressure from the hose prevented me from breathing properly. It was one of the worst agonies I have ever endured.

The leader finally ordered, "Stop!" The pressure hose closed. In between coughing, gagging, and gasping for that much-needed air, my head spun. I lost control of my stomach, and I vomited not only my breakfast but the terrible things I had been forced to swallow in that tank. The hooded men laughed, enjoying my agony. Without even letting me get back to breathing normally, the leader approached me. "What? Are you going to talk, or are you going to drown in fucking shit again?" I looked at him in disgust. Gathering all the crap in my throat, I spat with amazing accuracy, hitting him squarely in the mouth. I smiled at my luck. He swore and spat as he wiped his mouth with the back of his hand. He screamed like the chubby man had earlier. "Son of a bitch! Dunk him in the tank again!"

I felt the rope tighten once more around my legs. I took a deep breath, and was once more plunged into that noxious tank. When they finally pulled me out, they repeated the same treatment with the pressure hose. Once they closed the hose off, the leader screamed at me—this time from a greater distance—"You want more? Or will you tell us where you got that damned portfolio?"

In between coughing and spluttering for air, I said, "I don't know what the hell you're talking about."

He grew close to me once more. He covered the mouth hold with his hand. "What did you say? I can't hear you."

I repeated what I said before. He shook his head in frustration. He said nothing more, but signaled to the man holding the rope to lower me to the floor. The other men, though, moved the tank before I came down. When I was on the ground, they untied me. I felt a tremendous relief to see that, at least for now, they weren't going to make me swim in the human crap again. I had no idea, though, what they had in mind for me now. But I figured that anything else wouldn't be worse than what they had already been doing. I was very wrong. They brought me to the torture table and secured me once more to the chair.

The leader pulled up another chair and sat down in front of me. "For sure, you're going to force me to cut off your fingers. Or are you finally going to tell me what I've asked you so many times?"

I looked at him. I let him see how much I despised him. "Go ahead and cut my damn fingers off right now. I've told you before, and I'll tell you again—you're going to regret it, you goddamned son of a bitch!"

This time, he reacted violently. He hit the table with his hand. He shoved his chair away from the table at the same time with such force that it rolled back and away from the table. He yelled, "OK, I've had it with this fucking kid! Let's begin the show. He will talk or this is the last thing I'll ever do in my life!" The large men came over to me and put my hand into the guillotine to cut off my index finger. I closed my eyes and braced myself. I saw the leader ready to pull the lever. He stopped for a second when he realized I was expecting the worst and was going to keep my silence. "No!" he commanded. "Get his finger out of the guillotine. Let's do something better to this fucker. Let's cut his dick off!" I got goose bumps when I heard that. The leader instructed the chubby man, "Go. Get a pair of surgical gloves." He said to the others, "Pull his pants down."

The men raised me up out of my chair and started to pull my pants down. That was the moment I started to panic, and I screamed at the top of my lungs, "The dick! NO! Take off all of my fingers, you sons of bitches, but don't cut off my dick!" I repeated this with my eyes wide open. I looked at the chubby hooded man, who was pulling off my underwear, his gloved hands searching for my penis. He pulled it out, and I continued to scream in anger, fear, and desperation. They pulled me to the table and inserted it into the guillotine.

Once more, the leader yelled in my face, "The portfolio or your dick!" His hand was already on the handle of the guillotine.

I screamed with all my strength the same insult I had hurled before. "Cut my fingers off, but not my dick!"

Luciano had been watching in silence. Now he screamed, "For God's sake! Don't be such degenerates! How dare you do this to this poor kid? He might still be a virgin!!"

Those words reverberated in my brain like an echo. It was totally true. I never had sex before, and the only opportunity I had I declined to preserve the girl's honor. I reflected on that with great remorse. Even in my fantasies, I had dreamed about what it would be like, and in that moment, I thought of Yaneba. I looked at my sexual organ and realized what she probably felt as she nearly lost her virginity at the hands of that despicable sergeant.

One of the hooded men screamed at Luciano, "You shut up, you piece of shit, or you'll be the next to lose your dick!"

The leader repeated his question once more. "This is your last chance."

I replied, "I already told you! Damn you, I don't know

anything of what you want to know!"

"OK," he replied. "Good bye, ding-a-ling. Kiss your banana goodbye." He gestured as if he was about to throw the lever.

I braced myself and looked away. Out of the blue, I heard a familiar voice say, "Enough! Enough! Let him go. That's more than enough." When I opened my eyes, I couldn't believe it. My happiness and confusion battled to make sense of the reality before me. I saw in front of me what appeared to be the General.

One of the hooded men started to laugh. "Son of a bitch, my dick, no! But not even that could break this kid."

To my surprise, all the hooded men started to remove their disguises, even as they gave me each a thumbs-up. The leader came over to me and began to unstrap me from the chair. After he was done, he put his hand on my shoulder and said, "You are real man. You passed the test that many adult men fail. Congratulations!" He held out his hand to shake mine.

Still confused and not completely recovered from the shock of the ordeal, I worked on pulling my pants up and refastened them. I took his hand tentatively and shook it. I was happy that it looked like my ordeal was over, and I was coming out of it with all of my fingers as well as my little friend still in place.

The General stepped towards me. He shook my hand and said, "Congratulations! This is the grand day of your graduation. Today, professionally and officially, you are now a spy. Even though you've already been one in my eyes as well as the eyes of others, after today, no one can doubt you or your abilities."

My emotions were a mixture of relief, resentment, confusion, and shock. I tried to smile as I watched them untie Luciano, but knew that it was forced. Luciano, however, was smiling like someone in on the joke. He took off the apparently bloody bandage around his hand. I looked at the table and the fingers scattered over its surface. The leader, understanding my confused state of mind, stepped over to the table and picked up one of the bloody fingers. He put it in his mouth and started to eat it. I looked at him in nauseated astonishment. He smiled and held out one finger to me. "Do you want to taste it?" he asked, grinning broadly. "Luciano's fingers taste like a brisket with raspberry marmalade."

I looked at Luciano. By now, he had completely unwrapped his hand. As he washed his hands, I could see that all of his fingers were in place. I kept shaking my head unhappily. The General took one look at my expression and said, "I'm sorry we had to put you through this, but it was absolutely necessary."

I forced a half-smile. "I understand. This is part of the training."

The leader and his group were introduced to me. They all congratulated me, and the chubby one put his arm around my shoulder. "There's no doubt that you have nerves of steel."

I looked at him with resentment, but I could see the sincere admiration in his eyes. I tried once more to smile. "Thank you."

The General took me a few steps away from the others. "This is the last of your training. I want you to be sure of that, and I want you to understand that this is premature. We shouldn't have done this to you until a little later. Unfortunately, we had to rush your training because of the importance of what we are discovering in the documents you provided us. Your uncle and I both feel that it was absolutely necessary to prepare you for the worst. There is a very strong possibility that you'll have to go through this for real, and we wanted you to be ready for it. We don't even know what the reactions of our enemies will be; we do know that there is going to be a purge. But, given the damage you've done to them by stealing this information, we don't know what the extent of that purge is going to be. I want you to know the magnitude of the data you discovered. It's a huge treasure, not only nationally but also internationally. It will change the game not only for us; it will also change it for them. They have to assume that this is not a common burglary, and that it's now in the hands of their enemies. Even though we know for a fact that they will change some of the details of these plans, according to our calculations they have to continue with their objectives. They have too much already invested in these plans to completely abandon them. For that, we now have to start to figure out which details they are going to change so that we can be ahead of them, and be prepared. I'm sorry—but that is why we have to prepare you." He was very emotional, he patted my chest affectionately. He felt something semi-solid, and pulled his hand away to examine his hand. It was covered in fecal matter. He smiled, and I returned a smile, this time genuinely, and he pulled out his handkerchief to clean his hand. "Go behind that wall. You'll find a room with a large bathtub in it. Go, take a long bath, clean yourself as completely and take as long as you like. It will be an opportunity for you to relax and completely recover your sanity and composure. I will go and pick up your uncle. He's in town, so it won't be too long. We'll then take you to the ranch where you left your jeep."

"Very well," I said. We shook hands once more and

were about to hug, but he realized I was still covered in excrement and worse, and he pulled back. I nearly laughed, and we both smiled again. I went to the bathroom in the back as directed, and soaked myself thoroughly in clean water. I soaped myself everywhere, trying to get the smell of human waste that seemed indelibly burned into my nose. An hour and half passed. When I emerged from the tub, I saw clean clothes laid out for me, and I dressed. I put the soiled clothes in a plastic bag they gave me. I returned to the front of that strange torture chamber. I saw the front door was open, and could hear voices outside. I assumed them to belong to my supposed interrogators, and heard laughter among them.

As I drew near the table, I stopped and picked up one of the fingers. I examined it curiously, wondering how it could be made to look so real. I realized that it was made of bread, but even the knuckles and nails were so detailed that it looked like something out of a wax museum. They had covered it with something that looked like vanilla or cinnamon; it was very close to actual skin tone. It was an absolute masterpiece, worthy of the best Hollywood special effects.

As I replaced it on the table, I heard the chubby man say, "Is it not unbelievable work that our leader, Olirio, did with those? Don't you think so?"

I nodded. "He really did these himself?"

He smiled pleasantly in satisfaction. "That's nothing. You should see the complete hand. That was a masterpiece, the way he did it. You don't know how many people have freaked out to see an entire hand cut off on that table."

"I can imagine! Just the fingers are enough to freak anyone out—I don't want to see the psychological effect of someone seeing an entire hand cut off. That would damage somebody for life!"

"Well, in your case, we were the ones getting freaked out." He looked at me with amazement in his eyes. "When we saw that you had no fear, for God's sake, when we were going to cut off your fingers or even your penis—where the hell did you get this courage, kid?"

I smiled and touched my groin. "You don't even know that my balls went clear up to my neck when you put my finger in that guillotine. Fear? Of course I have fear."

He slapped my back with a smile. "But we couldn't break you. You might have fear, but you never showed it to us."

"I didn't have fear—I had panic. But the General taught me to control my fear. If I show my enemies fear, it will be worse for me. I'm not only going to lose my *chorizo*[13] but also my life, at that point."

He burst out laughing loudly. "You don't even know, but that is how my friends call me: Juan Chorizo."

"Why?" I asked curiously.

"Well, when these sons of bitches put my penis in that guillotine like we did to you today, and they couldn't break me like we couldn't break you, the only thing that came into my mind to scream was 'My chorizo? No, not my chorizo, you faggots!' Because of that, they've called me Juan Chorizo ever since." He laughed heartily at the memory.

I smiled and shook my head. The other men came over at hearing him laugh so loudly. The General had just arrived, and walked in as well. Juan said to the tallest and most muscular of the men, a mulatto with refined

---

13 Sausage

features, "Is it not true, Candelario? You guys couldn't intimidate me, not even when you were going to cut off my chorizo."

Candelario nodded and smiled. "Evidently, for you your chorizo was more important than your life."

Juan raised his right hand high and said, still smiling, "*Claro, chico! A quien carajo le va a gustar eso*[14]? Not even a homosexual would like that!"

The General laughed. "I'm glad you guys are getting to know each other better." He turned to me. "You can trust these men with your life, even as you've been trusting me. From now on, they will be guarding your back from the shadows."

I nodded appreciatively. "That is good to know." I shook hands with everybody, and we said our goodbyes. We left that place and drove for a while.

As we drew near to the ranch, he pulled over so that Leocadio wouldn't see him with me. That day, I learned that whoever looks like your enemy and executioner could wind up actually being your best friend. This was the case with these men, who wound up watching my back for around a decade until my cover was blown in 1971, and I was forced to scuba dive to Guantanamo Base to flee. I also learned that your best friend today can become your worst enemy tomorrow.

---

14 Certainly, man! Who the hell is going to like that?

Canen and Disa cutting their wedding cake

Godly and Ungodly Men

"It is a lot easier to find a man without principles who doesn't believe in God than to find a man without principles who loves God with all his heart and believes in His Son Jesus Christ."

Dr. Julio Antonio del Marmol

Chapter 7: The Wedding

The next day, very early in the morning, I went to my Commandos' Headquarters. I had already scheduled through Daniel a meeting with my officers. I told them officially the orders I had received from Fidel, even though Daniel had already at my request informally advised them, I tried to keep my cover by telling them they were welcome to enroll themselves in the new Young Communist Union. Every single one of them told me that they wanted nothing to do with that. Even though I didn't actually care, I tried to persuade them like a good, ardent communist that this was going to be a good thing. I didn't put a great deal of effort into it, but it was a little bit of theater for the benefit of any communist that might ask them later about this conversation.

Daniel said to me, "I believe in God. I'm sorry—I can't be a part of that."

"I understand that," I replied. He invited me to dinner at his house that night. His father was coming to visit him from Havana; it was a monthly routine following his father's divorce from his mother. I knew his father, and knew he was one of the leaders of the labor unions; he was also definitely a Marxist. He was one of the big honchos among the stevedores, and was in charge of the old Pan-American Pier docks. I told him it would be a pleasure for me to come that night and have dinner with his family and him. Daniel was a very lucky kid, because his parents were different from other divorced couples in that the pair maintained a cordial relationship. His father would spend a weekend in Pinar del Rio to avoid affecting his son psychologically as a result of that separation. Every time Daniel's father, Lazaro, came for a visit, Daniel would invite me to have dinner with them. His father enjoyed hearing my stories and anecdotes about the conversations I had with Fidel and Che. He knew how close I was to these people; in consequence, his son was, as well. Our contact was something not everyone was able to have, since it was on a daily basis that we saw these men.

Daniel and my other officers assured me that, in only a few more days—certainly before the weekend—that the move of our offices to the new building would be completed. Daniel gave me the time for the dinner that night, and I went to my house for lunch. Mima and Majito had been reprimanding me for not coming home to lunch more often. They said they never saw me anymore, and the implied suggestion was that I like military food better than Mima's meals. As I drove in my jeep towards Avenue Cabada, I saw in my rear-view mirror a local police car following me with its lights on. I considered not stopping, my recent abduction still fresh in my memory. I wanted to make sure I was in a busy place before pulling over, but I saw in the mirror that the Transit Authority car behind me was that of my other brother-in-law, Guerrero. He motioned with his hand to turn into the Jupiña factory parking lot that we were passing at that moment. After I pulled over and got out of our cars, we greeted each other. He told his assistants to go inside to the factory. They went in and came out with boxes of soda pop into his car. He asked if I wasn't in a rush if we could load my jeep with some boxes. The owner had, as a courtesy, offered some complimentary boxes for the upcoming wedding. The gesture from the owner was not directed to Guerrero—it was directed towards Canen, who was a local Pinar del Rio native, and the two of them had gone through accounting school together. Guerrero continued, "We will have all the soda we want, not only for Canen's wedding, but also for mine."

I smiled and replied with a hint of irony, "Well, we have to use the opportunities that arise with these capitalists, at least while they're still around."

He smiled and looked slightly ashamed by his obvious opportunism. Guerrero was not from Pinar del Rio; he was from Camagüey. He served under the command of Huber Matos in the Rebel Forces. After Matos' accusation of treason, every officer under that command was sent to the extreme provinces of the island by Raul, Fidel, and Che in an effort to isolate them and so prevent the possibility of a mutiny. Every one of Matos' officers had been classified as 'not clear,' or whose loyalties were considered murky at best. Guerrero had no loyalties to Matos, or anyone for that matter, had joined the G-2 in order to clear his reputation to prove his loyalties and distance himself from Matos' activities. He attempted to justify his opportunism by saying, "Well, something we have to try and get out of these capitalist parasites' teeth."

I replied, "Thanks to those parasites' teeth and capitalism, we will have free soda pop at both you guys' weddings." He smiled again, this time maliciously. Both his assistant and driver came out with four cases of soda on each shoulder. I unzipped the awning over the back of my jeep. "There you go. See how much you can stick in here."

He turned around and said to his men, "When you guys finish with my car, fill this jeep up to the roof." I rolled my eyes and smiled. I didn't say a word, but I had no doubts about Guerrero's character. When his men disappeared inside of the factory, he put his arm around my shoulder. "Come on," he said, "I need to talk to you." He was trying to draw me away from the vehicles. "There's something I need to share with you that's extremely important. I want you to keep your eyes open. Our enemies are everywhere." We walked across the parking structure and stopped in the shade of a beautiful Poinciana tree in full bloom. His expression was grim, positively funereal. "I just came back from the capital, from an emergency meeting with Piñeiro, Ramiro, and Che. Everything's extremely hot right now. Just last February there were four attempts on the life of the Commander-in-Chief. Thank God we were able to detect and stop those attempts." He waved both arms exaggeratedly. "Can you imagine it? In less than twenty days, four attempts! Everyone in the meeting agrees that the headquarters of the CIA and the most dangerous enemies to our Revolution are on the Occidental side of the island, specifically right here in Pinar del Rio. Well, with the exception of Camagüey and the betrayal of Huber Matos— and even so in there, what happened there is nothing compared to what happened here. The theft from within the most secure military fortress, from even within the private office of the provincial chief!" He scratched his head in frustration. "Somebody stole the Che's attaché case! Everyone is asking how the hell that could even happen."

He lowered his voice conspiratorially. "Of course, we in intelligence are the ones from whom they are demanding answers. I told them loud and clear that we had no jurisdiction inside the military forces." His tone was imploring, like he was begging me for something. "You are by the side of all of these big wigs in the military. If you want to help me, and help yourself, you bring to me any information, any detail, anything you see. It might seem at the time of minor importance to you, but write it down and bring it to me. Anyone that is even remotely suspicious, anyone that you think might be capable of doing that, you let me know. I need your help, because everybody is in question. If we don't produce something, they are going to start thinking that we're not doing our job. This fucking spy they're calling 'the Lightning'--we know for a fact that he is one of the big officers. If you help me to get this guy, I will share the credit with you. I know he's in the regiment, but I need your help to entrap and arrest him. This can bring to me promotion within intelligence. Since I'm marrying your sister in a week, it won't be just of benefit to her; it will also benefit your family. The higher I go in intelligence, the more protected your family will be. You know the G-2 is the most powerful department in the government, including the Army."

"Of course I know," I replied with a smile on my face. I understood completely what Guerrero was proposing to me. He wanted to recruit me to be an operative for him inside the military in order to catch the spy who stole Che's portfolio. I shook my head slightly and silently laughed. If he only knew who he was talking to at that moment! This time, I patted his shoulder. "I will keep you informed and my eyes fully open. That is for sure. I will take note of everyone who is suspicious inside the compound. You can count on me."

The royal imbecile said with a pleasant smile on his face, "I knew I could count on you!"

I nodded my head. "Claro, chico!" I had known for a long time I had to be careful with Guerrero; but after this conversation, I knew how dangerous this individual could come to be. After this moment, I knew that this man was capable of selling his mother for a couple of boxes of Jupiña. I was able to corroborate this when, as we walked back to the cars, I saw him give a very strong hug to the owner of the factory. His extreme fawning attitude towards the man who just a few minutes before had been described as a thief, parasite, and capitalist showed what a hypocrite he was. Over the next three hours, Guerrero used me to make five trips conveying cases of soda out of that factory. I finally excused myself, telling him that I hadn't even lunched yet, and that my mother and Majito were waiting for me back at home. After that, I had important business to take care of at the military regiment, and I finally was able to get rid of him. I thought that if one let this man run rampant, he would take the entire factory to his house.

When I reached my home, Mima and Majito had a big surprise for me. A friend of my father brought as a gift to the house a beef liver, and they had prepared for me my favorite dish, liver and onions with fried plantains. Even though I had arrived late, I ate like *señor cura*, or like a priest. After lunch, I went to the Regiment to speak with Commander Argibay about what happened to Yaneba and her friends. As soon as I reached the HQ, I went to the Military Auditor, and found him in his office. I told him in detail what had happened earlier that day. To my surprise, Argibay told me, "Yes. I spoke to the sergeant, the corporal, and some of the soldiers who were the witnesses to that incident. The version they told me is very different from the way you are telling me now. According to your version, they are the bad guys. According to their version, the women are the bad people, trying to smuggle drugs and contraband."

I reclined back into my seat, uncomfortable with what I had just heard from him. I had another impression of him, and wasn't expecting this out of him. In an unfriendly tone, I snapped, "Is the sergeant your friend? Or do you have some kind of relationship with him, or any reason to protect him? Or any of the other men involved in this incident?"

He looked at me gravely. He said evasively, "No, no. Why do you ask me that?"

I said very seriously, "Because it is the only way you can justify what these degenerates tried to do to these kids—we can't call them women, because the eldest of them is not even fourteen." I pointed right at my eyes, "I saw with my own eyes how they were running behind them along the riverbank like dogs behind the rabbits." I was becoming extremely irritated as I thought about it once more. "I could also see a large bump one of them had on her head from a rifle butt. There were other small lacerations, and it was very clear to me that if I and my friend had not arrived at the time we did, the best scenario was that they would have raped all three of those girls. No matter that you and I have known each other for a long time, I'm not asking you to take my word. I ask you to do your job and to investigate all the way to the bottom of this situation." I took my uniform hat off and slammed it onto his desk angrily. "That sergeant is not only dishonest and a sexual predator, but he's also a huge liar. This Revolution was made because of these same abuses and indecencies that the Batista police and soldiers did to our people. We should not allow our new Army to do exactly the same that the Dictator's police and army used to do."

Argibay understood my irritation, and tried to calm me

down. "Well, well, Commandantico. Calm down. Don't make a big deal out of this. I know the sergeant very well, because he used to be my personal assistant during the Insurrection."

I shook my head and raised my arm. I could no longer contain myself. "Ah-ha! That is the reason! We cannot give too much importance to this—the sergeant is your friend. In other words, it's not really important that he tried to rape an under aged girl and bring his corporal and soldiers to be accomplices. It could have ended in murder—they could conceivably have killed those girls to cover their crime. And you try to cover up this despicable action done by supposedly honorable Rebel Army soldiers. They are supposed to protect and defend the new Cuba!"

Argibay reclined in his seat and smiled cynically. "Commandantico, Commandantico, please! These little worms, *cubanitas gusanas*[15], they are all going to the USA to give their asses to the gringos. Maybe they'll become prostitutes there to earn their living. You don't think it's better to leave their virginity here, in Cuba, with a Cuban? If it's a Rebel soldier, so much the better. At least they'll have something good to tell when they get to Miami. They're going to tell horrible things about us there, anyway, and that will include you, since you are a part of this Revolution."

My blood rushed to my head and I could feel the heat on my face. I had to control myself, because I had an extremely strong urge to grab him by the neck, put my pistol to his head, and blow his brains out, right there in his office. I put my hand on the handle of my pistol. I thought about it twice, but contained myself. I looked at him in

---

15 Little Cuban worms

revulsion. Until that moment, I had never felt so ashamed and saddened by the uniform I was wearing. I had to admit, though, that what he was saying was true—whoever in the town didn't know my true thoughts and feelings would look at me with the same despite and disgust that I was looking at Argibay with right now. They lumped me in with this same band of delinquents, with no morals, principles, values, or respect for human life. Other people probably thought I was an atheist like these men as well. Everyone who looked at me on the street viewed me as guilty by association.

My expression grew sour, and I understood that any further conversation with Argibay wasn't going to get me anywhere. Clearly, he was no different than anyone else I had met in that circle; I couldn't imagine why I thought he would act with any honor. I shook my head, controlling my violent impulse, and remembered what the General had trained me for. I stood up from my seat, grabbed my hat off of his desk, and looked him in the eyes. "You really, really disappoint me. I believed in my heart that you were a man with dignity. I see now that I made a big mistake with you." I smiled cynically, nodded affirmatively, and said, "The only thing I wish to you is that, one of these days, you have a little girl, and that when she reaches thirteen or fourteen years of age, that one of your glorious Rebel soldiers hunt her, hit her in the head with the butt of his rifle, drop her in the sun someplace in the river or the ocean, and rape her like these bastards tried to do to those girls. Then maybe you'll understand that whatever is immoral and indecent is not good either for us or our enemies."

I put my hat on, still staring into his eyes in anger and disgust. I could barely control my irritation. Maybe I wanted to believe that I touched a little nerve of decency in him, hidden way down, but he put his hand on his chin, and looked ashamed of himself. I thought that he might be thinking to himself that this thirteen-year-old kid just gave him a moral lesson, and would remember that the same principles I was talking about had been taught to him by the elders in his family. Maybe he had forgotten them in the middle of the Revolution and all of this. Before I reached the door, he said, "Let me see what I can do." It was a vague promise.

I turned around and shook my head negatively. I remembered a conversation he and I had before about his family. He had a young sister that lived on the extreme Oriental side of the island; he might perhaps have had a nerve touched as he thought about how he would react had this happened to her. With my hand still on the doorknob, I replied in a tone dripping with irony, "For sure, you will do whatever you can. After all, none of these girls is your daughter or a member of your family. As you told me before, they are little worms and future prostitutes." He gulped, his shame clearly growing deeper. Giving him the benefit of the doubt, I thought I could even see some sign of repentance in his face, but I didn't give him any more time. I left the office. The deception and frustration created a painful knot in my chest, and I seethed at my impotence. I had made a promise to Yaneba and her friends that this outrageous act would have consequences to the soldiers involved. What was I going to tell them now? It also went against one of the earliest lessons I learned from my father, that a man should prefer to die before he fail to live up to his word. Though I had controlled my violent impulses in front of Argibay, my anger and frustration grew by the minute as I walked out of the building towards my jeep.

I looked at the sign on the building: "Military Auditor." I shook my head and thought sarcastically that they only audited whatever was convenient to them. I could see the sergeant and two of his soldiers walking towards the building. As soon as he saw me, the sergeant screamed, "Atten-HUT!" The soldiers pulled themselves to attention and saluted me. I looked at them disdainfully and didn't even slow as I went by them. As I perfunctorily returned their salutes, none of them would meet my eyes. They knew that if looks could kill, my glare would have put them in their graves immediately. As I walked down the stairs, I stopped. The pain in my chest was so bad that I couldn't breathe. I placed both hands on the back of my neck, leaned back, and took a deep breath before I continued on. Behind me, the two guards who were at Escalona's building the night of the robbery were on duty. I didn't even look at them or recognize them in my disturbed state of mind.

The jovial man asked, "Are you OK, Commander?"

I recognized him and said, "Yes, I'm fine. Just a little bit of stress." I breathed deeply to get rid of my anger and the bad influence of my dark intentions. I looked at the pair of them. "I thought you guys had been punished and were in jail because of the incident in Escalona's office."

He nodded. "Yes, but your brother-in-law, Captain Canen, took away our punishment."

The other one said, "Yeah, that is very unfair. We had nothing to do with the robbery. Whoever did this came from the back of the building. We were on the front—how could we know?"

My jovial friend said, "The only reason we knew about it was that I had gone to the back of the building to urinate, and saw him come out of the open window. The rest you know from all the commotion. That's why they've put two guards on the back of every building. Everything's changed now."

I nodded. "That is a lot better. Before, it was like you were washing your face but leaving your ass filthy." They both laughed at that. "Well, I'm glad to see that Canen removed your sentence. It's not because he's my brother-in-law, but I think he looks like a decent man with good principles."

"Yes, yes," the big one said with a big, satisfied smile. They both agreed and added that he was a fair man as well as good. They saluted me, and I left towards my jeep.

That afternoon at my house, I took a long bath in the large bathtub. It was my refuge, up on the second floor. I dressed in civilian clothes and went to dinner. I had told Mima and Majito that I wasn't going to be home for dinner, but that I would be dining at Daniel's with his father. My mother gave me a flan to take with me to the dinner, as it was the custom to never show up as a guest empty-handed. Daniel lived with his mother, Esmeralda, and his grandmother, the very wonderful and lovely Doña Carmen. She was over eighty years old, but her spirit and liveliness was that of a forty year old woman. She was known in town as a healer and a medium. She frequently read the future to my mother and Majito. She built herself a name not only in our neighborhood but throughout the whole town because she had been able to foretell events with astonishing accuracy. She predicted exactly the day the Revolution would win and the Dictator would be deposed. In the past, she had predicted a major hurricane that caused the river to flood. She managed to give winning numbers in the lottery to several people in town, including

Mima and Majito, enabling them to win large amounts of money. This validated her completely as a medium, and established her as a member of the fabric of the community. Even prominent businessmen came to her for consultation before making important business decisions or taking long trips.

She was a short, plump woman who always dressed in white with a matching turban on her head. She usually wore large, white loop earrings. Her friendly character earned the love and respect of everyone who had dealt with her over the years. She didn't like Daniel's father, Lazaro, very much. She said that Lazaro was both a communist and an atheist. She might also have harbored a resentment against him for failing to maintain his marriage with her daughter. According to Doña Carmen, who was old-fashioned in this regard, a dignified man should have continued the relationship in spite of the problems for the best interests of his son, rather than being selfish and leaving as he did.

When I arrived at Daniel's house, everyone was waiting for me. They welcomed me with joy and hugs, as they always did when I visited. After I gave them the delicious flan that my mother had decorated beautifully, both women told me to make sure to thank Mima for that lovely gift. They rushed me so that the food didn't get cold, since the table was already set. We sat down in the dining room. As we were sitting and food began to be served, Daniel asked his father, "Papa, do you want me to tell Mom and Grandmom, or did you want to tell them?" Both women looked at them in wonder and surprise. Daniel and Lazaro stayed silent, however, as they began to eat. They continued to eat, even though the women weren't, and instead stared the interrogative at them.

Lazaro couldn't take it anymore, and finally said, "Well, Esmeralda, the truth is that Daniel wants to come back to the capital with me on Monday next week, because he wants to work with me on the piers at the port. I told him the work is very harsh and heavy labor that he isn't accustomed to. He's insisting, because he wants to explore the capital and live with me for a while, since there's not too much for him to do here in Pinar del Rio." It was clear that he was sugar-coating the words, that he didn't want to start an argument with Daniel's mother and grandmother; he was trying to persuade them that he had nothing to do with Daniel's decision. On the contrary, he had tried to dissuade Daniel from doing so.

Esmeralda didn't even touch the food on her plate. She looked straight in Daniel's eyes. "Daniel, what about your schooling? And the Commandos?"

Daniel stopped eating for a second and put down his fork. He wiped his mouth with the napkin, and said in a conciliatory tone, "The school I can continue at night, as many of my friends here do. They work during the day and attend night school." He looked over at me. "As for the Commandos, you can ask him." I had been listening quietly, eating without making a comment. "Unfortunately, they will not exist anymore. Fidel has decided to convert it into the Young Communists." He raised his arm apologetically. "With all my respect, Father, because I know your ideology, I believe in God and His Son, Jesus Christ, and don't want anything to do with the Young Communist Union. I don't want to be involved in anything that even slightly smells communist to me."

Doña Carmen looked at him, smiled, and touched his shoulder. "Amen to that, my boy." She looked at Lazaro in recrimination.

Lazaro raised his arm as he looked around condescendingly. "I've told you before—your ideas are yours, and my ideas are mine. You believe what you want to believe. The only thing I ask from you is that, if you come to be with me, that you don't make those ideas public. Keep them to yourself. I don't think it will be prudent to tell anyone how you're thinking, taking into consideration that I am one of the high leaders of the Port Union. That is not going to be too smart."

Daniel shook his head. "Papa, you don't have to worry about that at all. I don't have to tell anyone the way I think."

Lazaro shifted in his chair uncomfortably, due to my presence. He looked at me nervously, still smiling, though the smile was partly forced. "What do you think of all this, Commandantico?"

I smiled. "More than anything, I think this is family business, not mine at all, or that of anyone else, for that matter. One thing I always loved about Daniel was his honesty. We should all live by that code. That is why he is one of my best friends. To me, it doesn't make any difference if he believed in the Devil," at that, both women crossed themselves, but I continued on, "that is his business, and not anyone else's."

Doña Carmen looked at me admonishingly. "God with us! You should not mention the Enemy at the table. It is blasphemy."

"I'm sorry," I said at once. "Please forgive me. It's only an expression, it's not my intention by any means to offend anyone." They calmed down a little. "Maybe my reaction is a little improper and out of line, but it's because that never before in Cuba has anyone been persecuted, even during the Dictatorship, for his religious sentiments or beliefs. Today, though, the fashion is to dishonor anybody who expresses his feelings towards any religion. This, in reality, has started to bother me very deeply. My father is a Mason, and he only believes in the Supreme Architect of the Universe. My mother is a Catholic, and she believes in God, Jesus Christ, and all the Saints and virgins that exist and will be existing in the future. No matter how huge the difference they both have in belief and ideology, I never heard them in all my life disrespect each other or even argue between them. I believe it's because they respect each other. That is more important than anything. My question is, why our Revolutionary government cannot do the same?" As I said this, I put my fork down on the table, a little angrily. I frowned and massaged my forehead. "Are we going to do the same thing the Dictator used to do? Are we going to persecute the opposition and everyone not thinking like us? Why did we build the Revolution that so many people died for, if that is the case?"

A very deep silence followed my words. No one even moved in their seats. Perhaps my words touched an indelible reality on what had been slowly happening in Cuba as the government instituted the new socialist regime instead of the democracy for which people had so thirstily fought. Indeed, the first thing that had been implemented in the grab for power was the limiting of freedom of expression.

In the midst of that silence, Doña Carmen brought both hands to her head. Slowly, she reclined in her chair, resting her neck on the back of the chair. The rest of us watched her in surprise. She remained like that for a few minutes. Lazaro was about say something to Esmeralda, but she checked him with an outstretched hand. She brought it back, placed her finger on her lips, and shook her head to indicate that no one should speak. She then circled her index finger in the air to communicate that something was going on. Lazaro impatiently shifted and rubbed his face in exasperation. However, out of respect, he maintained his silence. We all kept our eyes glued on Doña Carmen. She began to move her head as if she were speaking with someone, nodding and shaking her head in affirmation and negation. She then brought both hands and placed her fingers on her temples. We weren't expecting her to scream loudly, "NO! NOOO! AAAAAGGGGHH!!!" At the same time, she brought her hands down to slam on the table, her head breaking the plate on the table. The glass of water fell over from the impact, rolled off the table, and shattered on the tile floor. We were all taken by surprise, and were a little frightened. Lazaro, who was sitting closest to her, jumped out of his chair. The chair flipped and would have fallen over had he not caught it.

Doña Carmen stood up and opened her eyelids, but her eyes were rolled so far in the back of her head that the pupils didn't show. As she stood over the table, she looked to me in that moment larger than normal, as if she had somehow been raised up. She began to speak in a voice that was clearly not hers, a deep voice of a man of African descent, it seemed to me. It demanded of Esmeralda authoritatively, "Light me a Habanos cigar! You know the ones I like."

Esmeralda bowed submissively, and got up quickly. She replied with humility, "Yes, Massa. Whatever you want, all you have to do is order." She turned around and went to the china cabinet against the wall. She pulled out one of the drawers on the bottom and removed a box of very refined Monte Cristo cigars. She hurriedly lit one and handed it to Doña Carmen.

Doña Carmen took it and smelled it like a seasoned smoker. She then put it in her mouth and inhaled deeply. She took two steps and blew the cigar smoke in Lazaro's face. She then waved her hands through the smoke, while Lazaro stood paralyzed in wonderment. She unwrapped her turban, revealing her white hair. She snapped the turban like a whip in his face repeatedly as she walked around the table. She then draped the material over her shoulder like a shawl, and then walked toward the china cabinet. When she reached the wall, she leaned her head against it. She took another deep draft out of the cigar, tilted her head up, and expelled it. She said again in that deep, sepulchral voice, "Lazaro, you are sentenced. The death is around you. If you really love your son, stay far away from him. On the contrary, he will be an innocent victim in your misfortune. Go far away from the capital. La Havana is your death sentence. If you go far away from her, you will live many years and reach old age. But if you don't listen to me and insist, your destiny will catch up with you. You will die. Your days are counted. You will die, and will bring death to everyone close to you." She half-turned and came back to the table. She sat down in her chair, shook her head, and crushed the cigar out in the piece of flan Esmeralda had cut for her. Her eyes rolled forward. She said in astonishment and in her normal voice, "Who the hell put that nasty cigar in my dessert?"

We were completely in awe, paralyzed by the whole scene. It looked like she hadn't even been there, and had just come back from some trip, and her body had been taken over by someone else. Esmeralda was apparently accustomed to it, and rushed to clean up the table. She threw away the cigar and the piece of flan, cut another piece, and gave it to her mother.

Doña Carmen laughed with satisfaction. "This is very good flan! Your mother makes an excellent flan." She continued to eat it as if nothing had happened, while we looked at her in fascination.

Lazaro took his piece of flan, reclined in his chair a little bit, and shook his head with a smile of disbelief. He looked over to Daniel and said with irony, "Your grandmom evidently doesn't want you to come with me to the capital." The Doña threw him a puzzled look, but said nothing. Lazaro shifted back towards the table, dug his spoon deeply into the flan. Before he put it in his mouth, he said, "Remember, my son—it is your decision, and nobody else's if you want to come with me or not. Don't let anyone manipulate you in any way or form."

Daniel looked at his father with a smile. "I already made my decision. Like I told you, on Monday, I go with you to Havana, no matter what. There's nothing for me in this city anymore. My mom and grandmom have to understand that. Yes—it's my decision."

Esmeralda looked at him with tears in her eyes. She leaned forward and touched his cheek. "My boy, if that is what you want, that is what you should do." She nodded. "Go to the capital with your father." She crossed herself and looked toward Heaven. "Even though my mother is very seldom wrong in her predictions, I pray to Jesus and the Holy God, His Father, and the Holy Spirit, to guard you on your trip and hope that my mother is wrong."

Doña Carmen was still eating. She looked up in surprise. "What am I wrong for? What is wrong? What are you talking about, my daughter?"

Esmeralda could no longer control herself and began to cry very hard. "Excuse me," she sobbed, and walked away. As she walked away, her sorrow increased, and she began to run as her sobs grew louder. We remained at the table in silence.

Doña Carmen stood up, leaving a small piece of flan. She glared angrily at Lazardo. "What did you say to my daughter to make her cry? You always make her cry, what did you say this time?" She stormed away.

Lazaro looked in absolute astonishment at me. "What did I do?"

At that precise moment, I recalled the vivid nightmare I had a few months before as I convalesced at Tite's house from that high fever. I could see once more Che cutting the heads and torsos of men, women, and children. I asked myself if that revelation that Doña Carmen just had was in any way connected with my nightmare. I felt a hand on my shoulder and jumped.

It was Daniel. "Did you want some more flan, Julio Antonio?"

"Yes," I replied. "Please put a little coconut on it, if you could."

He smiled and said, "Sure." After he cut a piece for me, he got one for himself. "You want another piece, Dad?"

"Sure." Daniel got his father a piece as well, and the three of us sat in silence, eating the second serving of the flan. We could hear the sound of Esmeralda wailing and sobbing in her bedroom. After he finished eating his flan, Lazaro said irritatedly, "I hate this rubbish voodoo. Only ignorant people believe in this kind of stupidity."

Daniel pointed at me. "Papa, remember what the Commandantico said just a moment ago. The respect of other people's beliefs is one of the most important things in life."

Lazaro shifted uncomfortably and forced a smile. "Well, that's true. I don't disagree with that. It just bothers me how people try to manipulate others. If your mother and grandmother don't want you to come with me to the capital, there's no need to make all this drama. All they have to do is sit down with you, communicate to you their displeasure at the idea, and attempt in a good way to persuade you."

I reclined in my chair and stroked my chin. "You will forgive me, Lazaro, but does it not cross your mind that there's a small possibility that all this we see is not really theater. It could be a spiritual revelation. We have to keep an open mind. It could be one of your ancestors taking the body of Doña Carmen. Maybe he wants to prevent you from experiencing some future misfortune or tragedy."

Lazaro smiled and shook his head incredulously. He raised his arm and said, "Oh, please, Commandantico—don't tell me you believe in this kind of stuff."

I shook my head. "I don't believe and I do believe. In the short years of my existence in this world, I've learned to maintain my open mind in everything. Sometimes you think you know something only to discover later that you know nothing. There are so many things that don't have any logical explanation. For so many people, even for us, out of the blue, something happens and on a beautiful sunny day something lands in your hands from someplace you can't imagine, and you see the clear answer to all the things you didn't understand and others that you didn't believe. Clear as that." I pointed to the glass of water to highlight my point. "Only in that moment, when you see the answer, do you realize that you've had it in front of your eyes all this time, but you couldn't even see it. It sounds to you incredible, and your brain isn't capable of digesting it."

Daniel's father held his right hand to his face in surprise.

"Can you give me an example of what you're talking about?"

I raised my eyebrows. "Yes, I can give you an example." I paused. "Let's use, as an example, the death of Camillo. It doesn't seem to you extremely strange they never found anything—not the plane, none of the people who were in the plane, no pieces of them, not even his hat, for God's sake—and everybody believes what they've been told."

He said hurriedly, "Yes, but that has a logical explanation."

I shifted and smiled. "That is what you think. In reality, that logical explanation has no logic to it at all. It's very far away from the truth." I touched my chest. "I know. In reality, if I told you that truth, in this particular moment, it might sound so incredibly crazy and bizarre that you would probably choke. It's so bizarre that it would resemble to you the theater Doña Carmen created for you. In your brain, you could not understand why someone would be lying and fabricate something so crazy to make you believe something that's not the truth. That is why my personal advice to you is that, if I were in your skin, I would maintain my distance from the capital. You never know what is cooking in Havana. My father used to tell me, when I was a little kid, if they tell you not to put the broom upside down because it brings bad luck to your house, why are you going to ignore it? Why fool around and change the broom, and leave it instead in the normal way it should be resting? Just in case, it's better to be safe than sorry, because maybe some kind of adverse or strange thing could occur. I would maintain my distance. If you don't want to believe for yourself, then at least believe it for the security of your son, if you want to bring him close to you. But what do I know? I'm only a thirteen-year-old kid." I stood up and put my napkin on the table. "Well, it's been a pleasure to see you again, and I hope to have the pleasure of seeing all of you guys at the wedding tomorrow. Daniel, please say goodbye to Esmeralda and Doña Carmen. You all have a beautiful night."

I left the house with an extremely deep, powerfully sad feeling in my chest. It was like the day when I was ten years old that my best friend, Andresito, died of leukemia. I passed by in front of the funeral home at least ten times with the intention of coming in to say my final goodbye and giving my condolences to his mother and the rest of the family. But I never had the courage to enter. Every time I stopped at the door of the funeral home, I was so devastated, and the painful knot in my chest made my entire body tremble. Tears would run uncontrollably down my cheeks, and I felt I was going to bring more sadness and grief to the family more than anything else. I finally decided to go home, and that day I made for myself a resolution. I would never visit anyone I loved after death at a funeral for the rest of my life. Instead, I would give the best of myself every single moment of every day of my life to everyone I love and care for, to my friends and my family. After they pass, I would leave it in the hands of God.

The next day, the suburban country club in which the wedding was to take place was decorated rustically with large trunks of wood, thatched palm leaf roof, and rope wrapped around the wooden columns. The location was breath taking, near to the river and some waterfalls. The gardens had palm trees, coconut trees, bougainvillea, and the groundskeepers had constructed an artificial lake with channels of water containing koi. It was a location frequently used for *quinceañeras*[16] parties, weddings, and other major festive events that would have large groups of people in attendance. There was a stage with lighting set up for musicians, dance floor before the stage, and the tree trunks were wrapped with strands of small lights. The tropical gardens were extensive, and one could easily get pleasantly lost in them. There were hammocks hanging near the river, and the gardens also included jasmine, roses, and other fragrant flowers that added to the exquisiteness of the surroundings.

They had rented the entire club for the wedding, and my family spent the entire day running back and forth from the house to make certain that everything was on hand and in order, so that the day would truly be a special one for the entire family. Around twilight, the Baptist minister performed the ceremony that married my sister to Canen. People were celebrating, pictures were being taken, and everyone was walking around with a piece of wedding cake and a bottle of soda or a drink. I was curious, and looked behind the bar. I noticed only a few cases of Jupiña; most of the pop behind the bar was Coca-Cola. I decided that Guererro had kept most of the gifted cases for himself. I drew near to Canen and gave him a big hug. "I wish you guys much happiness," I said.

My sister was very emotional, and looked at me with tears in her eyes. She hugged me and whispered in my ear, "With thanks to you. You introduced us."

I smiled and gave her a kiss on the cheek. I turned and walked over to my table where all my friends were sitting. Before I got there, I felt a hand on my right shoulder, stopping me. I turned back saw it was Canen. He looked

---

[16] A girl's 15th birthday party.

at me gravely and said, "What is wrong? Don't tell me that it's nothing, because your sister and I both noticed that you've been a little depressed all day long. What's bothering you?"

I shook my head. "I don't want to bother you with my problems on your wedding day. It's not really anything important. When you come back from your honeymoon, we will talk."

He took me by the arm and demanded in a pleasant tone, "No—we will talk now. I don't want you being depressed or worried for the two weeks we'll be away on our honeymoon. Follow me. Let's go behind the dressing room so we can talk." I followed him to the small salon behind the reception room that was used as a dressing room. He closed the door behind us, sat down, and said, "Sit down. I want to tell you something important. A few hours ago, we were very good friends. Actually, we've been friends for a long time. I appreciate very much your company and your input. Now, we are brothers. I need to know more than ever when you have a problem, since we're members of the same family." I summarized the incident that Yaneba had with her friends along the river, my encounter and disappointment with Argibay, and the burden I had carried since leaving his office. He listened to me very patiently. When I finished, he said, "Wait for me here. Don't move—I'll be back in a minute." He opened the door and disappeared. He came back almost right away, and returned with a tall mulatto. His face looked familiar, but I didn't immediately recognize him in his civilian clothes. When he held out his hand to me and smiled at me, I saw the gold tooth in his mouth, and knew who it was.

He said, "How are you doing today, Commandantico?"

I shot up out of my chair as if I had been stuck by a fork. "This is one of the sons of bitches with the sergeant and his group that tried to rape my friends!" I advanced on him, shaking my finger almost in his face. "You cannot lie to me like you did to that accomplice you guys have, that stupid Argibay!"

Canen saw my agitation and moved between us. "Wait, wait, wait—you are mistaken."

I turned around abruptly. "No, I'm not mistaken." My expression grew very sour. "What are you telling me?" I demanded in confusion.

"Hold on," he said, "for God's sake, calm down." He pointed at the man. "Mayari is the only one who defended your friends."

"What!?" I said in astonishment.

"Yes," Canen said. "He is also the only one who didn't go along with the lies to Argibay. Did you see him in the building?" I thought about it for a moment, and it was very true. I had not, in fact, seen him there. "He is the only one who came this morning to the tribunals to tell me the details of what happened. He actually told me that you are a witness. He waited for me outside the District Attorney's Office, and gave me the details of the incident."

The tall mulatto man looked at Canen and nodded affirmatively. He looked at me and said, "If you don't believe me, go and ask the girls at your table who it was that tried to stop the sergeant." I took a couple of steps back, looking between the two of them still a little doubtfully. Mayari said, "I told the sergeant that I didn't want anything to do with that abuse. I turned around and sat down in one of the jeeps. When they hit one of the girls with the rifle, I couldn't control myself any more, and I got out of the jeep and screamed at them that what they were doing was indecent and improper, that they should be ashamed of what they were doing. Then the sergeant screamed back at me to go back to the jeep or sleep in the jail that night for disobeying his orders. At that moment, thank God, you guys showed up with your horses."

I glanced at him once again, and remembered at that instant, that he was the only soldier who smiled when I reprimanded the sergeant. It was that gold-toothed smiled that I remembered. I then also recalled him not only smiling but also nodding in agreement. I had wondered at the time why he was behaving that way, since I had been including him in my admonishment. Mayari repeated, "If you don't believe me, ask the girls."

"No need; I remember now that you were agreeing with me when I said that they were a disgrace to the Rebel Army. I believe you." I turned to Canen. "What are you going to do?"

Canen replied, "I'm going to sign a detention order right now. Mayari will deliver it tomorrow morning to the military police. We will put all of them in jail, including the sergeant. There they will remain during my fortnight honeymoon, and when I return, they will be prosecuted in a military court. I assure you these sons of bitches will pay for what they tried to do."

I considered that, and nodded my head. "I'm not the one getting married today, but if I were, this would be the best present you could ever give me. I gave my word of honor to my friends that this crime would not go unpunished." I stepped up to him and gave him a big hug. "God bless you, and bless all your sons. You are a dignified man. Evidently, this is fading slowly these days in the military circles."

Mayari showed his gold tooth with another large smile.

"Amen to that!"

Canen stepped over to Mayari. "Negro, for your honesty, I will recommend you to be promoted to sergeant. You are more deserving to have those stripes than that degenerate man who was your sergeant."

Mayari shook his head in embarrassment. "That will not be necessary, Captain."

Canen said, "Seriously—do you like the idea or not?"

Mayari smiled. "Claro, Capitan! Thank you very much."

"I will also recommend for you a position in the Tribunals, so that you will work directly with me." Mayari positively grinned from ear to ear upon hearing that. "I like to surround myself with decent people." Canen smiled at me. "Now that everything is in order, let's go rejoin the party. Your sister will be looking for me, and wondering if I've run away."

* Amplísima zona de parqueo.
* Pista super-gigante.

Y en los jardines del tipicismo Tropical de nuestra Isla

"Rumayor Night Club"

Km. 2½, Carretera a Viñales

Pinar del Río, Cuba

Magazine ad promoting Rumayor

The waterfall at Rumayor

Chapter 8: Sandra's Departure and Threat

I felt at that moment a great weight released from my shoulders. All day long I had been wondering what I would tell Yaneba and her friends when I faced them and got questioned about this subject. I had, in all honesty, been circulating around the party and avoiding sitting at the table. Both Canen and my sister knew me well enough to realize how out of character this was for me, and I figured that she had sent him after me to find out what was wrong with me. Even though I had been sympathetic towards Canen from the moment I had met him a couple of years previously, from that day forward an intensely strong bond of sincere caring unified me with him until his death separated us in 2012. I received that news with the greatest sorrow, as I had not only lost a great friend, but a great member of my family. I still feel the pang of his passing, which proves that this is one of those eternal bonds. I know we shall see each other once again in Heaven.

We came back to the party. I was very happy in the knowledge that the situation would be resolved. I not only had complete conviction in this, but I also had complete trust that Canen would do exactly as he said he would. I not only went to the table at last; I virtually rushed to it. My friends were all seated and waiting for me. They had been enjoying the exquisite Cuban meal that the waitresses had been serving as they circulated among the tables. From a distance, I could see Sandra, looking beautiful in a mint green dress. I waved hello to her with a smile on my face. To my surprise, she did not even acknowledge me, let alone return my greeting. She half turned and walked towards the door to a salon on the extreme opposite side of the room. At first, I thought she might not have seen me, and that she was going that way to look for the rest room. As I drew close to the table, I noticed that, instead of going towards the bath room, she was heading towards the exit door. I was confused, but I went ahead and went to sit down at the table. I was embarrassed at the way she didn't return my wave, and tried to ignore the whole thing. I said hello to everyone and sat down next to Tite. He handed me a sealed envelope.

"S-s-sandra told me to g-g-give you this." The pink envelope was sealed with my name written in large, capital letters.

I took it in confusion. In order to avoid creating a scene, I excused myself to the others. Yaneba was sitting right in front of me. She clearly wasn't missing any detail of anything that was happening. She smiled at me, and I returned her smile. As I pushed back my chair, she said, "Don't take too long. They're already serving the food, and it will get cold. It's delicious!" Doña Carmen, Lazaro, and all the others agreed, and urged me to come back soon.

I nodded. "I'll be back right away." I walked to the salon. There were public phones located there, and I looked for a quiet place with decent lighting to read this mysterious letter. I sat down on one of the long benches in that small room. A quick glance showed me a young lady, who I thought was one of Canen's sisters, was in one of the booths. She waved at me, and I returned the wave. I opened the letter and started to read.

"My lovely Julio Antonio," it read. "I only came to the wedding to say goodbye to you. I'm leaving very early tomorrow for Moscow. I'm going to the Nautical Superior Military School. We probably won't see each other for years, but I think this is best for both of us. I've been observing how slowly you have been choosing to separate yourself from the political principles of the Revolution and not embracing where it is going. This is really a pity, because I thought that, until a few days ago, for a long, long time, that you would be the man who would take me to the altar, and that we would have many sons and be together for the rest of our lives. But it was with sadness that I finally saw that you can only see the negative side of this Revolution, and not the good things, which are many, that it has done for our people. With all the enemies and worms with whom you maintain friendship and keeping close to yourself every day, including that blonde glass of milk that probably will be leaving with all her family very soon to join the rest of the worms in Miami, I can tell you that you are guilty of treason to this Revolution. I'm not going to judge or condemn you, but I will give you this advice as the good friend you've been in the past, before I finish this letter: walk very carefully. If you tell me who you hang around with, I will tell you who you are. Maybe other eyes that aren't good like mine might be observing you. Remember, you are very close to all the leaders of the Revolution. Associating with their enemies is not precisely a good thing. To me, it would be very sad if you ended up being accused as a traitor and executed by a firing squad. Please, I will ask you one single thing. Don't write to me, don't look for me, ever. I want to forget you. If you do this, it will make this task more difficult for me. That is why I want you to please forget about me and never look for me ever again. Thank you, with all my heart, Sandra."

I read it twice through; I couldn't believe it. The words were harsh, and could be interpreted as a death threat. When I had finished, I reflected for a few minutes. I thought that I had known Sandra since we were little kids. She could put her finger on me and tell the G-2 or her father what she thought. Even though there was no basis, I couldn't help but wonder if she was capable of accusing me to the authorities and making trouble for me. I knew all it would take would be something little like that to cause an investigation of myself and my family. It would be very difficult for me to move freely in the military circles if that happened. A dark shadow of worry cast itself on my brain and soul, and I realized from that moment I had to be very careful about to whom I revealed my feelings and thoughts. I had to be careful not only for myself, but for the lives of my family and my closest friends. They depended on how good I could be in the future to convince not only my enemies, but everyone else, that I continued to be a Revolutionary, but I also had to convince them that I was a communist. That thought disgusted me.

Deep inside, however, I received Sandra's decision with joy. I was already sick and tired of pretending with her that I liked the Revolution, while the reality was that with each passing day I despised the system more and more. I considered every single one of them, starting with Che and finishing with the Castro brothers, as opportunists, liars, and hypocrites, with egos that wanted to be even greater (in their minds) than Adolf Hitler ever was.

I was so abstracted in my thoughts that I hadn't even realized that Yaneba had come with a plate of food for me and sat down next to me. When she touched me, I jumped. "I'm sorry," she said, "I didn't mean to scare you."

"No, no—you just startled me."

"Bad news?"

"It's not so bad a piece of news, after all," I said. I shook the letter. "Sandra just broke up with me, but I think it's best for both of us. We're completely different in many things, especially in the way we see where this Revolution is going. I think that for you, this is also good news."

She grinned broadly, showing her beautiful teeth. "Yes, that is good news. It's not good—it's stupendous! But why don't you eat the food before it gets cold? It's been sitting there too long, as it is. We'll talk about Sandra later."

"There's nothing to talk about Sandra at all." I nodded. "Very well, Mama. Let's go back to the table, and I can eat this food in a more comfortable place. Thank you very much for bringing the plate over here. You shouldn't have bothered yourself. Where is your food? Yours is the one that's going to be cold."

She smiled and touched her belly. "I doubt that. Mine is very warm in my stomach."

I smiled. "Boy, you're a fast eater! I left you five minutes ago, and you ate all your food."

"No, you haven't been gone five minutes. You've been gone half an hour!"

"OK, Mama," I said, and we went back to the table. After we sat down at the table, I asked one of the waiters if he could take the food and warm it up for me. He nodded, and I said, "And so you don't make two trips, when you come back, please bring me an ash tray and a book of matches." Everyone, especially the adults at the table, looked at me in surprise. Even my friends were surprised; as a kid, if I was going to smoke, I shouldn't do it in front of the adults. Doña Carmen kept looking at me in admonishment. "Grandmother, don't worry about it. The ash tray and matches are to burn this letter, nothing else."

She smiled. "Of course—I knew that."

When the waiter came back with my food, ash tray, and matches. I burned the letter, as I didn't want to take the chance of that letter winding up in the hands of my enemies. It contained some things that I most certainly did not want them to know about. By the time I finished my food, everyone save for Doña Carmen were on the dance floor. Yaneba also stayed at the table, waiting patiently for me to finish eating. My family were also all dancing to the music of the jazz band. The current song was "Summer of Love." One of my father's brother Masons, a great saxophone player, had offered to bring his band to provide live music to the celebration at no charge as a gift to my father.

Once I had finished, I walked with Yaneba to the dance floor to join the rest of the group. We danced for a while, until the music ended. The next selection was more fast rock, a style called presumida. It translates to English as conceited or vain, but it was a very fast, energetic kind of music of the 1960s. In the middle of the music, Daniel and the others came over and showed me a box of Salem cigarettes. He said, "Let's go to the river. Here, in front of my grandmother, and all of these adults, they're very restrictive." He had to come close to speak in my ear over the loud music.

I turned to Yaneba and said, "He wants us to go to the river to smoke."

"OK," she said.

"You guys go ahead," I said. "I need to go to the bar and get something first, and I'll join you there in a bit."

Daniel and Tite went with Yaneba to look for Chandee and Marlina. I went straight to the open bar. Because we were underage, I and my friends of course couldn't order any alcohol. I grabbed a tray, however, and filled it with Coca-Cola and Jupiña soda. Jupiña was a pineapple soda. Because I was a part of the family, I was able to go behind the bar without question. To give myself some legitimacy, I handled a few drink orders while I was there as a show of helping out. While the bartenders weren't looking, I grabbed a couple of bottles of Bacardi rum, and concealed them under each arm upside down under my coat. I held the tray of sodas against my stomach, enabling me to maintain my grip on the bottles. As I went by our table, I asked Doña Carmen, "You want a soda?"

"Oh, you're so kind. Where are the other boys?"

"I think they're outside by the garden. Did you want to come out there with me?"

"No, no—it's far too cold. You children go ahead and enjoy yourselves outside."

I went down the gentle slope, and I saw my friends in the distance under the huge tree on the rocks by the riverbank. They were all smoking cigarettes, laughing, and making jokes. When they saw me with the tray full of soda, Tite and Yaneba ran to take the tray from my hands.

"Oh, you're so nice," she said. "You brought drinks for all of us!"

"You don't even know how nice I am," I said mischievously. I whipped the bottles out of my coat like a magician. "Look at what else I brought!"

They all exclaimed delightedly, and Daniel said, "Oh, man—we are going to get in trouble! Why did you bring two bottles? One bottle is more than enough for us."

"Whatever we don't consume, the rest I will bring to

Leocadio."

Tite smiled. "You always think of your friends."

I smiled back. "Claro, chico!" For a long time, we sat down on the rocks and drank rum and Coke that Yaneba and her friends prepared. Each time we finished a drink, the girls prepared another one. The music could still be heard clearly, as we weren't too far away. However, we were effectively invisible. While we could see the rest of the party very clearly, where we were sitting was so dark that we could not be seen from the main room. Should anyone head our way, we would have plenty of warning and time to hide the evidence.

I was never a smoker. I didn't like the smell left on your hands and clothing, but in the case of the Salem cigarettes, it was different. The menthol smelled better, and so I tolerated it. I shared a cigarette with Yaneba. Daniel offered us another one when we saw the one we had was almost done. I checked with Yaneba, who didn't want another, and so declined the offer. Yaneba must have been putting more rum in my glass than anyone else's, because, in spite of my not being a heavy drinker in the first place, I began to feel like I would be able to raise the large rock on which we were sitting with one hand on my own. Yaneba was giggling, also a little tipsy, as she took occasional sips from my glass as well.

All of our friends were sitting around, minding their own business. Yaneba grabbed my hand, and we looked at each other briefly before giving each other a passionate kiss. When we finished, she whispered in my ear, "Why don't we go for a swim in the river?"

I opened my eyes wide in tipsy surprise, but said, "OK." I looked at my friends, and said, "We'll be back in a while. We're going to go for a walk."

They told us to go ahead with vague gestures, and we walked along the riverbank far enough away that we would have safety and some privacy in a grove of weeping willows. We took off our clothes. There were several small creeks that were tributaries that joined the river at that point. We put our clothes under the tree and concealed them under leaves and dead branches. We were clad only in our underwear, and ran over to a large rock that sloped into the river. We jumped from the rock into the river and swam to the waterfall, perhaps five hundred feet or so. We got underneath the waterfall, and kissed for a while with the water splashing down over our heads and shoulders. We didn't notice, but the current beneath the fall took us to a cave under it that was concealed by overgrowth. The cave was dimly lit from the party lights through the curtain of water. The current of water made the dim light dance intermittently, like a neon sign in the city flashing on and off outside a darkened room. We continued to swim to what appeared to be a small, sandy beach. The lighting was very romantic and exotic, and we both lay down on the refined sand, trying to catch our breath. I noticed Yaneba's small breasts that seemed to me to grow larger on a daily basis. Her beautiful body was petite but very well-balanced. Her wet hair made her look very appealing to me. Her breasts under her wet, cotton halter were entirely visible. She noticed my excitement and observed me in silence. She saw how I was taking in her breasts and body. We looked each other in the eyes. Her fingers started walking over the sand, creeping towards me. Her hand drew near my hand, grabbed it, and drew it onto her breast. She squeezed my hand. I felt the wet fabric and the warmth of her breast. I moved closer to her, accepting her invitation.

We kissed each other passionately for a few minutes, until she turned around in the sand and jumped over my knees and onto my waist, taking off her bottom of her underclothes. With a smile on her lips, she slid her hand inside mine. She said, "Ooh, I know this is supposed to hurt, but it will hurt more than I thought it would. But I know also that this will bring us together for the rest of our lives." She raised herself up slightly, and then settled on top of me, accommodating herself. She slowly let herself go down, very slowly. Her face was at first discontented and dissatisfied in her momentary discomfort. As she continued down, her face changed to satisfaction and pleasure until she sat. She bent over and kissed me, long and passionately. We both felt chills, full of love and passion. We smiled and embraced together.

Julio Antonio's parents, Verena and Leonardo

Chapter 9: Al Erbuoc

Majito, Julio Antonio's beloved nanny

The morning of the next day, I woke up with a huge headache. My mother, Majito, and my uncle were by my side. Luckily for me, my father had left town for Guane to his business. My mother had called my uncle to the hotel, because she was so worried. I had passed out completely. They looked very concerned. It seemed that, after I had come back with Yaneba to rejoin my friends, we were so happy that we continued to drink some more. I had gotten intoxicated to the point of passing out, and my friends had to bring me home. According to Mima and Majito, I had been delirious all night with a high fever and vomiting. In consequence, no one in the house had been able to sleep. They had to put ice bags on my head and my testicles. My uncle calmed them down, saying that I would be fine in a few more hours. It was no wonder that, once I was able to finally get up to go to the bathroom in the morning, that I could not find my penis after that ice bag treatment. I never urinated for so long in my life. While I was in the bathroom, I listened to my mother asking my uncle if I was going to be all right.

"Don't worry," my uncle replied. "This is simply the first time, and the first time is the worst."

"Why did he have to drink alcohol, when he's a little kid?"

"He might not have drunk that much," my uncle said, "but he's not accustomed to it. That's why he was so intoxicated."

When I came back to bed, Mima and Majito had both prepared me some *caldo de gallina vieja*[17]. They took turns admonishing me. I put my hand to my head, and said, "Oh, God! My head! Please, I didn't drink. Maybe it was the punch—they might have put some rum in it. I only had a couple of glasses."

"Oh, my God," my uncle said, coming to my defense. "I only had two glasses of that punch myself, and it nearly knocked me down. If you took two glasses of that stuff, it's no wonder that you were knocked out by it."

I winked subtly at my uncle. "Yes, that must have been it. You know me, Mima—I don't like to drink. I don't even like beer!"

"OK, my son, OK. But when you go to a party in the future, don't drink the punch, OK? Some people can get brain dead from alcohol."

"OK, Mima."

---

[17] A soup of broth made from an old hen

"Yeah," Majito added, "your liver can even rot out from alcohol."

When Majito and Mima left the kitchen, I used the opportunity to thank my uncle. He likewise used the opportunity to let me know that he needed to speak to me in private, and that he would be at his hotel in an hour. "Very well," I replied. "I'll be there in an hour."

After I finished my delicious soup, my head was much clearer as well as my stomach being much happier. I felt like it had given me greater energy, and I jumped in the shower. I then went to meet with my uncle at the Hotel *Globo*[18]. The hotel was in the center of town, on Calle Real. After I arrived at the small shopping center in which the hotel was located, I passed by a small stand of stores and entered the building. Inside were a number of small stores, one of which was the Discolandia record store. I noticed the presence of Olerio and Juan Chorizo. They acknowledged me, but didn't say anything to me or wave. I understood they were probably there to protect my uncle and ensure our privacy. I continued on inside, got to the elevator, and went to suite 292. I rang the bell, and my uncle opened the door. He embraced me. "How do you feel? Feel better?" he asked.

"Yes, much better, thank you." We sat down in the small sitting room, he on the sofa and I in an armchair in front of him.

"I know you were with your friends last night, but in future be extremely careful about drinking and who you drink with. This is one of the ways our enemies use in order to get to us: drinking and women. This is how they can neutralize us." I reclined a little bit uncomfortably, and

---

18 Spanish for balloon

nodded my head without saying anything. He stroked his chin thoughtfully. "Under no circumstance, never drink out of an open container, unless you were the one to open it."

"Very well," I replied with another nod. "You know, I'm not used to making irrational decisions or behave in an irrational way, but," and I smiled a little bit, "last night was a special night for me. It was my first time, not only for me but for the woman who was with me."

He reclined a little bit in the sofa. "Well, well! Why doesn't this surprise me? I should have been expecting this. You've come into the university before you've gone to high school." Still seriously, but still understanding perfectly what I was saying to him, he asked this time, "Was it a nice experience? Did you have a good time?"

This time, I grinned broadly. "Not a pretty experience—a beautiful and unforgettable one. It was a very special night, one that I will remember for the rest of my life."

He grinned broadly himself and nodded. "Congratulations. That is very important. The first experience is the one we never forget. Even though I think you're still too young for this, I believe you're too young also for the rest of what you're doing right now with us, risking your life every day. I personally believe that this is the reason you've been growing up and maturing so soon. I always knew you were mature before this, at a very early age. But I want you to remember something," he added, raising his right arm high, "no matter what you will be feeling the need to share almost everything, particularly with that girl, don't ever make the mistake of telling her what you're doing with us. Without exception, no one should know what you're doing. Not only are you putting your own life at risk, you're bringing that person into the same risk. You're also putting the lives of everyone one of us involved with you in jeopardy."

I grew very serious. "Of course. That is the first thing I learned with you guys, when I started my training a while ago. You know how I'm accustomed to follow the rules strictly. If something bothers me extremely, it's improvising." I shook my head. "Even though sometimes we have to improvise, because there's no other remedy, it's not really something I enjoy doing. Our secrets belong to ourselves, and we don't share that with anyone unless it's absolutely necessary for our survival."

My uncle smiled in great satisfaction and relief. He nodded and took an envelope out of his pocket. It had large capital letters on the outside. He gave it to me. "Yes. This is one of the codes and schematics in one of the documents from Che's files."

I looked at him in surprise. The letters read, "AL ERBUOC."

"Do you know what that signifies?" he asked me.

I massaged my forehead with the fingers of my left hand. "No, of course not. That's why I put question marks in front of it."

"That is the name of the French ship that should be arriving to our port in a few days, loaded with weapons and artillery from Belgium, but her name has been written backwards. The real name is *La Coubre*. Our analysts brought us the report, and we are completely certain that this ship is going to be sabotaged by Che's men in agreement with the Castro brothers."

The mysterious ship at the center of Che's sinister plot

I shook my head in confusion. "But why is Che going to sabotage a ship of weapons coming to Cuba? They need these weapons too much; this has no logic. Are you sure your analysts aren't wrong?"

He shook his head and raised both his arms to slow me down. "Let me explain to you." He reclined back in his seat, shifting into a more comfortable position. "These weapons are of Belgian manufacture. They will be completely obsolete in less than a year from now. They're coming from a capitalist country, and in a very short time Che and the Castros aren't going to want any association with them. They already are expecting a big shipment from the Soviet Union. These weapons will be more important than any other weapons. From now on, they will supply themselves from the Communist countries. The Belgians didn't sell those weapons to Fidel Castro and his team of traitors to democracy. The weapons were sold to the Dictator Batista in the 50s. Since the Cuban government is the one that paid for them, the new government demanded the money back from Belgium. There was a stipulation in the contract, however, that in the case of cancellation no monies would be returned."

I said, "I believe that this idea is probably conceived by Che. I'm not surprised, since there's a huge insurance policy on those weapons. Unfortunately, they're not considering the cost in human life and the suffering they'll bring to the families of the dock workers." It clicked together in my mind at that moment, and I remembered Daniel and his father, Lazaro. I put my hand on my mouth and said, "Oh, my God!" I shook my head and stroked my chin. "Oh, my God," I repeated.

My uncle moved forward in his chair suddenly. "What's up? What are you thinking?"

I looked at him. I compressed my lips and shook my head in disbelief. I still didn't fully accept Doña Carmen's prophecy. "My driver and my great friend, Daniel, is on the way to the capital or already there with his father. To make matters worse, he's supposed to be working on the pier with his father, who is one of the big honchos in the Port Union."

My uncle shook his head. He brought his fist to his mouth in thought. "You know the worst part of this thing is that you can't say a single word to your friend or anybody about this. If you try to alert them to the danger, you'll blow your cover. Your identity will be exposed, and you'll expose all of the rest of us. Oh, my God—what a dilemma!"

I asked, "Is there any way at all to foil this plan, prevent it from happening?"

He looked at me, understanding my frustration. He opened his arms as part of the question. "How can we detour this when we don't know the details? We don't know who will be executing this—it could even be one of the workers in the harbor. It could be anyone. It's marked in the schematics that the main operative is classified as the X Man, but we don't know who he is. Perhaps some of the G-2 have been planted inside the union to keep the government informed of what is going on in the worker's movements. We know that Che is behind this, and we know generally what will happen, but we don't have any specifics. We know what results they expect to achieve with this success as well as many other things, but this is like looking for a needle in a haystack."

"I ask myself what they could obtain through a sabotage of this magnitude," I said.

My uncle stroked his chin. "From this sabotage, believe it or not, depends the future of Che and the Castros' grip on power. It is entirely a power play so that they can retain their power indefinitely, not only here, but also to ensure their power to be able to manipulate the destiny of other countries from this tiny island. With this sabotage, they are looking to gain the backing from all the communist countries around the world. Remember, they have to destroy the bond that exists now between the Cuban people and the North American people. What better way to implicate the CIA and the US government than from this horrible sabotage?" He stopped and breathed deeply. "Can you imagine it? We are two years into the Revolution, and look in your pocket. What do you have for your currency? Probably half or more is in North American coins and dollar bills. US currency circulates in Cuba as frequently as our own. They will never convince the Cuban people to give this away. It's like a marriage." His voice grew increasingly frustrated. "They have to create an anti-North American sentiment in order to break those bonds.

They have to convince the Cuban people that we have to break with these capitalists because they are evil and have no respect for human life. They have to paint the Americans as the worst criminals on Earth."

I shook my head, desperately trying to think of a way to alert Daniel and his father to their danger without giving away my position as a spy. But I could think of no solution to such a complex situation. My uncle looked at me, guessing my thoughts. "Just remember what we were talking about a few minutes ago, about your girlfriend. That goes along with everybody the same—family, friends, everyone in general. For God's sake, don't make the mistake of opening your mouth with your friend Daniel, because this could be the last thing you say to him. The rest of us would probably wind up getting terminated, as well."

I nodded gravely without saying a word. My uncle looked into my eyes deeply, understanding my pain and frustration. He raised his right arm. "Let me think of some way that you might be able to do this without compromising yourself or any of us. Maybe we can find a way to take your friend and his father away from the danger, at least until it's over. You have to also contemplate that unexpected things happen in life, and maybe they'll wind up aborting the operation for some reason."

I smiled and shook my head. I knew he was trying to cheer me up. "Thank you, but you know as well as I do that when Che creates a plan, he probably has plans B, C, and D in place. It will be very difficult to properly frustrate their plans. You cannot forget that he has all their sources at his disposition and the full support of the Castro brothers."

My uncle thought for a second and then nodded. "Yes, unfortunately, you're right. Do you know what today is?"

"Claro! It's February 15, the day after my sister's wedding and the day after Valentine's Day. How could I forget the day? Did you forget my sister was married on February 14?" I added mockingly.

He smiled. "No, I'm not referring to that. I was referring to something else, but you are very young, and you may not yet know the entire history of your country." He scratched his head. "Today is the anniversary of the United States battleship, USS Maine, getting blown up in the Port of Havana on February 15, 1898. 260 crewmen died; ironically, it is because of this historical day that Che and the Castros came up with this idea for this criminal act. Only a morbid mind like theirs would like to repeat history in this way." He coughed. "The communists for a long time have been trying to fabricate a story accusing the US government of sabotaging their own ship and killing their own people, only for political benefits. According to them, the Americans wanted to declare war on Spain in order to take away their colonies in Cuba and Puerto Rico. Unfortunately for them, there's no shred of evidence to prove this conspiracy. The explosion was proved by demolitions experts to have come from the outside—this is undeniable proof that this came from a mine used by the Spanish in the port. That is the way history records it, as well."

He leaned back into the sofa, trying to get comfortable once more. "Yes sir—these Machiavellians. Che probably proposed this idea to the Castro brothers and they received the notion with joy."

I squeezed my lips with my fingers. "I will stick like glue to Che. I will try to see what I can find about the little details we need, and then perhaps we can handicap their plans."

My uncle looked a little worried. "Be careful—if you think you can do this in a way that will be safe for you, and won't compromise yourself, then do it. But remember, he's very smart, he has no scruples, and is a very dangerous man. There is nothing more terrible than a man with a Napoleon complex and no scruples. It's a double whammy, and makes being close that man extremely hazardous."

I nodded. "I know, I know. I know him from the inside out. That is why it will be very difficult for him to catch me by surprise."

My uncle stood up, and I followed suit. We hugged each other, and he said, "Look very carefully how you walk. After what you did in the Military Regiment," he took one of the pages and shook it with a satisfied expression, "you can be extremely sure that you will find more than one trap in your road. Maybe not precisely for you, but you could still wind up getting caught by it."

"Don't worry—I know. I'm prepared, and I will walk like a sniffing dog whenever I get close to them."

He smiled and said, "I'm sure you will." We left the room, and I walked towards the elevators. While I was crossing the small shops on my way to the exit, I saw Luciano had been added to the team. He pretended to look through a magazine on one of the stands opposite Discolandia. When I came near him, he looked at me very seriously. With the magazine still in his hand, he winked at me very subtly. In case I was being observed by somebody, I didn't reply. I just ignored him and continued on without making any gestures with my face or my body. After I left the place, I drove towards Daniel's house in the hope that maybe my friend had changed his mind regarding his trip to the capital. Perhaps I was torturing myself, and then when I got there I would be told he was still there. Maybe his mother and grandmother had convinced him to not go through with the plan to leave for Havana with his father. I knew in my heart that, no matter what, I couldn't communicate anything with him about this matter, but still mechanically drove to his house with that wish in my heart. In a wistful voice, I prayed to God as I drove.

When I finally arrived, I was greatly disillusioned, as I found both Esmeralda and his grandmother very depressed. They told me that Daniel had left very early that morning for the capital, and had probably arrived there already. They both told me with tears in their eyes that it had been impossible to persuade him, since his mind was so completely made up, and they had to let him go. I attempted to comfort them and said, "Maybe it's all for the best, and he'll find a great future there." I tried to get Lazaro's phone number, just in case I wanted to communicate with Daniel when I was in the capital. I had the idea that I might be able to approach him in some way that would allow me to get him away from the danger. They told me that Lazaro had no phone in his house, and that the only neighbor they used to leave him emergency messages had left the country a while ago with her family, and the government had expropriated the house as they had with anyone who abandoned Cuba. The new bureaucratic department the Revolution created called Urban Reform oversaw these seizures. Unlike Castro's promises that these houses would be given to the poor, the houses were rented, which effectively made the government the landlord of the people. It was a move that was very similar to what the Nazis did in pre-World War

Two Germany. I bit my lips against saying anything further, however, and I left the place.

Very worried and deep in my thoughts, I drove the jeep towards Leocadio's ranch. As each day went by, I had fewer friends in town. The ones who didn't abandon the country to flee from the communist system were leaving by some kind of student grants to another socialist country. It looked like the idea of the new system was to consistently divide the families, no matter what the cost. I remembered the slogan used throughout history: "divide and conquer." Claude Fauchet played both sides in the French Revolution, though it came back to bite him, and ultimately led him to the guillotine.

When I got to the ranch, Leocadio received me with his usual happy countenance. I noticed that a bunch of the dogs barking by the wheels of my jeep that we had a small addition to the pack. My little Kimbo had already been adopted by the other dogs. I thought for a minute with a smile on my face that there was a new musician in the band. The little one identified me as soon as I got out of the jeep and followed me all the way to the house. After I exchanged greetings and hugs with Leocadio, I gave him the bottle of Bacardi I had concealed beneath the seat of my jeep, along with a case of Jupiña that I had taken from the party for myself.

Leocadio received the bottle of Bacardi more than anything else with joy. He clapped me on the back and said, "You never forget your old friend! Thank you. Not too long ago, Captain Francisco Lemus stopped by and asked me if you had been here or if I knew when you were going to stop by. I asked him if he looked for you at your house. He said he had, but you had left the house very early. I asked him if he wanted to leave any message for you." I stayed silent and tried to remember him. I realized he was the first assistant Escalona had, and Fidel had promoted him to one of the positions in the Prime Minister's office in Havana. My expression was indifferent as I picked up and held Kimbo. Leocadio took his hat off and scratched his head. "This guy looked to me a little weird, the way he looked at me up and down, like he was examining me. He made me feel uncomfortable."

"He didn't tell you what he wanted?" I asked.

"No, he only told me in case you stopped by here that he needs to talk to you. He has something from Che to share with you. He will be in the Military Regiment, look for him there. He said he would most likely be in Escalona's office."

I nodded and said, "Well, that can wait. I have a bunch of other things I need to do before I go to the Regiment. I'll stop by later." I went to the jeep and took two empty five gallon tanks and handed them to Leocadio. He knew what they were for without asking. He put them by the side of the jeep, next to the gasoline tank, and went to the porch. He took a transparent hose, opened the tank to the jeep, and stuck the hose inside. He put the other end of the hose and sucked on it until the gas started to flow into the tube, and then stuck it into one of the tanks, siphoning the gas. He smiled in satisfaction in that he only had to suck twice before the fuel started to flow. "Please, fill up both and put them into the back of the jeep when you're finished, and cover them with the blanket back there. I'm going to saddle up Diamante and walk him around for a bit, so that you have time to fill up both tanks."

"Go, don't worry about it. Have your ride with your horse. When you come back, everything will be done."

I went to the stables, saddled up my horse, pulled

bottles of Jupiña from the pockets of my uniform and filled the saddlebags with them. I left the ranch towards the river and realized that Kimbo was following me. After a little while, he couldn't continue any further and lay down in the sun, panting heavily. I decided to let him rest for a while, and dismounted. I went over to the creek and let my horse drink. I went and brought little Kimbo over to the creek as well, and he drank thirstily. Clearly, he was too small yet for this adventure. I tried to make him walk behind me, but he continually lay down after a few steps. I finally put him into one of the saddlebags, leaving the flap open so that he could breathe.

I decided a little while later to turn around, and went to the riverbank. Far ahead, I saw something on the same road along which I had all-too-recently had such horrible experiences. It looked like a wagon drawn by four horses headed towards me. As I grew closer, I realized it wasn't in motion, but stationary, on the left side of the road. I slowed my horse to a walk. I didn't know what this meant, but I was very nervous about the situation. Slowly, I continued onward. I saw a couple of tarp-covered military personnel trucks approaching. They stopped by the wagon on the opposite side of the road.

As I drew near, I noticed that the wagon looked like a paddy wagon. It was very strange, since it looked very solid in construction, painted in a black camouflage. I could see the soldiers moving men from that wagon. They were all dressed as Rebel soldiers, but they were handcuffed and manacled. They were very young, the oldest appearing to be perhaps twenty-five years of age. They were chained together, and pulled out of the wagon in pairs. They were then transferred into one of the trucks, where they were once again restrained. The guards were moving them only two at a time, keeping them manageable. It was all very methodical, with two guards performing the transfer out of the wagon, two into a truck, and two on guard with semiautomatic rifles. I wondered what this was; I had never seen anything like this before. As I came up to them, I realized that the highest ranking officer was a lieutenant. He recognized me immediately and bellowed, "Atten-HUT!"

I returned his salute and said, "Continue." The lieutenant was of medium height, dark skinned, and had thick eyebrows. I had seen him frequently in the Regiment. He was a friendly man, and very pleasant, a good friend of Canen. I drew close to him so that we could speak.

"God, you guys blew the roof off!" he said. "Unbelievable wedding!"

I smiled and said, "Yes, indeed. My father likes to do things right. He always says that if you can do things right, why would you do it any other way?"

He smiled and came close to my horse. He started to pet Kimbo. "He's a cute little puppy. Where did you get him?"

I smiled again. "It's a long, sad story. One of these days, I'll tell you."

"Changing the subject, they called me this morning very early to assign me to this duty. We're escorting this group of Counterrevolutionaries they captured last night. Imagine it!" he said as he wiped imaginary sweat from his brow. "I still had a huge headache from last night, but that is the military—you cannot say no, even if you're drunk as a sailor."

"I have a great remedy for that hangover: a delicious bowl of *caldo de gallina vieja*. That, for sure, my friend, will make you feel like new."

He grinned broadly. "What? You say that from experience?" It was clear that he was thinking that, at my age, I hadn't yet had my first hangover.

I nodded my head. "Believe it or not, but I can tell you properly from my most recent experience, Lieutenant Bordon. A very unpleasant experience, by the way, and so recently that it was this morning."

He burst out laughing. "I see, I see."

All the soldiers turned and looked at us at his laughter. The two soldiers by the wagon were untying the last three prisoners. They took the chains out to wrap up and put back into the coach. They were distracted by our laughter. The other two guards took only two of the prisoners, as they were accustomed to doing, assuming the remaining prisoner was still locked up. The third prisoner, a tall, young, dishwater blonde with freckles stayed squatting on the ground. He noticed that his release was completely unnoticed by the four guards. He looked at me, as I had the greatest elevation and would be able to see what was going on. Lieutenant Bordon had his back to him, and the remaining two guards were distracted by our conversation. The young man looked the question at me. I maintained eye contact with him, but my face did not change expression. I put my arm on the saddle horn and bent towards the back and said loudly to Bordon, "If you guys want some soda pop, I've got some Jupiñas in my saddlebags." I tried to reach the bottles, but it was throwing my balance off too much to easily get to them.

The young prisoner realized that this distraction was his chance. He stood up and began to move towards the bushes. As soon as he was far enough from the group, he began to sprint towards cover. As I saw him walking towards the bushes, I got off my horse to start handing out the soda. The two soldiers on watch came over to get the bottles.

However, one of the soldiers in the wagon realized the prisoner was running. Before I gave the last soda to one of the corporals, he started to fire his gun into the air. "Stop!" he screamed. "Halt!"

As soon as they heard the gunfire and shouting, the others dropped the sodas and began running in pursuit. The prisoner was close to the dikes surrounding the river. One of the soldiers noticed that the prisoner wasn't about to stop. He brought his small machine gun to bear and started to shoot at the youth. Pieces of wood, rock, and dirt started to spray around the running man. He was almost to the top of the dike, and suddenly he clutched his right shoulder as if he had been hit, and fell into the river and out of our view. Everyone save for the guards on the prisoners already loaded into the truck started to run after him, followed by Lieutenant Bordon. They hoped to find the prisoner on the other side of the dyke, either wounded or dead. I tied my horse to one of the bushes and ran to see what happened. When I got to the top, I kept my expression neutral to conceal my joy at the revelation that the young man had gotten away. There was no sign of him anywhere.

Lieutenant Bordon looked scared and worried. He came back from the river bank with a bunch of leaves and branches in his hand. They were covered in blood, indicating that they had indeed wounded the prisoner. He looked at the corporal. "Send men up and down this river immediately! We have to find this prisoner, or we're all in major trouble!" He looked at me in shame. He looked at a sergeant, a white kid with a cauliflower nose. "How the hell did this prisoner get away from you guys? What is wrong with you guys?"

The sergeant rushed to defend himself in the face of this reprimand. "It's not us, Lieutenant. The ones in the paddy wagon—they released three this last time, instead of following regulations and releasing only two. They should know by now, given the number of prisoners they've transported. How the hell could they release three and leave the third unsupervised? My men assumed, as is logical, that the third one, the last one, was still tied up. They took the chains and started to roll them up into the wagon before we finished the work. How many times have these people been doing this this month already?"

Lieutenant Bordon took his hat off and scratched furiously at his head in indignation. "I don't give a damn about who is at fault, Cojones, goddammit! We have to find the goddamn prisoner, even if we stay here all day and all night!" He threw his hat onto the ground and began to stomp furiously on it like some child throwing a tantrum.

The sergeant looked at the frustration and irrational behavior of his lieutenant, and decided not to say a single word further. He took his men and began to search for their invisible prisoner. We went back to the wagon and the trucks. Bordon walked close to me and tried to excuse himself.

"You have to believe me, Commander—this has never happened to me before. I don't know how these men can be such idiots."   I listened to him swear and ramble his excuses. He screamed to the corporal by the wagon. "Who is the one who took the chains off the last prisoners?"

The corporal tried to defend himself. "I don't know—I was the one putting the chains inside of the wagon."

I said goodbye to Lieutenant Bordon. "I have to go. I hope you find him." I walked to my horse in silence, and rode to the ranch. I had to put some distance between myself and them quickly to hide the smile of satisfaction on my face. I prayed to Jesus Christ for the life of that man and shook my head as I spoke to myself out loud. "I hope he's not badly wounded."

Shortly after I got to the ranch, I told Leocadio of the incident I had just witnessed. The good Leocadio said, "Let's pray to the Lord for the life of that young man. Go ahead and go. I'll take the saddle off for you."

I gave him charge of my horse, jumped in my jeep, and drove to Yaneba's house. About half a block before my destination, I could see her riding her bike. She had a basket on the front of her bike, and it was loaded down with two bags of groceries. She didn't notice me behind her, so I kept my distance so that I wouldn't scare her by blowing my horn or anything like that. She turned to look behind, noticed it was me, smiled, and motioned for me to follow her. I drove very slowly behind her until we got to her house. I parked my jeep in front, and saw her pantomiming to me to wait while she picked up both bags and walked into the house.

She soon came back outside and jumped into the jeep. She kissed me on the cheek and asked curiously, "Are you repentant or very well satisfied?"

I smiled. "Repentant for what? Are you repentant?"

She smiled mischievously. "You see how I receive you, with a kiss? How can there be any repentance? I'm very repentant, yes sir—for not doing this with you a long time ago! That is the only thing I repent."

I smiled again and shook my head. "If we did it any earlier, we would have been doing it in kindergarten."

She hit me on the shoulder. "You are too much!"

I turned around in my seat and stretched behind me to lift the blanket and show her the gasoline tanks. "Where is Josue?"

She answered, "He is in Las Canas in the beach house."

"OK," I said. "Did you want to leave the gasoline here, or did you want to bring it all the way there?"

"I'm sorry to bother you, but I think it will be a lot safer if we take it over there. Can you do that?"

"Sure—let's take it over there. It's only half an hour."

"It's just that if they catch him with those tanks, he could wind up in jail. They would know what they are there for. In your military jeep, though, they might not search."

"Don't worry about it."

"Please, wait for me a few seconds. Let me tell my mom that we're going to the house on the beach. She might want to send something to my dad."

"OK, don't worry. I'll wait."

She went inside the house, and came out soon with a bag of groceries. Her mother, Maria, and her younger sister, Elena, both came out onto the porch to say goodbye to us. We left towards Las Canas.

Las Canas was a beautiful, sandy beach in Pinar del Rio. Everyone liked to enjoy the ocean, and most of the people from the middle class, even people just a little under the middle class, had houses there. The land was inexpensive and affordable to many. Most of the people enjoyed spending the summers there. Most of the houses were very middle class, with only a small enclave at one end of luxurious housing owned by the very wealthy. Most of these luxury houses were now empty, their owners having left the country earlier. The most politically savvy rich individuals knew what the Revolution was trying to do, and made sure to leave, taking all their money with them. This was one of the reasons that every day there was less work available and increasing unemployment. Even the people who supported and applauded Castro and his accomplices in their speeches against the "fat cats," "capitalist landowners," and "the richest" were starting to realize the big mistake they had made in following the false prophet and let themselves drift down the current of filth, envy, and division, not only of class, race, and religion, that the Revolution created. Instead, it ended in something that resembled nothing of what was promised and completely had turned towards the left and communism. The Castros didn't need the support of those naïve fools anymore. The brothers now had the power.

The trip to the beach where Yaneba's father worked in secret to fix the outboard motor of their boat to remove the family from Cuba took around twenty-five or thirty minutes from the city along the neglected one-way roads. The only things that grew along either side of the road were small palm canas, the reason the beach had earned the name. The beach itself was lovely, situated on the southern coast of the island. In summer, the waters were very warm, but still very cooling in the hot tropical weather.

Yaneba reclined a little in her seat and stroked my cheek with her fingers. "What are you thinking? You've been silent for a long time. I realize you're kind of worried. Can I help you?"

I smiled and said, "You know me very well. Yes, I'm very worried. No matter how hard I think, I'm not finding any solution to my problem. My head is going to explode at any moment."

"If you told me, maybe I could help you find that solution."

I shook my head. "That is part of the dilemma. I cannot communicate with anyone what this is all about, unless I implicate myself and others who are involved with me in this situation."

"Oh, God! Well, I don't think you should worry so much. The more you worry, the less solution you're going to find. All you have to do is tell me without giving me any details. Tell me using comparative examples, a movie, or some other subjective or figurative way, so that you don't compromise anybody and still let me understand what the issue is. You can even use other names or change the specifics to protect the identities of the people involved." She touched my forehead with her fingers. "A lot of times, when you can't find a solution with your mind, even though you're very intelligent, you are too overloaded from many other things. When you trust another person, even though that person might not be as intelligent as you, that person's mind is fresh and not overloaded. Bingo!" she added, throwing her hands up, "that person can give you a solution in a few minutes while you've been having nightmares about it for days, weeks, or months."

I nodded in agreement. "Well, that bit about intelligence, I thank you for that. But the less intelligent— if you refer to yourself, I don't believe you are less intelligent at all. If anything, you might be more intelligent than me, because you suggested something I hadn't even thought of yet. Because you're a woman, probably, and are sensitive to your woman's intuition. If men have intuition at all, I think our testosterone buries it or it got asphyxiated by our machismo. Society injects that in us when we are little kids. Because we are boys, we're not supposed to cry; if we cry, we're sissies. If we get hurt, we're supposed to hold it in, because we're men. You girls, though, can cry for anything, even a little tiny scratch on your skin, and your mom and dad come and kiss you and say 'poor little girl'—" At this point, Yaneba kicked me. "You see? That is why you are more sensitive. But you, in particular, deserve great merit, as a person and as a woman."

She grinned from ear to ear. "Your Mima gave you great values. She taught you to love women. Not every man possesses this quality. Since you know your weakness in your sex, and you also admire the qualities in the opposite sex."

"Claro, chica! If it wasn't for one of you, none of us would be around."

"OK, OK—are you going to tell me or not?" she asked me impatiently. "Stop beating around the bush! We're going to be at the beach house in a little while. If you don't tell me about your dilemma, I'll jump out of the jeep, I'm so full of curiosity."

"OK, I'll tell you," I said in surrender.

She smiled. "Finally! Come on, start—I'm all ears."

I looked into her big, blue eyes that were so full of curiosity. "OK, I'll use you as an example."

"OK."

I grew very serious. "You and your family will be leaving Cuba very soon in an illegal and clandestine way." She nodded. "Well, what if somebody gave me some information that you all were going to be assassinated, because the government knew already what you guys were planning? But think very carefully. This information could only be obtained by somebody inside of the government, and that person stole it. That person not only has the danger of being discovered, but also puts in danger all the others that helped him obtain this information." I paused. "Let's consider for a moment that person is me."

"OK," she said, looking at me very serious and a little frightened.

"What if I wanted to prevent you and your family from the tremendous danger you will incur by going on that trip? Of course, I have to explain to you and to your family where that information came from, or you guys won't take me seriously. Add to that, let's say maybe that I doubt your father. Maybe out of fear or because he wanted to clean himself from the guilt of what he's doing, he goes and betrays me and informs the government that I was the one who provided you with that information. You follow me?"

"Yes."

"OK, in this case, the situation not only gets complicated for me, but also for everyone behind me. Just because I want to protect you from the danger you and your family will be exposing yourselves to, by trying to help keep you from getting hurt, I drag not only my friends and associates but also my family into a dangerous dilemma."

She looked at me gravely and replied quickly, "Don't do it." She shook her head and repeated, "Don't do it. It's very sad to know ahead of time that you can prevent the death or misery of other people. It's absolutely devastating to have to sit on that information and not do anything about it for those people's well-being." She leaned back in her seat and touched my arm. She shook her head once more. "Poor Julio Antonio. I don't want to be in your shoes for one second. What a dilemma! But I can tell you with no selfishness at all, you have to analyze this from the logical point of view. The risk is too great, not only for you, but for your family and those who are behind you. If something goes wrong, you will be like a traitor in their eyes. Even though your act is altruistic, generous, and extremely brave, it's completely stupid. It's like playing an unnecessary game of Russian roulette, not only with your life but also the lives of all those around you. This can be considered extremely irresponsible on your part."

We passed the sign that welcomed travelers to Las Canas. I rubbed my forehead with my free hand. "What if you and your family," I asked gravely serious, "are the ones who are in danger? And this supposition you asked me in reality is the truth, and you, your dad, your mom, and your sister are the ones who might be killed?"

She returned the gravity of my look for a few seconds before replying. "Don't do it. That is my answer, even if it's my family."

I nodded reluctantly and said in a tone of admiration, "Every minute I'm around you and know you better, I feel prouder of you."

She moved forward in her seat and kissed me on the cheek with a beautiful smile on her lips. "But it's not me and my family you're talking about, right?"

I shook my head slowly with a smile. "No, it's not you or your family. Don't worry."

We approached the house on the beach. Yaneba got out of the jeep and went to knock on the door while I sat and waited for her. A few minutes later, she came out onto the porch and gestured for me to go around to the back. Josue came out behind her and walked in that direction as well. He opened huge wooden doors on the patio and gestured for me to drive through. In the back was a large dry-dock that looked like a warehouse—long and narrow, with a high roof. Both roof and walls were covered by corrugated aluminum siding. It looked like it had been previously used to build small fishing boats. After I drove in, he closed the wooden gates and opened the door to the workshop, allowing me to drive the jeep inside. Once I was inside, he closed the large doors. It had been built behind the beach house, but was connected to the interior by a small hallway. Yaneba had come through the house and entered the workshop. She opened the cover on the back of the jeep and threw back the blankets covering the gasoline tanks.

Josue came up to me, a large, happy smile on his face, and gave me a big hug. "God bless you, my boy." He pointed at the tanks. "This is the most difficult to find and transport in these days—not only because the government is rationing the gas, but because some people are using it to make Molotov cocktails to burn the cane fields and perform other acts of sabotage against this government." He rubbed his forehead with his right hand as his expression changed to one of discontent. "But we will need at least 30 to 35 gallons to make sure we can make this trip without any problems." He raised the tarp that covered the small boat that looked like he had been working on. It was freshly resurfaced and had a huge Mercury outboard motor. His expression became satisfied. "This horse should take us to Miami without any problems—it's very powerful. But it will also drink gasoline the same way an elephant drinks water."

"How much gasoline do you already have?" I asked him.

He smiled and pointed to the two five gallon tanks I had brought. "You see it there, right in front of your eyes."

I nodded my head. "Don't worry. Just empty those tanks into other containers, and I'll continue to bring them until you're satisfied that you have enough."

His eyes looked doubtful and he raised his arms as if to ward off danger. "You're sure you won't have a problem? I appreciate tremendously what you're doing." He took a couple of steps towards me and put an affectionate arm around my shoulders. "I don't by any circumstance want you or your family to get into any trouble because you're doing this for us."

I smiled and said, "Even though I can't tell you anymore than what I'm going to say now, but I can tell you for sure that the least of the worries I can have at present is to bring you a couple of tanks of gasoline every two or three days."

He thought about that for a minute, and grew very serious. "I don't know what you're doing or what you're involved in, but no matter what your objective and your plans are, be extremely careful. There have been too many young men that have been executed at the firing wall by this Revolution. I don't want you to be one of those. Remember, after all," he added in an unconvinced tone, "why risk your life to remove the Castros when you could wind up putting someone worse in their place? How many people died in removing the Dictator, and look at what we ended up with? My personal advice to you is to not let anybody use you as a ladder for any political idea, no matter who that person is or what he promises, because they're all the same dog with a different color. That is the reason, my boy, I will take my family," he said, gesturing towards Yaneba, "to another country. I don't care if it's the United States, Canada, or wherever—so long as it's far away from the communist idea. I'm tired of fighting, and tired of seeing people die for nothing. All that I want is to be able to live in peace with freedom and democracy. I'm willing to risk my life and that of my family in the process of that pursuit."

I smiled and replied, "Is this not how we all want to live? But who can assure you in the country you select to go and live in to pursue that dream of peace, freedom, and democracy, that after you establish yourself in five or ten years these communist bandits won't follow you all the way there and steal once more your freedom and democracy?" I shook my head. "What will you do then? Keep running all your life, all around the world? Every single time you abandon one of those countries, you leave behind your friends, your accomplishments, your home, and start again—for how long do you think you can do that?" I rubbed my forehead in frustration. "I don't criticize anyone who wants to leave the country, because maybe in the end, someday, maybe they'll force me to do the same. But I'm going to do the most damage I can do in my power against these unscrupulous sons of bitches. And please excuse my language," I hastily added, remembering that I was a kid speaking to an adult.

He looked at me and shook his head. "I admire you kid. I used to be like you, but I don't have enough strength to fight anymore. I wish you well, from the bottom of my heart. You will grow up to be a good man and a great patriot. You don't have to apologize for the swearing—this is their real name."

Yaneba saw how red my face was getting from this conversation and my frustration. She had been listening in silence, completely understanding that this conversation wasn't going to get anywhere. She knew very well that I didn't share the idea that every one of us should leave the country in the hands of the Castro brothers and their band of communists. She knew I didn't believe in leaving them to do as they please, completely clear of any opposition— in my view, that was simply doing them a favor. For this reason, she interrupted and said, "Listen—why don't we go to the beach? It's a beautiful day: sunny, no wind. In the time it will take my dad to empty that gas, we could go snorkeling, and maybe you could release your tension a little bit before you return to the city."

Josue smiled, a little embarrassed by the conversation. He didn't want to get into an argument with me, and so said, "Sure, sure—you guys should enjoy yourselves. Go and have a good time." He might have worried about compromising his supply of gasoline, as well, and added warmly, "Take your time, kids." He was happy with Yaneba's interruption of a friendly argument between different opinions. "By the time you guys get back, I'll probably be done with this," he said, pointing to the gas tanks, "and I'll put the empty tanks in the back of your jeep, exactly in the same way you brought them in."

I nodded. "OK, why not? A little bit of distraction and relaxation after all of the things I've got in my head right now will be good for me. Maybe this will help me clear my mind and think more clearly about how I will handle my problem over the next few days."

We both left the workshop through the hallway and went into the house. Yaneba was enthusiastic about going snorkeling. She hit me on my shoulder. "Come on, it will be good! Let's go!"

Martina, their housekeeper, was inside. She was a great and hard worker. She greeted me when she saw me. She always had a big smile on her face; she was not only the caretaker of that house for them, but had been the nanny for both Yaneba and her sister since the day they were born. Yaneba loved her as much as she loved her own mother. She was a plump, black lady. She gave me a kiss on my cheek. "What a pleasure it is to see you! You haven't been here in a long time."

"The pleasure is all mine," I answered. "It's true, I haven't been able to come around for a long while. Between all this craziness with the Revolution, the Commandos, and the military training, I don't have time anymore for anything. I don't have time to study, much less have a vacation."

She frowned at me and shook a finger in the air. "Uh, oh—the studies come first. You don't let anyone take you away from your education. If you don't get a good education, my boy, you don't have anything."

I smiled and said, "Don't worry about it, Martina. I hear the same thing in my house at least forty times a day—twenty from my Mima, and twenty from Majito."

With a huge smile, she said, "Claro, claro! They are very, very right. You should listen to both of them, because they both want the best for you. You should only listen to them, not to those flea-infested, long-bearded military types. They're almost all illiterates. What do you expect from them? Of course they're going to tell you to drop school." She noticed my uniform. "I'm sorry, my boy, I don't want to offend you or the Revolution. But it's the truth, and the truth will set you free."

I couldn't hold it in any longer and started to laugh. I stepped in to her and gave her a hug and a kiss on the cheek. I wanted to tell her that she was right, but I didn't say anything. Yaneba returned with the snorkels, fins, and mask in hand. "Where is your swimming suit? When are you going to change?"

"Well, I didn't bring a swimming suit?"

She spread her arms. "How can anyone come to the beach with a swimming suit?"

"Remember, it wasn't exactly in my plans today to come

to the beach. You suggested it." I tapped my temple with my forefinger.

She smiled, a little concerned that she might be aggravating me after the near argument with her father. "Come on, I was just joking. Don't worry, Martina will find you something to wear. You have to relax—you're too tense."

I smiled. "I was joking, too."

Martina looked me up and down and shook her head. "I don't think you will look good in Josue's swimming suit. But wait a minute—I might be able to find something for you. The other day, I was sorting his clothes and found in his old clothing a pair of shorts from when he was younger and skinny. Maybe you'll be lucky, and one of them will fit you." She turned around and went into one of the rooms. A few seconds later, she came back with duffel bag, which she emptied onto the sofa in the living room. She looked at a few shorts, shook her head each time. Finally, she picked three of them and held them out to me. "Try these—maybe one of them will fit you."

I looked at the shorts that looked so large to me, and shook my head dubiously. I didn't say anything, but went into one of the bathrooms and tried on all three. I could dance in every one of them, but after a while I picked the one I thought might perhaps look the best. I finally came out of the bathroom to find both Yaneba and Martina waiting anxiously outside. They both laughed when they saw me—I looked like a clown! I immediately turned around to go back into the bathroom to change.

"No, no, no!" Yaneba said as she took my arm. She handed me a large towel. "No one will see you—just put this on until you get into the water. It's the middle of the week, so no one will notice. We're going snorkeling, and the fish won't care if your swimming suit is too big or not."

I nodded reluctantly. "Yeah, you're right." I wrapped myself up like a tamale in the towel, picked up my snorkeling gear, and said goodbye to Martina. We walked outside and down the short distance away from the people.

After we walked a little way away from the house, Yaneba took my hand and said, "Let's walk all the way to the extreme end so that we have some privacy. Then, if you want, you can even take off your shorts once we're in the mangroves if they bother you. I actually don't like to swim with clothes on. I usually leave them on the beach when I go swimming."

I smiled mischievously. "Oh-oh-oh—this egg wants some salt, and maybe a little pepper!"

She hit me on the shoulder. "Oh! You always make me turn red!"

"It's not my fault that you're so white," I teased.

We walked all the way to the far end of the beach. It was undeveloped, no houses, just rocks and mangrove trees. We walked in among the trees, looking for a private place that would allow us to leave our clothes and do whatever we wanted in seclusion. We were on the Caribbean side, and so normally one could walk easily a half mile in the shallows before finding some truly deep water. Here, we found a small cove with deep water fairly close in. It was perfect, both from the perspective of our desire to go swimming in deep water as well as the desire to swim naked. We were very glad to find such a perfect place, and we took our clothes, including my humongous shorts, wrapped them in towels, and camouflaged them as best we could in the bushes, so that they would not be seen by a casual passerby. We put on our masks and snorkel tubes, and waded into the water. The beach was completely deserted, as we were there in the middle of the week as well as the middle of February. Even in the summer, most people only came to the beach on the weekends. It was a beautiful day—the sun was harsh and there was a light, fitful breeze. Because it was February, the occasional breeze was cool, but the harsh sun made the water bearable after the first shock. We hugged each other to warm ourselves up with our bodies. We laughed, and in a few minutes, our heat and the warmer currents changed our mutual outlook, and we didn't notice the cold any longer.

We kissed each other a few times, Yaneba noticed that I was getting excited. She said, "Uh, oh! We'd better snorkel now, or we won't have any energy left to do it later."

"OK," I said. We put on our fins, and then began to snorkel, swimming out towards the horizon, enjoying the marine tropical vegetation. Multicolored banded fish swam by, and splendidly-colored algae covered the bottom. I had brought with me my Commando knife, a sharpened, double-edged blade given to all of my unit by the Army. They had been made from the swords of Batista's old cavalry units. The handle was the hilt of the original sword, with an eagle's head on the pommel. The knife was sheathed on my cartridge belt—I had brought it along in case I needed to defend us against a shark attack.

After we had been snorkeling for a while, ever going deeper into the ocean, I could see that we were about 40 to 50 feet beneath the surface. I could see something moving along the bottom below us. I motioned to Yaneba that I was going down, and dove further down to investigate. It was a big lobster—from its size, it must have been the grandparent of all the lobsters in the area. Yaneba was swimming behind me. I took my knife out, stabbed it in the middle, and turned it around to hold it up to her. She gave me a thumbs up and gesticulated with her arms in excitement. She signaled that she was going to surface. I nodded, but saw that I could see something else moving in the seaweed, and so delayed to investigate further. With my free hand, I parted the kelp and saw nine or ten lobsters of varying size concealed in a mound of underwater vegetation. I had only caught the motion out of the corner of my eye, and smiled happily. They were perfectly camouflaged, as the kelp was very nearly the same color as the lobsters' shells. I didn't have enough room on my knife for all of those lobsters, but got an idea and started to swim towards the surface. When I broached the surface, she was waiting for me with her snorkel beneath her chin and her mask pushed up on her head.

"Well," she said, "I think we we're going to have a wonderful dinner. Martina knows how to make a wonderful *enchilado de langosta*[19]."

I removed my mask and snorkel. "You don't even know—down there, there's a lot more!"

"What do you mean?" she said, "I didn't see anything else."

The lobster was still moving on my knife, and I held it over my head. "There's at least ten more down there!"

"Where did you see that? I didn't see anything."

"They were under a kelp bed. They're the same color, very difficult to see. I only caught a little movement shortly after you left. At first, I thought it was the current moving the leaves of kelp, but when I explored, I saw that there

---

19 A very special Cuban dish, a lobster fricassee.

were a lot in there. I need you to stay right here and not move. I'm going to swim back to where we've got our clothes, drop this lobster there, and see if I can find some wood that I can use to pin as many as I can. I promise I'll be back in a few minutes."

"Don't worry, take your time. I'll stay right here."

"Don't move," I repeated. "We need to be able to find that place again."

"Don't worry, I'm not going to move. Go—if those lobsters are there, as you say, that will feed your family and mine for a few days."

I smiled and said, "OK." I put my mask and snorkel back in, and swam back to the coast and our little cove. I put the lobster inside the large shorts, tied the legs shut, and secured it with the string. I hung them by a branch, and went in search of some wood. I was able to find one that I could cut the length of a sword, and that had a slight J shape at one end, which would help secure the lobster at the bottom, enabling me to pin several lobsters and drag them along to the beach. I took this long stick and tested its strength across my knee. After I realized that it wouldn't break under that weight, I re-entered the water and swam back to where Yaneba anxiously waited for me. When I got there, she received me with a smile that betrayed her concern at how I might have left the other lobster. I smiled and said, "Don't worry—your father's enormous shorts make an excellent cage." I then described to her how I had tied the legs, and finished by saying, "At least those large shorts served something practical." I then showed her the stick I was going to use, and she voiced enthusiastic approval. "OK," I asked, "are you ready?"

We dove back down. It didn't take long for us to find the kelp bed, thanks to Yaneba taking great care to not move an inch from where we had been, even with the swell. I smiled and thought what a good soldier she was. I drew my knife, parted the leaves, and stabbed the first lobster. Yaneba held out the stick, and I transferred the lobster to it. I repeated this operation several times, until Yaneba signaled to me that she was running out of breath. I nodded, and we headed towards the surface. We removed our snorkels and mask, and as we gulped in the air, we counted eight lobsters total on the stick. We stayed there for a few minutes, catching our breath. I asked her, "Are you ready to go again?"

"Yes," she said. We put our snorkels and masks back on, and dove back down. At the bottom, I continued catching lobsters until I didn't see any more crawling around. When we reached the surface, Yaneba squealed, "Whoo! My father's not going to believe this! We've got twelve lobsters here! Boy, have you got a good eye!"

I smiled and said, "Have you forgotten the one we have in the shorts? Add one more."

"Thirteen? Oh, that's a bad number!"

"Don't be so superstitious. There's no such thing as a bad number, only bad people."

"My father is not going to believe it," she repeated.

"Well, then we'll be two liars. Very good liars, since we have the proof!"

She nodded and smiled mischievously. We each took an end of the stick and swam back to the shore. When we got ashore, we climbed up among the mangrove trees and wedged the stick between two branches near the one from which hung the shorts. I removed the large one that I had in my mind named the Grandmother, and put it with the other lobsters. I cut some branches and put them at the bottom of one of the trees to create a cushion. I then put one of the towels on top to make it soft. We hadn't felt the cold before, but now that we were out of the water and in what breeze there was, our teeth began to chatter and the muscles over our stomachs began to shiver uncontrollably. We lay down on the improvised mattress and covered our bodies with the other towel. After a little while, our bodies warmed up and we began to kiss. I massaged her hands under the towel. Finally, the cold dissipated in the warmth of our caresses. We made love very slowly. It was one of the most beautiful and unforgettable moments, due to our innocence of these, our newest experiences with each other—now, we were growing to know each other and learning through repetition of that beautiful adventure. It was something still new to us, but something that grew more profound and momentous each time we explored one another. Time stopped for us, even though a long while had passed. We suddenly realized that it was near sunset. Neither of us wanted to go back, but good sense told us otherwise when we saw how low the sun was on the horizon. We knew we needed to get back before they started looking for us. We wrapped each other in a big towel, grabbed the stick-filled lobsters, each with one end in a hand, and our diving equipment in our free hands, and walked along the beach back towards the house. As we drew closer to the house, we saw Martina heading in our direction, waving at us with both arms. Clearly, she had spotted us.

When we got close to her, she looked at the stick of still-moving lobsters between us, clapped both hands to her mouth, and said, "Oh, my God and all the virgins! How did you get all those lobsters? You didn't have any traps or anything." She kept looking back and forth between the two of us.

Yaneba smiled proudly and said, "My Julio Antonio is an expert scuba diver. If anybody doubts it, we have the proof here."

I shook my head and said, "If it weren't for you staying there like a stick staying in that exact place, we would have wound up only with that one lobster." I pointed at Grandmother. "They were hiding in a very strategic place."

"OK, OK," she said, "You both got it! Now give me that stick." She took the heavy stick and began to waddle cumbersomely towards the house. "You are both angels—you're both sent by Heaven. We've had nothing to eat, only lentil soup. Even then, with no spices. It tastes more like the water leftover from a dog's bath!" We all laughed at her joke. We walked along with her, and she began to bellow, "Don Josue! Don Josue!" In between calling for him as we walked along, she muttered to herself, "He's not going to believe it. He's not going to believe it. No sir, he's not going to believe it."

Josue came out of the house, putting his shirt on and looking concerned. From the urgency in Martina's voice, he had thought something bad was happening. When he saw what Martina had in her hands, he rushed out to help her with a huge smile on his face. We all went into the house and gathered in the kitchen. We related our adventures in lobster catching in detail, and Josue looked at me and said, "Wow, kid! You brought me three great things today. You brought me the gas, you brought my daughter, and now you've brought me food! Thank you!"

"You're welcome sir," I answered, "no problem. It's a pleasure for me."

"You guys go and clean up," Martina said. "I'm going to prepare our dinner."

We each went to a different bathroom and took a

shower, changed back into our clothes, and prepared ourselves for dinner. After the dinner, Josue told me as we sat on the porch outside and looking at the ocean, that the little boat was almost ready and that they would very soon be able to leave on their trip. He also told me that a friend had traded in exchange for some tools a few more empty tanks for the gas. He reasoned that this would make it much easier to transport the fuel to the boat once it was in the water.

We were silent for a few minutes. I watched the waves crashing on the shore not more than thirty feet away from us. Even though I was never happy at the thought of anyone abandoning Cuba, those words from Josue hit me hard. I realized that if the boat was almost ready, Yaneba was only days or at most weeks away from leaving, and I would probably never see her again. Realization washed over me like a cold bath, and that sad thought sobered me. I looked through the dim light at the shadows beneath the porch at her, at her father, and at Martina, who also sat with us, watching the ocean. A strong frustration and pain started in my chest and created a knot in my throat. Two tears escaped my control, and rolled down my cheeks. The beautiful relationship and the deep union Yaneba and I had created in the past weeks made me, for the first time, want to leave with them, where ever they were going, where ever my Yaneba was going to be. At that moment, I no longer cared for anything else. For the first time, I could truthfully say I was tasting the flavor of love. I learned from my adult friends and others that love can break your heart into tiny pieces. I dried my tears with the back of my uniform's sleeve.

Yaneba, perceptive as always, saw me do that. She couldn't really see me, but she could tell that something wasn't right with me. "What's the matter? Everything OK? Do you feel OK? Is something wrong?"

Almost immediately, I replied, "No, no—I think one of those gnats flew into my eye." I stood up and said, "Well, the company is wonderful, and I'd love to stay with you guys here for a long time, but unfortunately I have to get back. I'm supposed to meet with one of the big officers in the Regiment. He apparently has something important," and I made quotation mark gestures around that word, "to tell me. I don't know what you put in those lobsters, but they were delicious."

"I hope you don't mind, but I had to give one of the smallest lobsters to one of my neighbors in exchange for the spices that made it so good."

"No, not at all," I said.

"And thanks to you for bringing those lobsters to us." He caught himself. "I mean, thanks to you, Yaneba," he added to include her. "Take this cooler with you. I put half of them in ice, so you can take them to Majito and your Mima."

I said my thanks, and we hugged and said our goodbyes. It was already getting dark as we drove away from the beach on our return trip to the city.

Dr. Julio Antonio del Marmol

Chapter 10: The Predatory Pedophile

After I dropped Yaneba at her house, I stopped by my own place to drop the lobsters off with my family, who received them with joy. I then drove to the Regimental HQ. I asked around, and was told that Captain Francisco Lemus, or Franco, as we all called him, was in the Officer's Mess. When I got there, he had just finished his dinner, and the place was empty save for a few officers who were eating late.

He said to me, "Let's go to Escalona's office. We'll have more privacy there for what I want to tell you." We went into the main building and sat down in Escalona's office. "I've been working on some very secret plans with Che. I actually prepared under cover some groups to liberate Santo Domingo and some other nations that are under military dictatorships. I have other duties as my cover, but this is what I'm doing for Che. We're recruiting internationalist soldiers. They are in the position to risk their lives in liberating the Americas from the Yankee capitalists, the same patriotic idea that Simon Bolivar, the greatest patriotic guerrilla leader the Americas have ever had."

I reclined in my seat and observed him keenly. I thought to myself about how I had read in history how Simon Bolivar was nothing more than a cocaine addict and the biggest instigator the Americas ever had. I said nothing, however, and let no expression show on my face. Instead, I crossed my legs and patiently listened without interrupting him.

Captain Franco had been the First Assistant to Commander Escalona in the Pinar del Rio Province before his promotion that moved him on to more important duties in Havana. Even though we hadn't known each other for very long, I had dealt with him frequently for a while. He was the first person I had met when I first received my appointment as the Commander-in-Chief of the Commandos. At that time, he was the one who handled all the military logistics and was the one who provided me with all of the supplies, buildings, and materials that I needed for creating my unit. He was a peasant with little education, tall, brunette, pleasant looking, and impressively built at a 6'6" frame and a lean, muscular 300 pounds. His character was friendly and so was generally an easy person with whom to deal. This helped his career immensely, because he was very clever and stuck to the high level leaders of the Revolution. Evidently, he had now been brought into the closest international clandestine operation by Che. Up to this day, I had looked at this man with admiration. From my youthful perspective, this man was a giant. Now, however, I was slowly realizing that his greed for power had gradually changed him through his ambition to step higher on that ladder. A new class in the Revolution had been created, to whom the most important things were not integrity, intelligence, or any sacrifice that an individual had incurred. Even education was disregarded. The most important thing they took into account for future promotion had come to be to say only 'yes' unconditionally to whatever the Castros and the other big leaders following their orders said. The first time you said no or hesitated to obey one of their commands, you got isolated from their circle and classified as 'not clear,' which was enough to end a career.

When he finished speaking, he paused. He asked me, "Not too bad for a man like me, eh? To be in this position now? You're a lot younger than me—you could go higher."

I shrugged my shoulders and asked, "Well, I see you're doing great. Congratulations. Che is very selective, and I don't think he would bring anyone close to him unless they went through a thorough testing, and he must have extreme confidence in you. I don't understand, though—what does all this have to do with me? Could you please explain that to me?"

He reclined in his seat, crossed his legs, and placed his hat on the desk. He ran his fingers through his hair to fix the mess left by his hat. I continued to observe him. Finally, he said, "Che needs very much younger men for this internationalist army to accomplish these missions. Who better than you to recruit these men for him? You've already recruited thousands of youngsters into your Commandos for us. Who better to do this work for us?"

I stroked my chin. "Oh, I see, I see. Che wants me to recruit these youngsters as his internationalist soldiers for these missions." He smiled and nodded. I continued, "There's only a small problem that maybe you don't know."

"What is the problem?" he asked in surprise.

"Well, I don't know if you know, but Piñiero and Ramiro both came here not too long ago to communicate to me that Fidel wants to send me to the Soviet Union to train me into an intelligence officer for Cuba."

He stood up with both hands waving in the air. Smiling, he said, "Don't worry about it. We'll give some excuse to

Piñiero and Ramiro, and I don't think Fidel will care if you're coming to work with us. In fact, he might even look at it in a better way." He began to walk towards me slowly. He sat down by me on the sofa. Still smiling, he crossed his legs and said, "This is between us, please. Don't even repeat this to Che. Che wants to talk to you personally, but I wanted to prepare you and give you a heads up as to what the whole meeting is about. But I want you to maintain this as a surprise, as if you hadn't heard this before. I just wanted to let you know in advance, so you can think about it carefully, so that you can give the proper response. This is a great opportunity for you. Remember, Che is the President of the National Bank—he oversees the entire monetary system here in Cuba. Imagine what we can do with the power we will have! We will leave early tomorrow to Havana. I will pick you up at your house at 6:30. Be ready."

"I will be ready," I said.

He uncrossed his legs and leaned in towards me. He put his right hand on my leg and looked at me in a way that made me feel uncomfortable. "I will like very much you coming to work with us. Who better than you, with all your experience and charisma? All the youngsters in Cuba will follow you. That is why you are the Commandantico." He squeezed my leg with his hand. He shifted a little closer, so much that I could feel his breath on my face.

I jumped up out of the sofa. "Well, well—we will see each other in the morning, and I will find out exactly what Che has to propose to me." I didn't expect any further answer, so I walked towards the door. I wanted to get out of that place, and my heart was beating hard in my chest; for a moment, I thought that this huge man was becoming a woman, not just in the way he looked at me but also in his demeanor. I thought that his intentions may not be honorable, and the way he got so close to me, putting his face so close to mine, and the way he looked at me made me feel the same way Yaneba had been looking at me for a long time, before we finally kissed each other. I was confused and surprised. I didn't know if it was all in my mind; this person was the last man on earth from whom I would expect something like that. Without even hesitating for a further second, I went to the door. "I will be waiting at 6:30. Good night."

"Good night, Commandantico," he said in an uncomfortably effeminate voice.

I rushed down those stairs, almost jumping two steps at a time. I was very worried about the next day, as it was a long trip to Havana in the car with that man. I hoped he didn't come by himself; if he came by himself, I would pretend to be sick, and go to see Che by myself. After I responded to the guards' salute, I got into my jeep and drove from the Regiment towards my house. I kept thinking about what a strange experience I had just gone through. That man, even if he were a homosexual, what could he possibly be attracted to in me? I was a kid, still very undeveloped and skinny. It didn't make any sense to me. I tried to think that my mind might have been overreacting, and that I was wrong. Maybe he was just trying to be friendly and overdoing it. I shook my head, but I realized that there was no way I was overreacting. The man, when he had his face so close to mind, had a morbid fascination, and that was why I was so uncomfortable. It was like he was about to kiss me. Once I got to my house and had gotten into my bed, I couldn't sleep. The more I tried to sleep, the more my thoughts dwelt on that embarrassing situation. What was going to happen the next day? When I finally did get to sleep, I had a horrible nightmare that both Franco and Che were chasing me naked, and both trying to kiss me with open mouths. They had me caught between them, like a couple of predators sharing their prey.

I woke up drenched in sweat. I looked at the alarm clock and saw that it was 4 am. I sat on my bed and wondered if it was possible for Che to be a homosexual, as well. It would explain why he hated these men so badly and persecuted them in his desire to put them in jail or in labor camps. I scratched my head in confusion and worry. I said aloud, "Well, anything is possible. Maybe Che is still in the closet like Franco. Birds of the same feather fly together. These two are very close now, so close that Heaven alone knows what else they're doing."

I jumped out of bed and took a shower to cleanse myself of the memory of that horrible nightmare and calm my nerves. I was so tense that my nerves felt like I was on steroids. Perhaps it was because of the night before, the way Franco had completely caught me by surprise. As I showered, I thought that I had to control my nerves and focus on relaxing. I was going to be walking next to lions from now on. I didn't care if they were homosexuals as long as they left me alone. It crossed my mind that if this man stepped out of line on our trip to Havana that I would put my pistol to his head and stop it, once and for all. This thought gave me courage. The shower was long and hot, and when I was done, I dressed and had a breakfast of oranges and assorted fruit. I packed a couple of changes of clothes, underwear, and socks into a travel bag and sat down on the porch of the house to wait patiently for Franco.

It started to grow light, and I saw a car approaching in

the empty street. It was a beautiful, brand-new 1960 light mint green Buick. It stopped in front of my house, and I looked inside the car to see two men had come with Franco. I breathed a sigh of relief, and felt the tension flow out of my stomach. I picked up my bag and walked down to the sidewalk. The chauffeur was a sergeant I had seen a couple of times before with Che. I had never been presented to him, but he was powerfully built and had red hair. He wasn't a pleasant-looking man at all. He saluted to me and said, "My name is Claudio, Commandantico, but we've never been properly introduced."

"Nice to meet you," I replied as I returned his salute. I handed him my bag, which he put it into the trunk of the car. I was going to open the door in the back, but he prevented me by opening it for me.

I sat in the back seat of this luxury car, and Franco said with a smile, "I see you're ready like a good warrior—you're up early."

"My father taught me that it's better to wait for somebody than to have them wait for you," I said.

Franco introduced me to another man dressed in civilian clothes who sat in the front seat, a skinny man with blonde hair and refined features. "Sergeant-Major Paco Vanti."

"Nice to meet you," I said to him.

"Do you like my new car?" Franco asked.

"Very beautiful," I answered.

"A little present from the Revolution and the Minister of Transportation for my good work." He paused and then added, "With a little push from Che. Maybe you'll get one like this pretty soon. All you have to do is say 'yes' to every single thing Che asks you to do, and you'll see the results."

I smiled and answered, "I see. I see." I stayed silent,

thinking that Sergeant-Major Paco, with his white skin, blue eyes and young age, might be Franco's partner. I could see how they occasionally looked at each other—though I could have imagined it, due to my suspicions about Franco. It just seemed like they knew something I didn't know, the way they would look and smile at each other. Maybe he preferred lightly built men. It made me feel better—if he had someone he was already with present, he wouldn't bother me. I leaned back in the comfortable seat. It still smelled of the fresh leather, as if no one had yet sat in it. I could only wonder at how much sweat it had cost somebody to buy this beautiful car. This man, through the new government's arbitrary laws, had gotten to enjoy this new vehicle without working a single day in his life.

I thought about what my uncle had told me not too long ago. In the end, sometimes you didn't know who you were working for, and suddenly find out that someone else was enjoying something that had been obtained through all of your hard work. He had also told me that if we try not to get involved in politics at all, we can wind up losing everything we had worked all our lives for.

Paco turned in his seat to look back at us. "Commandantico, your friend, Nicolas, told me to say hello to you. I ran into him yesterday at the Havana University. We've known each other for a long time, and he told me when I explained that we were coming to pick you up, and his exact words were, 'Say hello to Morrongo'." Franco and Paco looked at each other maliciously. "He told me they gave you that nickname when you were a very little boy as well as why." I remained serious. I never cared much for that sobriquet. He might have realized that I wasn't very happy with it, based on my continued silence. He smiled and said, "I would think you would be proud of that. Not every man is born into this world with an organ of such a large proportion. If you do, and so they call you like that, you could be proud, since you don't have to worry about people laughing at you when you take your clothes off. It's nothing to be unhappy about."

I looked at him gravely. "I never said I'm not happy about it, and I'm extremely thankful to God for everything He's given me: my family, my friends, my health, and everything physical and mental, including the size of my penis. But that doesn't mean I have to hang around my neck a big sign that announces to the world my size, even in inches. That includes having your friends screaming to you that name 'Morrongo' in the middle of the street." Franco burst out laughing. I fixed Franco with my serious stare. "It's especially embarrassing when you're walking with a girl out of the school, of course leaving in the air that girl's curiosity as to why you're called that by your friends. "I gave him an incredulous look and frowned in anger. "What am I going to tell her? I believe that is crossing the line from friendship and into what I consider a lack of respect. That is the reason that I haven't been on speaking terms with Nicolas for a long time now. I asked him repeatedly not to call me that, especially in front of people in the street. The others followed his example, and he thought it was a joke. To me, it was embarrassing. That is why I don't consider him a friend anymore. The next time he says something like that to you, tell him that I don't send greetings back, because he's not my friend."

Franco smiled and crossed his legs. "If it's not embarrassing to you, since it's just us and you're among friends, you could tell us the story how that came about."

"I'm pretty sure Nicolas has already told in details to

Paco the whole thing," I replied. "You tell him to tell you the story if you're that interested. I'm very tired; I didn't sleep well last night. If you don't mind, I'm going to close my eyes and sleep for a little bit." Franco could see I was angry, and so didn't insist. I reclined my head back against the seat, pulled the armrest down, and tried to let myself fall asleep.

I was not even remotely comfortable with the idea of explaining to Franco the reason I got saddled with that particular name, and why Nicolas Peres, one of my big brother's best friends, had thought of it when I was only nine years of age. However, my own mind went back in time. It was at Roosevelt Park, where we would go to play baseball. The older boys were around seventeen or eighteen years old, and they saw a girl who had a reputation for being loose walk by. They started to flirt outrageously with her—even though they were definitely crossing some lines of decency, she was enjoying the attention, and kept walking by to elicit more reactions from them. Her name was Madela, a pretty girl with a large posterior as her outstanding attribute. I started to join in with them as Madela started to swing her hips even more provocatively. She was wearing elastic white pants, and it was clear that she was not wearing any underclothes. I started to mimic with my hands and waist like the other boys how I was going to get her. It looked more like a dancing dog, perhaps, but I was so distracted that I hadn't noticed that the older boys had stopped yelling at her and started to look at me, hands on their mouths in astonishment. They started to laugh. When I finally realized that I had a big audience and that they were laughing at me, they started to ask me more directly, making fun of my size due to my young age. Nicolas put his hand in his pants, undid his fly, and stuck his pinky out to make fun of me. I grew angry at his taunts. And then Nicolas motioned to Madela.

"Hey, Madela—we've got a really big man here for you! Julio Antonio wants to make love to you!"

She smiled and started to come over to be a part of the joke. The other boys started to copy what I had been doing as they made fun of me. Even my brother joined in with them—I had no defenders. Madela came close to me. "With what?" she asked mockingly, gesturing to me with her pinky. "Please, this little kid's not going to do anything with me. I couldn't even use him for a suppository."

I turned red and was utterly humiliated and furious, especially with comments like that from a girl who had no decency to begin with and so was, in most people's estimation, very nearly a prostitute. How dared she compare my anatomy to a suppository? I was beside myself, and had to gain revenge, so I went behind the statue of President Theodore Roosevelt. I looked up, and it seemed like Roosevelt was watching me, so I went to the other side. I couldn't concentrate with that thought, and what I was going to do required privacy. I dropped my pants down to my knees, and I started to create a fantasy in my mind that would get me excited. I could see in the distance that Madela had returned to her usual route, on her way back from the store with a bottle of soda in her hand and a small bag with a few groceries. Patiently, I waited until she drew close, my weapon at the ready. I raised my pants up to my waist once more, but did not fasten them. Holding them up with one hand, I walked back over to the bunch of boys that were sitting on the bench. This time, Madela came back and stopped to flirt with the boys. She was joking around and still making fun of me. I used the opportunity to get very close to her.

The others saw me behind her and started their chant. "Oh, Madela, here comes the big man again." They started their mocking dance in imitation of me. "He's going to do this to you, and he's going to do that to you."

She turned around with a big smile. "Honey," she said to me, "how can you break a horse when the horse hasn't even been born?" She raised her pinky high and fluttered it tauntingly at me. "The horse hasn't even been born!"

In front of the surprised eyes of all of them, I got on top of the bench and let my pants fall down. "Here's your suppository, Madela," I said. Everybody looked at my erection.

Madela smiled maliciously. "Oh, my God!"

I did the dance on top of the bench. "Yeah, I'll do it to you like this and like this!" This time, nobody laughed. They were all struck mute, their eyes popping out of their heads in disbelief. Madela had her hand over her mouth and was smiling.

She said, "My God! This kid isn't a kid—he's deformed! This is not a boy—this is an alien from outer space!! That, or he has a little alien between his legs. My God! What a morronga this little boy has! My mother would never believe me if I told her. I'll bet you a hundred pesos that none of your guys has anything that big—pull down your pants right now!"

Everyone looked at my frenzied dancing on top of the bench in surprise. Nicolas said, "Morrongo! Oh, my God! We're going to get arrested here. He's not a kid—he's a donkey!!" He started to bray like a mule.

I thought I might have hurt a few of the egos in that group, especially that of Nicolas. I pulled my pants up and fastened them. "I told you," I said. "I'm not a liar. If I said that I would do this and that to Madela, it's because I have something to do it with."

I was very satisfied with myself in remembering all of this, and fell into a deep sleep. It lasted for quite a while, because when I woke up to car horns, it was because we were entering Havana. Franco looked at me when I opened my eyes. "Welcome back to the land of the living. You've been in dreamland for two hours. You must have been very tired, and had a great dream. You were snoring like a tractor."

I smiled and said, "I'm sorry if I bothered you with my snoring. But yes, I had a nice and relaxing sleep—no dreams at all. I didn't even feel the trip."

"Are you hungry?" Franco asked.

"Yes, very hungry. I only had fruit for breakfast."

Paco and Claudio replied almost in unison, "We're in the same club. We haven't had anything."

Franco smiled and said, "Well, let's eat like kings. First class, and the best quality—we'll lunch at the Hotel Capri. I have a lot of friends in there, and we'll get royal treatment." He continued to smile with satisfaction. "What an irony—truly, we are the kings here in Cuba now. Since we are the kings, we will eat like them!" He rubbed his stomach with his right hand to emphasize the point.

We crossed the streets of Havana, and I thought about Daniel, and how I could protect him from the danger that was so imminent. I could, however, still find no solution to that dilemma. It had bothered me since my uncle had shared the information about that situation with me. Completely lost in my thoughts, I abruptly realized that we were in the entrance to the hotel. The Capri was a famous cabaret hotel and restaurant chain, famous for its unique and controversial entertainment. One of these controversial acts was a sexually-charged scene called Superman, in which a black man with a disproportional penis would engage in pornographic acts on stage with women of different races. It was one of the famous shows in Cuba, not only as an attraction to the locals, but as the preference of the tourists from around the world. One of the reasons Havana in particular, and Cuba in general, had been nicknamed the Paris of the Americas and the Pearl of the Caribbean were shows like these.

The Hotel Capri and Cabaret

When we drove into the valet parking of this luxury hotel, I realized that Franco was a regular there. Everybody knew him, and all received him with affection. The maitre d' received him with a big smile and asked if he wanted his usual table, or if he preferred a different one. Franco smiled and said, "No, no—that is great. That's my favorite table when I come here, you know that. Thank you!"

After we sat down and ordered, Franco ordered sides of green bananas, yucca, anchovies—all kinds of extravagances. After a while, our table looked more like a buffet table than a regular one. He also ordered a bottle of Cinzano vermouth. Fortunately, we got there early—not too much more time passed before the place was full. Most of the people were tourists, and even though it was now packed, the maitre d' continually came by our table to make certain everyone was satisfied. In the middle of this conversation, a very tall, skinny, young man with tanned skin and platinum-dyed hair came close to our table. He said hello to Franco with great affection.

Franco stopped eating and stood up to give the man a big hug. He looked familiar, and I knew him—I just couldn't remember where we had met. His look was very distinguished, and his manners very effeminate.

"Please, please, please, Captain," he said in a mincing way. "Don't stand up, your lunch is going to get cold. I don't want to interrupt your lunch," he said to the rest of us, "I only came over to say hello."

Franco introduced him to us as Fernando Alonso, and I could remember who he was. He was a very famous Cuban dancer of international fame. He danced in the national ballet, performed in television, and danced all over the world in representing Cuba. He had even been in several Cuban and international films, and had been interviewed by Desi Arnaz and Lucille Ball on their program. He forced Franco to sit down, gently pushing him by the shoulders.

Franco turned to him and said, "That was a beautiful show you put on last Sunday."

Fernando clapped his hands very effeminately. "I love that you liked it. It gives me a very great pleasure to know you did." A little more familiarly, he added informally, "Can I expect to see you this coming Sunday?"

Franco replied, "Of course! Thank you for the ticket."

"Don't mention it, please." He winked at Franco, and it occurred to me that his eyelashes were too long, like they were fake. He ostentatiously checked a beautiful gold watch. "Oh, I have to go—I have only ten minutes before I'm due in rehearsal. I'm going to be late." He reached out, held Franco's shoulder, and squeezed it. "Well, I'll see you Sunday. Maybe we can have dinner afterward?"

"OK," Franco said. As Fernando turned to leave, Franco reached up with his left hand and grabbed Fernando's rear end. The others stared at the gesture—Paco glared darkly at Franco. Fernando obviously loved that expression of affection from Franco, and walked away swishing his hips in a way that reminded me of Madela. He walked in between the tables with a huge, satisfied smile on his face and past the astonished eyes of the other customers. Franco smiled and grabbed his napkin from the table. "We have to keep these little faggots happy so they don't leave Cuba. They're a great attraction and a good asset to the economy—they bring the tourists here."

Paco was still obviously unhappy and shook his head. "Whatever you do," he admonished Franco very informally, "what you did was not prudent. Especially not here, in front of everybody and in public. If somebody starts to gossip and it reaches Che or Fidel, you'll put them in a very difficult position, especially after Fidel's last speech only a few weeks ago, attacking homosexuals and referring to them as a social disease and a menace to society. We're going to have to cleanse the new socialist youth of that immorality. Can you imagine what will happen if someone goes and tells them that you're squeezing a homosexual's butt in public, especially in this place, where there are so many diplomats and high-ranked people coming to eat and socialize? I think that could jeopardize that star on your shoulder."

Franco smiled again. "Calm down, man—calm down. This is just a joke. Besides, what Fidel told to the people, all that bullshit—he doesn't even believe it himself." He gestured dismissively with his hand. "What about Raul? He's the biggest homosexual in Cuba, and he's in charge of the Armed Forces. Take it easy, and don't be so stressed. Whatever Fidel tells to the regular people in his speeches doesn't apply to us. We're above the law—we can do whatever the hell we want!" By now, his smile had dropped off his face. "Do you understand? I know what I'm doing, and I know what I can do!"

Paco replied, this time more respectfully and with resignation, "Very well, Captain. You know better than us what you can or cannot do." He shook his head ironically. He draped his napkin over his plate in displeasure. "I just lost my appetite. I'm going to the bathroom to wash my hands. Excuse me." He stood up.

Claudio also stood up. "I have to go to the bathroom, too. Please excuse me."

I looked at Franco very seriously. He shrugged nonchalantly. After they left, he said, "I don't care. If they don't want to eat, more for me." He started eating like a pig. I had my last piece of chicken on my fork and was about to put it into my mouth, when I felt some pressure between my legs. I shifted back, and saw that Franco had his hand there, trying to squeeze my genitals. I looked at him in astonishment, and I saw him wink slyly at me. All doubt vanished from my mind, and I realized that he not only was a homosexual, but he was also sick. He continued to explore between my legs, clearly still searching. My fork was still in my hand, and I draped my napkin onto my plate to cover it, slid the chicken off, and quickly jabbed it down onto his hand. I spit my half-chewed food onto my plate. He yelped in pain, yanked his hand back and said, "Are you crazy?!"

I said, "No, but you are a deranged pedophile. You try that again, I'll break your teeth with one of these bottles!"

In the midst of his pain, he had to pretend for the people that were looking at his cry of pain. He put his napkin to his mouth and moaned to one of the ladies, "Oh, I think I broke my tooth!"

I looked at him deadly serious. "You keep your hands to yourself, OK?"

He showed me his hand. "Look at what you did to me!" The four holes were clear on the back of his hand, bleeding profusely. He continually had to wipe the blood off with his napkin, and finally just wrapped the napkin around his hand.

Paco and Claudio had returned from the bathroom and looked at the blood on Franco's hand and he unwrapped it once more to clean it with some water. Paco asked, "What happened?"

Franco didn't reply, but continued to fuss over his hand, putting ice on his hand, and wrapping the napkin once more.

When Paco had no answer from Franco, he looked at me seriously and said, "What happened, Commandantico?"

"Ask Captain Franco," I said. "Tell him to explain to you why he has the holes in his hand from my fork. Ask him where the hell he put his hand, and where he shouldn't have." I shook my head in disapproval. "I think you should take your captain to the hospital."

"Why?" Paco said. "For those little holes?"

"No, not for those little holes. They need to check his head. I think he has a disease in his brain."

Claudio involuntarily laughed and lowered his head to stifle further outburst. Franco glared at him, daring him to comment. Claudio stopped, fearful of any retaliation he might face. Paco looked at Franco accusingly and shook his head in disgust. He understood what had happened in his absence, but didn't say a word. Franco took his white linen handkerchief and wrapped it. As if nothing had happened, he asked, "You guys want dessert?" We looked at him in utter disbelief, but remained silent. Franco signaled to the waiter. "Please," he said, pointing to the dessert display case, "I want a piece of that chocolate cake with two scoops of vanilla ice cream."

"Very well, Captain," the waiter replied. He went into the back and brought Franco's order back out. Franco began to eat, only commenting that we should have ordered pieces for ourselves, because it was delicious. We watched him eat with his wrapped handkerchief now very bloodstained, as if nothing had happened. It only reaffirmed my opinion that this man needed psychiatric help from a professional.

After we finished lunch, he asked for the bill, but the maitre d' told him that the lunch was on the house. Franco smiled and said, "Thank you," as he placed a generous tip in the man's hand. The maitre d' gave him an elegant smile and very graciously declined the tip. Franco insisted, only to be politely refused again.

Utopian Dreams

"Marxist ideas are the most Utopian and romantic dreams for those fed up with the occasional corruption within the political systems in capitalist societies. Unfortunately, these dreamers wake up to a worse nightmarish reality that they now have to live with: the greatest deception that any man in his right mind could ever conceive of having to deal with for the rest of his life."

Dr. Julio Antonio del Marmol

Dr. Julio Antonio del Marmol

Chapter 11: The First Two Keys to the Enigma of the JFK Assassination

We left the hotel and drove through the Havana streets in utter silence. We went to the National Bank and entered the building after the routine security procedures—they knew Franco, but in order to see Che, the rest of us needed to be identified. We were sent to a large, private salon outside Che's office. The lady who walked us there informed us that Che was in the middle of a meeting with a group of foreign representatives, but should be with us shortly.

We sat down in silence around a huge table. It looked more like a conference room. I picked up a large magazine from one of the tables. The cover photo was Fidel wearing a straw hat with the Cuban flag in front, cutting sugar cane in the country with a machete. He was dressed in his Army Commander's uniform. I thought that the sugar cane photo op lasted ten, at most fifteen minutes to pose and make people believe that he had gone to that plantation to work—the leader sacrificing himself for his people. I smiled cynically, noting out of the corner of my eye how Franco still worried at his injured hand. I contemplated how this man didn't have any shame—he displayed no worry or discomfort about his obvious injury. Che must have already known about the man's deviancy; if it were me, I would have been worried that the kid with me would immediately tell Che everything. Instead, he appeared cool as a cucumber. He was cleaning his nails with a small nail clipper, whistling a tune called "Besame Mucho." I thought that, on top of being a pedophile, this man must entirely be lacking any moral restrictions, a cynical man with no compunctions, a point that would be verified shortly.

After almost half an hour to forty-five minutes of waiting, Che finally opened the door that connected that salon to his office. With a big smile on his face, he apologized for the prolonged wait, and he invited us to come into his office. We had not yet entered his office when there was a light tap on the large door on the opposite side of the room. It opened, and a man of middle height with greased hair said something to Che in Russian. He pointed to Che's desk with an idiotic smile. He picked up a gold cigarette case off of Che's desk, grinned helplessly, and started to leave. This time in perfect Spanish, he said, "I'm sorry for the interruption—I forgot my cigarettes."

Che said, "Yuri, stop. These comrades have my complete trust. You don't have to go—hold on." Che introduced him to us. Even though his origin was Russian, he could pass for any nationality, including Cuban. He was dressed sloppily, and his hair was a terrible mess. I felt like he looked goofy, and so thought that this man wasn't very important. He was friendly enough, his eyes were kind, and his arching eyebrows were unusual, catching my attention. I had never seen bushy eyebrows like that before. He spoke with us briefly, but he had to leave the office, apparently under a time constraint.

Yuri, Che's Russian contact

After he left the office, we sat down in comfortable armchairs. Che looked at Franco and asked what had happened to his hand. Franco didn't hesitate, blink, or look at any of us. He raised his arm and said, "Oh, this morning, I tried to get one of the rolls of bread out of the oven in the officer's mess. That heavy door landed on my hand and poked holes in it—look, you can see them. It's nothing important."

Che walked around the desk to him and said, "Let me see—let me see." He examined Franco's hand for a few seconds. "Hm—it's very strange. Four lacerations—it looks more like a pair of snake bites. Even though they are very small, in this area are many veins. That's the reason it's been bleeding so much," he added, as he looked at the blood soaked handkerchief. "Paco, take him to the infirmary. Have them put an antiseptic and a bandage on that hand. That way, it won't get infected."

Franco said, "It's nothing—don't worry about it."

Che said, "Listen, take care of it. You have some things you need to attend to in your office, anyway. I have some things I need to discuss in private with the

Commandantico." He looked at Claudio. "Claudio, make sure the cars are ready and the escort is prepared. We will leave the city in a very short time."

"Very well, my Commander," Claudio said.

After they left, Che turned to me and said, "Sit down, sit down. We've got a lot to talk about. You have a good trip?"

"Yeah, sure—I slept all the way here."

"Do you want to come with me? I'm going to leave for Santa Clara in a little while. I want to show you something extremely important there. We can talk on the trip without any interruptions."

"OK," I replied.

"Have you had lunch already?"

"Yes, I just had some a little while ago when we got into Havana. When are we leaving?"

He smiled and gave me a tap on my boot, as I was reclined back in the chair, my ankle resting on my knee. He didn't squeeze my leg or anything like Franco had done, and I relaxed. "That's what I like about you—you're always ready for the campaign!"

I smiled and said, "As true Revolutionaries, we should always be prepared and sleep with our boots on."

He beamed at that. This time, he slapped me on the knee. His expression grew more serious and he said, "There's something more important that I have to ask you, and this is completely confidential. Whenever we talk, whatever you observe, whatever happens when you're around me, don't repeat it to anyone. Your loyalty is to me, not to anybody else." He leaned back in his chair, settled in more comfortably, and lit a cigar he had removed from one of the pockets of his shirt. I didn't say anything, but just nodded my head. He took a long draft of the cigar and exhaled the smoke. He looked at the cigar and smelled it, thoroughly enjoying it. "Fidel has his own team, and they are loyal to him. Raul has his own team, and they are loyal to him. Everyone in this Revolution that's a leader has his own people, but my people only respond to me and nobody else. Just to me. That way, we don't create any misunderstandings. If somebody asks you anything, you tell them, 'ask Che.' If they say, 'well, I'm asking you,' you reply, 'I don't know anything.' You understand?"

I nodded. "Claro. I understand perfectly, Commander."

He smiled, full of satisfaction. "Che. Only Che. That is how my intimates call me, and I want you," he stood up and came over to me, clapping a hand on my shoulder, "to be one of my intimates. OK? Remember—Fidel, Raul, all these people, they have tremendous egos." He stroked his chin. "Nothing wrong with that. Everyone can have an ego the size of this building, if they want. To me, that is not important. More important than our personal egos is whatever we can accomplish not only in here, but around the globe, before we leave this filthy, nasty world in which we live today. Whatever we can accomplish, that is what history is going to say about us and judge us by." I nodded once more. He went over to the table and tapped the ashes from his cigar into an ashtray sculpted to look like the globe. He made a circle with the hand that held the cigar. "It's too bad, but unfortunately, we are surrounded by spies. We have to be very careful who we associate with, and with whom we trust our secrets. This Revolution hasn't consolidated itself in a firm basis yet. Considering that we're only ninety miles from the gringos, this is going to be a very hard battle. They will be doing the impossible to destroy us. That is why we have the duty to destroy them first. How we do that? We take away all of the countries in Spanish America, who are the ones that provide them with their economy. Without them, the Yankees are nothing."

I nodded again. "We are in complete agreement."

He grinned in satisfaction. He walked over to his desk. "Come on—follow me. I want to show you something."

I got up out of my seat and followed close behind him. We left the office with two guards standing at the door. They followed us down the long hallway. We came to a huge room with many desks and people working there. We walked through, everyone looking at us, and the person apparently in charge of the vast, bank vault, opened the door for us. He looked to be about forty, balding and bespectacled. I could not believe my eyes when I walked inside—it looked like Aladdin's treasure, with paintings from Van Gogh and Rembrandt, even Leonardo de Vinci, vast amounts of gold statues, rubies, golden and bejeweled goblets—the shelves were overflowing with them. There was a second vault beyond this one that was filled from floor to ceiling with gold bars. The door was still open, so that any additional loot could be stored there.

Che pointed at all this wealth. "Can you imagine how many Revolutions we can make with this? It was all confiscated from the fat-cat Cuban capitalists."

"I've never seen so much money in my life!" I marveled. "There must be millions of dollars in here!"

He smiled and said, "No—trillions."

I shook my head in disbelief. "I know Cuba has been a very wealthy country and well-known around the world for its ostentation, but," I said with wide eyes, "I never imagined to what point, until today."

He continued to smile and put his arm around my

shoulder. "Can you imagine, when we get all the countries of Hispano-America in our hands? No more rich people, no more classes, and in the end—we get the richest country in the world without shooting a single shot: Gringolandia!" He laughed in satisfaction. "But first," he continued, pointing at the floor, "we have to gain a foothold here. Then the rest of the world will belong to us."

We left that enormous vault and walked down the corridor. We saw Claudio, who came up to us. "Commander, everything is ready."

"Very well," Che said, "let's go."

We exited the building and got into one of three cars. The caravan drove off, our vehicle in the center. We negotiated the busy traffic and eventually left the city, heading towards a large avenue called the Via Blanca, a six-lane freeway that connected Havana with the next province of Matanzas. A very beautiful hard top red and white convertible passed in front of us, with four beautiful bikini-clad women. They leaned on their horn and blew kisses to us. I thought to myself that if they only knew what these guys had in mind, instead of kisses they would be throwing boxes full of feces at us. I thought that they should take a good look at their car, because if these people had their way, this would be the last year that anyone would see a beautiful car like that in Cuba for many years.

In our car, Claudio was driving, and another tall, dark-skinned, burly individual with a mustache and civilian clothes sat in the front. He might have been either Che's right hand or his bodyguard, I thought. The heavy escort, equipped with machine guns, were driving in front and behind our car, all men in uniform. We traveled for a while before exiting the central highway. The scenery was beautiful, lots of palm trees and tropical vegetation. We had already crossed the provincial boundary into Matanzas, and once in a while we could see a small house of modern architecture close to the road. The Batista government had built several of these around the island as gifts to those who supported him. However, he made sure they were built close to the highway so that the propaganda of his providing housing for the poor would be seen by every traveler. Looking at those small houses, all painted the same color, I thought to myself that history was repeating itself. The new dictator was using exactly the same demagogy of helping the poor and painting himself as the benefactor of the poor and helpless—the same dog with a different collar, I concluded. I smiled slightly as these thoughts went through my head. Claudio and the man in front started to whistle and scream cat calls. They rolled down the windows, and the entire caravan slowed down. I looked, and I saw the same hard top convertible stopped on the side of the road. One of the women was half-naked, apparently attempting to relieve herself by the side of the road. I thought she might have been doing this intentionally; while she seemed at first to be concealing herself, as soon as the commotion started, she began to cavort more shamelessly than ever.

Claudio screamed, "My God! Look at those beautiful breasts! Her nipples look like roses." He almost lost control as he yelled back at Che, "Look at this, Commandante! What a beautiful piece of meat. She doesn't even have any inhibitions, doing that right at the side of the road."

"Damn, Claudio!" Che replied. "Keep your eyes on the road!! Are you trying to kill all of us?"

"I'm sorry, Commander. It's been so long since I've seen a woman like that. I've been working too hard—the Army won't let me release my needs."

Che replied, very unhappily, "I think we'll need to give you a license for a couple of weeks, then, so you can go discharge your weapon. We don't want to be killed by the first woman who shows her tits on the road!" Che shook his head in resignation. "I have to agree with you about the woman, though—she is beautiful, like a sculpture." Everyone nodded their heads in agreement, clearly not wanting to anger Che any further.

I smiled to myself as I thought about Yaneba. The Army hadn't stopped me from finding my own releases. A very few minutes later, we heard once again the horns cars blaring as the car behind signaled once more. It was the convertible again, the women blowing kisses and laughing. As they drew next to us, they slowed down. I noticed that the girl who had been half-naked looked like she was bending down to grab something, but in reality, she wasn't grabbing anything—she was ducking. She was on the right, and one of the girls on the left was getting out of a bag something that shone in the sun. I thought it looked like a machine gun or a Thompson sub-machine gun. I grabbed Che's shoulder epaulette and pulled him down. I yelled, "Assassins! Watch out!!" It was an instinctive reaction, something purely out of self-preservation. He had an expression on his face of incredulity as he looked at my reaction. We both were reaching for our pistols, but Claudio slammed on his brakes, which caused us to be thrown into the back of the front seat. Even as this happened, I could hear the sound of automatic fire, and bullets sprayed from the front window and out the back window, shattering both, sending shards of glass like confetti spraying all around the interior cabin of our car.

Claudio screamed, "Son of a bitch!"

The other man was trying to take cover on the floor. He yelled, "Watch out, Claudio! You're going to hit the car in front!" The front vehicle had screeched to a halt when the gun opened fire on us.

Almost simultaneously, automatic weapons fire erupted from both the front and rear cars, rapidly turning that beautiful convertible into a sieve. When I raised my head to look, I saw the convertible flipping across all three lanes of cars, bodies flying through the air, and debris from the seat and interior spraying all over the road. It finally rolled to a stop, flipping at last onto its wheels. It completely blocked all lanes of traffic, forcing us to stop. Most of the guards piled out of the cars to investigate and look for survivors, while a small detachment remained behind to protect Che. Two the guards came over and opened the doors to inquire if we were all right. We looked at each other, saw that no one was bleeding or otherwise injured, and informed them that all was fine.

A short, plump man with bad teeth was in charge of the detachment in the rear car. He said, "Please stay in this car until we make sure everything is secure." He went over towards the convertible.

Che, his pistol in hand, didn't listen to him. He got out and walked towards the wreckage, the rest of us following behind him. The guards around the wreck were surrounding one of the women, the driver of the car. She was still alive, and they screamed at her to turn the engine off, throw the keys on the pavement, and to get out of the car. The engine was still running, and the woman didn't move. One of the doors was in the middle of the highway. A few feet further on the highway, another one of the women lay on the highway, her skull split open and her brain hanging half-way out. A small machine gun lay by her. A couple of soldiers came close to her, realized that she was dead, and picked up the machine gun. They continued to look for the other two women. One of them checked the woman in the driver's seat. He turned the engine off and reported that she was had died. Another woman lay moaning in the ditch by the right side of the road. We went over to her, and could see that it was our half-naked woman. Her legs lay at unnatural angles—clearly, she had multiple compound fractures in both legs. She had apparently crawled for a little way in that ditch, and now was resting against a small boulder.

Another soldier yelled as we drew near to her, "There's another body here!"

As we drew near to our living woman, her bikini was completely ripped off, and she was bleeding slightly from the mouth. Che hunched down onto his knees, took one of her hands and asked in a very paternal way, "You're dying. Why don't you tell me who sent you to do this and who you work for? Was it the CIA? They don't care—you're going to be dead in a few minutes. Where are they now? They're not here to help you, you don't owe them anything."

She glared at him with hatred in her eyes. She started to smile when he mentioned the CIA, but it hurt too much. It was clear that she wasn't able to talk, as she coughed and blood spewed out of her mouth. She looked each one of us closely in the eyes, as if she wanted to recognize us. She remained mute.

Another soldier screamed angrily, "Oh, my God! This woman isn't a woman—it's a man dressed as a woman! Son of a bitch!" Evidently, that soldier put his hand where he shouldn't have, and had an unpleasant surprise. Ch and the rest paid him no attention.

This time, the dying woman tried to laugh, but began to cough once more. Che was still holding her hand. "You're dying. Don't be stupid. Maybe we can do something for you if we call you an ambulance quickly. How did you know we would be crossing this highway today? Who gave you this information?"

She breathed deeply as if she were trying to draw strength from somewhere. She looked at him with a depth of hatred I have never seen in anyone before. She managed to gasp out with tremendous effort, "Go...to...hell...you...murderous...son...of...a...bitch!"

Che realized that she wasn't going to talk, and dropped her hand. Angrily, he whipped out his pistol. Without a word to anyone, he rammed the pistol into her mouth and pulled the trigger. We were sprayed with blood, brains, and bits of skull, so caught by surprise by his action were we. We started to wipe ourselves off while Che went over to the other body. We followed, and it was already dead. They checked the other two bodies, and the only real woman was the one we had spoken with by the side of the road. They inspected all the bodies for any other clues.

Che turned around and spoke to the tall man who had been in the front of our car. "Silvano, who besides you and Claudio knew we would be taking this trip to Santa Clara today?" he demanded.

Silvano quickly replied with a shake of his head, "Nobody, my Commander."

Che still had his pistol in his right hand, and stroked his beard with his left for a few seconds in silence. Claudio and Silvano looked at each other in confusion.

Claudio, in an attempt to relieve the tension, said, "It's

weird how nobody knew that we would be going to Caibarién."

Che raised his head in surprise and smiled. Then his expression changed in a weird fashion, a mix of incredulity and mistrust. "Well, the important thing is that none of us are hurt or dead from this attempt on my life." He turned to the escort. "Get all the bodies inside that convertible. Push it if that car won't start to the farthest part from the highway, and burn it." He turned around and started to walk back towards our car. As he passed Claudio, without saying a word, he whipped his still-drawn pistol up and shot Claudio in the temple. Claudio slumped to the ground, instantly dead. Without even stopping, he said, "Silvano, have the men put the body of this fucking traitor with the rest of our enemies, as well." As he walked, he said aloud, "How the hell did Claudio know we were going to Caibarién? I never told anyone the exact location of our destination in Santa Clara." Silvano, the rest of the men, and I were in shock. Claudio had been one of us, and yet Che had summarily executed him. Silvano looked at me in confusion, but we both followed him back to the car.

The short man with the crooked teeth said, "Commander, we have to switch cars. Yours has the windows all shot out."

I couldn't help myself and turned around. I looked at Claudio's body as a couple of guards picked it up off the ground like a potato sack, one at the arms and the other at the legs. They swung it between themselves to gain momentum, and then flung it into the convertible. I realized that this could easily have been me, and I remembered my uncle's words about his paranoia and how easily confidence could turn into suspicion. I knew then how dangerous Che could be. My forehead started to sweat and my legs started to shake. They felt like rubber bands, and I wasn't sure that I'd be able to walk all the way to the car. I sat down on a small rock by the side of the road. I pretended to tie the laces on one of my boots. I took a deep breath and said, "I will wait for you guys here. I need to catch my breath." I tried to blank the memory out of my brain and erase the horrific memory of the scene of Claudio being shot right in front of me. Even though I scarcely knew the man, it was a shock to me to see someone lose his life like that, in the blink of an eye.

The soldiers turned on the convertible on the first try. In the midst of all this stress and crisis I was enduring right now, I remembered the words of my father, because he was a huge fan of Ford automobiles: "When other cars can't make it, a Ford will make it with a tongue on the floor." I smiled, and used it to work on blotting out the other images and regain my sanity. I wanted to forget Che's cruelty; for all I knew, Che had known Claudio for years, and yet he killed him like one would kill a chicken for lunch.

Che was walking towards me with Silvano, holding something in his hand. I put my hand on my pistol, expecting to have to defend myself at any second. The soldiers had returned from their task with the car. Behind them a long column of black smoke rose into the sky. As Che drew near, he handed me a bottle of water. "What? Is this too much for you?"

I made an effort to smile. "Thank you for the water. No, it's not too much for me at all. I was just sitting here wondering how the devil that Ford convertible could start on the first try, after it was torn to pieces and flipped all over the highway."

He raised his hands on top of his head and laughed. He

turned to the others. "You hear this kid? This Commandantico is unbelievable! In the middle of all this convulsion and death, the thing he's thinking about is how that Ford started so quickly!" Everyone laughed, though I wasn't sure at that point whether they thought it was really funny, or if they were worried about being the next to get his brains blown out. Che held his hand out to me. "Come on, get up."

"Thank you," I said.

He gave me a hug out of the blue, taking me by surprise. "I owe you my life. That's a big one—I don't owe that to very many people."

"Thank you," was all I could say. After he let me go, I added, "You don't owe me anything. I'm sure, before long, you'll do the same for me."

"I've got one question, though—how in the hell did you know what was going on?" he asked.

"Simple," I replied, "while you guys were all watching these women's tits and butts, I was wondering what they were doing. When she ducked, I wondered why, and I saw one of the others pull out something could have been a machine gun."

He laughed. "You see? While the rest of us were behaving like morons and watching their tits and asses, he was watching what was in their hands. They distracted all of us, except for the Commandantico. This is a good lesson for us today—our enemies will pick the most beautiful distractions, and that distraction can cost us our lives!" Everyone nodded. He put his hand on my shoulder. "All of you guys should thank him—if they had killed Claudio in the driver's seat, we would all have crashed, and we would all be dead. Maybe that was their intention—to kill the driver of the middle car and so kill the rest of us through the crash." The others all murmured their thanks to me.

The short, plump man yelled, "A car is coming! Move the cars!"

The three cars moved onto the shoulder to clear the freeway. A few minutes later, several trucks filled with civilians bearing straw hats in their hands and machetes on their waists passed us. They waved at us as they went by. They looked like workers from the factories or the plantations. The government called them volunteers—those who did the agricultural work that no one wanted to do any more due to the hard labor involved. The government made it a requirement that anyone who worked in any office, bureau, or business that had been nationalized, in order to help the economy, had to perform for at least 18 hours a week this kind of voluntary work. Those who didn't agree or were reluctant to volunteer lost their bureaucratic positions and nice, air-conditioned offices in consequence. The worst cases of reluctance were classified as 'not clear,' and lost all benefits from the government. This enabled the government to force even brain surgeons, musicians, actors, television celebrities—anyone who worked directly for the government—to cut sugar cane or be involved in other heavy agricultural labor. The shortage was caused because those who previously worked on the plantations moved out of the provinces and into the cities when the Revolution won—precisely to avoid the hard work.

As I watched the long caravan of men, women, and even young children, I thought about how Castro could promise that there would no longer be any slave owners or slaves; but given this system, I had to ask myself who were really the slaves now. I waved back at some of the people. I noticed that some of the women, especially, had probably never been in the country in their lives.

After we switched the cars, putting our previous car in the back, we left that funeral pyre of the five bodies behind us to be buried in the history books. Che introduced us to the new chauffeur, Fausto, who was the chubby man, half bald; in spite of his ill appearance, his manners were very good. We rode in silence for a while until Che asked, "Do you guys know why I shot Claudio?" Everyone remained silent. I looked my question at him, but said nothing. That horrible scene replayed itself in my mind, and my right leg started to shake uncontrollably. I stretched in my seat, and crossed my left leg over it to stop it by putting pressure on it. I hid this by looking like I was pondering it, stroking my chin. This time, he asked me directly, "Do you remember, Commandantico, when in Pinar del Rio, we had the meeting in Commander Escalona's office? How just after we left the office, there was a break-in and my portfolio was stolen while we were dining together in the officer's mess?"

I nodded and said, "Yes, I remember very clearly. What about it?" I observed him closely, and saw that he was leaning over on the side of the car opposite me, and that his hand never left the handle of his pistol. I slowly started to bring my hand close to my own pistol. I never blinked or took my eyes off of him. I felt my palm rest against the pistol. Carefully, to not let the snap of the peace bond being undone be heard, I cleared my pistol so that it could come free quickly. I never took my eyes off him, expecting the worst after that question.

He continued very seriously, leaning over towards me a little bit, making my nerves more tense to the point that I was ready to pull my pistol out and shoot him in the head and both the guys in front if it looked like he was about to draw. I also had to think about what my alibi would be if I had to shoot the three of them. I thought that I could say that Che went crazy after shooting Claudio without any reason, and then, while we were driving, he pulled out his pistol to shoot the two men in front, and I had to shoot him in self-defense. If asked why he was going to shoot those two men and not me, I could reply that he, at that point, trusted me, since I had just saved his life, but he wasn't trusting the other two guys. All of this flashed through my mind in the time it took for him to lean in towards me. I was under a lot of stress; I didn't want to end up like Claudio with a bullet in my head. But I didn't want to overreact, either.

Finally, he said, "Well, the truth is that Claudio, at that time, was the only one of my team who disappeared for many hours. He was completely unaccounted for—we searched for him, but we couldn't find him. Several hours later, he showed up with the excuse that he was in the helicopter doing some small mechanical work. He was also the pilot, so it was part of his job. But nobody could corroborate that, since he was by himself. It was also very strange—why do mechanical work at night by a flashlight, when he could do it during the next day? Why didn't he come to find out what was going on when he heard all of the sirens? He said he had earplugs in so that the engine noise wouldn't bother him when he started it up to test it, but it's still very strange."

When I heard that, I felt much more relaxed. Che relaxed a little more in the seat, took his hand off of his pistol and started to scratch his neck. He said sarcastically as he pointed at his chest, "I've had that thorn in my chest from that day. I removed that thorn today, finally." He nodded in satisfaction. "I removed it today. Only in my portfolio did I have written down what we're doing in Caibarién. That showed me today that the only way this traitor could know of our destination today was because he had something to do with theft or he did it himself and read those documents. No one, except for Fidel and Raul, has any knowledge about what we're doing. That is why I gave him a one-way ticket to the inferno today. I don't have any more doubts that he is one of the traitors involved in that robbery."

I mentally said a prayer of thanks to God. I had not been considered a part of Che's team at that point. I also had a disappearance that night, and had he considered me on his team, they would have looked for me as well. My disappearance would have lasted for longer, as evidenced by the search throughout the island for me that had occurred. Claudio's excuse was probably actually valid, and Che had likely forgotten that, as an intimate, he might have mentioned to Claudio about Caibarién at some point. I breathed deeply to relieve my tension and replied, "I'm sorry, but you don't think it might have been more prudent to be arresting him and interrogating him before you shot him? Now, you'll never know if that is the truth or not."

He smiled and shook his head. "Commandantico, we cannot do that. We would put doubt in the heads of Fidel and Raul about the rest of my men. This man was one of my most trustworthy guys, and my personal driver. We completely would have lost our good reputation, and would have been all made ridiculous because of this son of a bitch. Fidel and Raul would never trust my people ever again. That is why I finished him off immediately. It was the only solution." He raised his index finger. "Remember what I told you before we left Havana." He made a motion like closing a zipper over his mouth. "Not a word of what has happened here to anybody—including Fidel. Unfortunately, Claudio will be a casualty of the Revolution, whether or not he's a traitor. He disappeared, just like Camillo. We don't know what happened with him—maybe he left the country with the internationalists to create a revolution in another country. Maybe after enough time passes, we can give out some medals to his family, and tell them we found out that he's been killed in one of the countries we're trying to liberate. Anyway, the Revolution needs good martyrs." He finished this with a very cynical and sarcastic smile, an expression I saw many times whenever he felt he had accomplished his objective.

I pantomimed zipping my lips shut and waved my hand. "Don't worry about it. My lips are sealed." Everyone else remained silent.

We entered the city of Santa Clara, and drove to another nationalized Hilton Hotel, the Santa Clara Libre. They gave us the penthouse; it didn't look like a suite of the hotel, it looked more like something belonging to a Donald Trump. The penthouse was a huge house-sized suite with five separate rooms. Each room had its own Jacuzzi, a bar, and a living room. The floors were of marble, the bathtub fixtures were gold, and we had our own private elevator with a security key. This provided, originally, accommodations for business executives and top corporate types, as it had a reception area and chairs around a large bar. There was also a large meeting room with a long conference table, around which were several comfortable leather-bound executive chairs. The sheer opulence of the place was breath-taking. Che took one room for himself, a room for me by myself that connected with his, and another room for Silvano and Fausto together, and the remaining rooms for the escort. I really appreciated the consideration Che gave to me—even though I was a young kid, he gave me the respect to be assigned a room to myself next to his.

After we refreshed ourselves, we ate a delicious meal Che had ordered from room service. He didn't want to go down to the restaurant and mingle with the people; he wanted his visit to Santa Clara to be a discreet one. Everyone knew who he was, and it would be the subject for newspaper articles and constant harassment for interviews if it got out that he was in town. We finished dinner, and he told Silvano and Fausto to stay put in there, as he was expecting some important visitors. He told me to come with him, and we walked outside and climbed a small stairway onto an upper deck and a terrace that looked out over the city. Two of the soldiers followed us. As we walked out onto the terrace, he took out one of his Habanos cigars, lit it, and contemplated the beautiful view from that height on the clear night. He looked down at the small pinpoints of light that marked the moving cars down at our feet. He told the guards to stay by the door.

We started to walk around, taking in the view. He put one of his hands on my shoulder. "If you stay by my side, I will teach you not only how to survive in this Revolution but also how you can get the best benefit out of it. The only thing I ask in exchange from you is loyalty and respect. And, as I've told you a couple of times already, to keep your lips sealed."

"I know, Commander—ah, Che." He nodded encouragingly with a tiny smile. "You told me three times already. Believe me, you only have to tell me things once. For me, that is sufficient. When we talk about respect, I even respect my enemies, but especially I give the very best respect to my friends. I expect the same respect from them to me."

He smiled and took a long draft from his cigar. After he exhaled, he said, "I will give you an advice. For your friends, yes—if necessary, give them your life. But real friends are very few. But for your enemies, to hell with them! You don't need to give them any respect at all, because they won't give you any in return. That is my advice—your enemies, eliminate them, squish them like you squish a cockroach on the ground. They won't have any mercy on you when they have you under their heel—they will squish you."

I tightened my lips and nodded. I didn't agree with him, but I didn't want to contradict him. Without doubt, we meant two different things when we spoke about respect and how to deal with our enemies and friends. I could understand where he was coming from, and I knew that he had no mercy for anyone. As the Bible says, whoever lives by the sword dies by the sword. In my mind, I thought that I would let time show to him the truth about the code of conduct he was suggesting that I follow.

We walked a short distance and stood on the veranda of the terrace. He stroked his beard with his left hand as he held his cigar in his right. "You know, Fidel, Raul, and I, we differ on many things?" he asked. I shook my head. "Well, I believe in the physical and complete destruction of the capitalist system, and it can only be obtained through the weapons of the terrorist and the clandestine fight in both the cities and the jungle, and bring destruction and unrest to all the population. Don't let people sleep anymore in peace, keep them not even being able to have the luxury of going to go watch a movie, because a bomb could explode underneath their seat. Use a heavy wind in a warm summer to start a fire that not only burns hundreds of acres of land, but also houses. The more distress and unrest you give to people, the more of them that will come to our side looking for peace and security, because the established government cannot offer it to them. The alteration of the daily routine of the citizens and the sense of a lack of security brings them to hate the establishment, creating labor disputes, protests for anything at all, accusing the government and the establishment of destroying natural resources and our forests—that is how we win in our Marxist ideas. We then take the power and force those ignorant peasants to die fighting for a better life."

I looked at him and smiled. He might have thought I agreed with him, but I thought to myself, You son of a bitch—obligating the ignorant peasants to die so that you can smoke that expensive cigar you have in your mouth and sleep in luxury suites like we are without paying a penny for any of it. All they are really doing is helping you to create your own feudal state. My smile was pleasant, and I nodded. He responded to my smile by patting my shoulder.

"You agree with me, eh?" he said with a nod. "Well, Fidel and Raul, they believe more in their version of corrupting a society from the inside, without violence, injecting all the youth with drugs, and using the instrument of indoctrination through the teachers and professors from primary and secondary school up through the university level, and using our great international propaganda machine to invite all the citizens of the world to come and visit us, since we will have the best free educational programs and the best health care with free medicine and free doctor's visits. According to them, people love free goodies, and when they leave Cuba, they'll go back to their own countries and convince their governments that they need to adapt and be more like ours. I believe this is too long a plan—it will take fifty, sixty, or seventy years to enact." He shrugged his shoulders. "By that time, we'll all be gone and with Papa Lucifer. Why the hell should we wait so long? To me, that is a Utopian dream and a waste of time." He took another puff on his cigar and smiled. "That is the reason I have my own ideas and plans—more effective and immediate, and I will prove to both of them that my radical ideas are better! Fidel dared me the other day to try my idea, while they try theirs. I told him that I will take that challenge and see who's right. We're going to change history, and my name is going to be forever in the history books while theirs will be forgotten, smeared and forgotten by time. Let's see who gets the best results in the end." This time, he smiled ironically, stroking his mustache. "I will prove to the two of them that, to win the battle for the world, the first thing you have to do is cut off the head of the serpent, then the tail where the poison is, and then you kill the small newborns they leave behind. That way, we leave no possibility for errors or repetitions of the stupidities of history."

One of the soldiers approached us. "Excuse me, my Commander. I'm sorry to interrupt you, but the visitors are here. They have been here for a while already."

"Very well. Did you guys take them to the conference room? You guys offer them food or drinks?"

"Yes, and they've finished. They're waiting for you, Commander."

"Very well." The soldier saluted him and walked back to the door. Che didn't rush himself. He took his time to enjoy the last of his cigar, smelling it appreciatively. He looked at me. "Do you agree with me?"

I looked him in the eye. "Totally." I saluted him. "You just tell me what you want done, and I will do it, exactly as you tell me."

He slapped at my hand. "Come on—I will groom you, and you will be even better than me. You are the next generation, and you will be driving those 2000s cars that we will be manufacturing in our nationalized factories in Chicago. You were admiring that Ford? You will be deciding whether that Ford will be manufactured or not. You like that?"

"I love it!"

He put his arm around my shoulder and said, "Come on, let's go. You're going to have your first international political lesson."

"OK, Professor," I said. "I'm right behind you." We walked down the small stairway and back into the suite.

The two guards followed us back down. We walked into the conference room. Che asked Silvano and Fausto to come in, as well. Two guards remained outside the conference room, while Silvano and Fausto took up positions on either side of the room, stationing themselves behind the visitors. As soon as we came in, Che introduced me to the two men. The first one I almost recognized at once, but I kept my silence—he looked exactly like Yuri. I was surprised when he extended his hand and said, "*Mucho gusto*, Marko Trotski" in perfect Spanish.

"The pleasure is mine," I replied. Then I asked, "Are you Russian?"

"No," he said emphatically. "I'm Yugoslavian."

"Oh!" I exclaimed. "It's nice to meet you." I looked at him closely when he said that. He looked so closely to Yuri, but I noticed that in his left eyebrow he had a tiny pockmark, like the remnants of chicken pox. Because of that, the left eyebrow was slightly shorter than his right one. I thought to myself that I would never have even detected this had it not been for the training provided me by my uncle, the General, and their people, teaching me to notice the smallest details that could be used to identify someone that I come in contact with. These small details were vital, because they could be key to my survival in my work.

The other was very muscular, barrel-chested—I thought he looked very much like a Secret Service or FBI agent. He wore a black suit with a silk black tie with a mint green paisley pattern, dark gray raincoat, even though it wasn't that cold, and wore a great white hat with a bandanna of the same color of his raincoat. He looked very elegant and tasteful. When he spoke, his Spanish wasn't as good as Marko's. "Mucho gusto—Jacob Leon Rubenstein, but my closest friends call me Jack Ruby."

Marko, Che's Yugoslav contact and Jack Ruby

Santa Clara Libre, formerly the Santa Clara Hilton

This concludes the first part of Rites of Passage of a Master Spy. Julio Antonio's adventures and trials continue in Volume II, The Havana Conspiracies. For even further adventures of the Lightning, visit our website, www.spymasterspy.com

The Greedy Parasites

Greed is the worst parasite that can invade the human mind without respect to gender. It makes people lose their minds. Greed makes people lose their morals, ethics, and decency that normal people have and make those previously wonderful people now act as if they are out of their minds. They no longer behave like a human being; they act more like a parasite. They are beasts possessed by greed. Now they start to act like common rats.

Dr. Julio Antonio del Marmol

CIA Document # 104-10015-10003, 12/17/63

Lee Harvey Oswald, our double agent, at the time was living in Minsk. "He noted in his 'Historic Diary,' he frequented the Foreign Language Institute on Ulyanova Street to meet women. By happenstance, the Institute was directly adjacent to the MVD school attended by Castro's young charges. Most importantly, Oswald added that he had befriended a number of the Cuban trainees being groomed there for leadership positions in Havana. Oswald hoped that he would one day end up in Cuba, where these contacts would prove useful to him. At one point he even bragged to Marina that he would become a 'minister' in the new government.

"Shortly after the Cuban Missile Crisis in 1962, Moscow invited 1,500 DGI agents, including Che Guevara, to the KGB's Moscow Center for an intensive training in intelligence operations."

Dr. Julio Antonio del Marmol

Other Works by the Author

Cuba: Russian Roulette of the World
The Cuban Lightning: The Zipper

Forthcoming
The remaining volumes in *Rites of Passage of a Master Spy*

The Havana Conspiracies
The Dark Face of Marxism
The Deadly Deals
The Evil Rituals
JFK: The Unwrapped Enigma

www.ingramcontent.com/pod-product-compliance
Lightning Source LLC
Chambersburg PA
CBHW031309150426
43191CB00005B/143